Other Books and S

*1901-1907 Native American Census S
Modoc, Ottawa, Peoria, Quapaw, and
School, Indian Territory)*

1932 Census of The Standing Rock Sio,
Deaths 1924-1932

Census of The Blackfeet, Montana, 1897- 1901 Expanded Edition

Eastern Cherokee by Blood, 1906-1910, Volumes I thru XIII

*Choctaw of Mississippi Indian Census 1929-1932 with Births and Deaths
1924-1931   Volume I*

*Choctaw of Mississippi Indian Census 1933, 1934 & 1937, Supplemental
Rolls to 1934 & 1935 with Births and Deaths 1932-1938, and Marriages
1936-1938   Volume II*

*Eastern Cherokee Census Cherokee, North Carolina 1930-1939
Census 1930-1931 with Births And Deaths 1924-1931 Taken By Agent L.
W. Page   Volume I*

*Eastern Cherokee Census Cherokee, North Carolina 1930-1939
Census 1932-1933 with Births And Deaths 1930-1932 Taken By Agent R.
L. Spalsbury   Volume II*

*Eastern Cherokee Census Cherokee, North Carolina 1930-1939
Census 1934-1937 with Births and Deaths 1925-1938 and Marriages 1936
& 1938 Taken by Agents R. L. Spalsbury And Harold W. Foght Volume III*

*Seminole of Florida Indian Census, 1930-1940 with Birth and Death
Records, 1930-1938*

Texas Cherokees 1820-1839 A Document For Litigation 1921

Choctaw By Blood Enrollment Cards 1898-1914 Volumes I thru XVII

*Starr Roll 1894 (Cherokee Payment Rolls) Districts: Canadian,
Cooweescoowee, and Delaware Volume One*

Visit our website at **www.nativestudy.com** to learn more about these
and other books and series by Jeff Bowen

.

STARR ROLL 1894

(CHEROKEE PAYMENT ROLLS)

DISTRICTS: FLINT, GOING SNAKE AND ILLINOIS

VOLUME TWO

TRANSCRIBED BY

JEFF BOWEN

NATIVE STUDY
Gallipolis, Ohio
USA

Originally published:
Baltimore, Maryland
2014

Reprinted by:

Native Study LLC
Gallipolis, OH
www.nativestudy.com

Library of Congress Control Number: 2020914749

ISBN: 978-1-64968-022-8

Made in the United States of America.

This series is dedicated to my longtime friend
and confidant, Kent Anderson.

Picture source: donated by Grant Foreman to the Smithsonian Institution Anthropological Archives. Treasurer E.E. Starr is seated at the center of the table. According to Foreman this photograph was taken shortly after distribution had begun for the Cherokee Strip payments. The picture is approximately 120 years old. Notice the armed guards, records and cash stacked on the table. Each eligible tribal member received $265.70.

Starr Family Tree

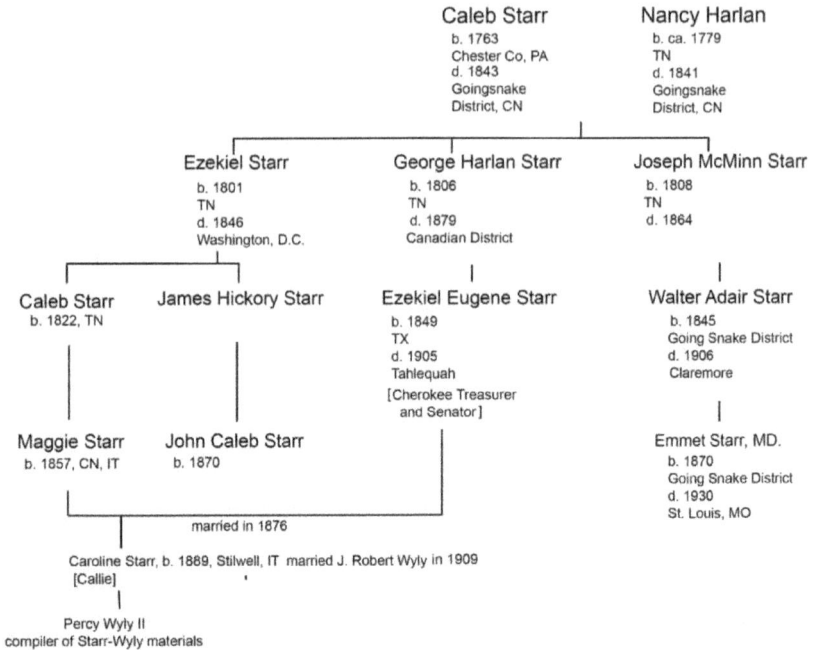

Caleb Starr
b. 1763
Chester Co, PA
d. 1843
Goingsnake
District, CN

Nancy Harlan
b. ca. 1779
TN
d. 1841
Goingsnake
District, CN

Ezekiel Starr
b. 1801
TN
d. 1846
Washington, D.C.

George Harlan Starr
b. 1806
TN
d. 1879
Canadian District

Joseph McMinn Starr
b. 1808
TN
d. 1864

Caleb Starr
b. 1822, TN

James Hickory Starr

Ezekiel Eugene Starr
b. 1849
TX
d. 1905
Tahlequah
[Cherokee Treasurer
and Senator]

Walter Adair Starr
b. 1845
Going Snake District
d. 1906
Claremore

Maggie Starr
b. 1857, CN, IT

John Caleb Starr
b. 1870

Emmet Starr, MD.
b. 1870
Going Snake District
d. 1930
St. Louis, MO

married in 1876

Caroline Starr, b. 1889, Stilwell, IT married J. Robert Wyly in 1909
[Callie]

Percy Wyly II
compiler of Starr-Wyly materials

Table of Contents

INTRODUCTION

The *Starr Roll (Cherokee Payment Rolls and Index 1894)*, is found in the National Archives film 7RA38, Rolls 1-5, under the heading Record Group 75. Many genealogists likely see the name Starr and think that these records were documented by the famous Cherokee genealogist Dr. Emmet Starr, (1870-1930), but discover that they were created by Ezekiel Eugene Starr, (1849-1905), who was elected a Cherokee Senator for the Flint District in 1883 and then Treasurer for the Western Cherokee Nation in 1891. Both Starr's were related but held different stations in life.

The background to the *Starr Roll* requires some telling. On March 3, 1893, Congress passed an act that authorized the sale of lands west of the Cherokee Nation known as the Cherokee Outlet, and later referred to as the 1894 Cherokee Strip Payment. The Cherokee Outlet, originally created by agreement with the Eastern Cherokee in 1835, occupied a strip of land 57 miles wide in present-day north/northwestern Oklahoma was intended as a "perpetual outlet west" for the Cherokee. After 1877, the Cherokee Nation leased the Outlet to the Cherokee Strip Livestock Association, who desired it for its rich grazing lands. Then in 1893, homesteaders were permitted to stake their claims to the land in the fourth and largest of Oklahoma's five land runs. In return for opening the Cherokee Outlet to white settlers, eligible members of the Cherokee Nation were paid a per-capita payment in the amount of $265.70.

E.E. Starr, then Cherokee treasurer, created the receipt roll for these payments and arranged it by each of the nine Cherokee Districts, and thereunder by each party's enrollment number. The contents of the receipt roll, transcribed for these volumes, includes the name of the head of household, names of other household members, name of person receiving the payment, as well as the name of a person that witnessed the transaction of record. The *Starr Roll* also includes an *Orphans Roll and Supplemental*, whose contents are self-explanatory within this transcription.

Jeff Bowen
Gallipolis, Ohio
NativeStudy.com

Flint *(District)*

Starr Roll 1894

We, the undersigned citizens of the Cherokee Nation, by right of Cherokee blood, do hereby acknowledge to have received of E. E. Starr, National Treasurer of the Cherokee Nation, the sums set opposite our names respectively, in full of our shares in the per capita distribution authorized by an Act of the National Council, dated _____MAY 3 1894_____ 1894.

Began Paying Flint District August one, 1894

Names of Head, and Members of Families	Amount	To Whom Paid	Witness to Payment	Remarks
1 Adair Chu-nu-lusky	*order* 265.70	Chunooluucky Adair	L B Bell	*order withdrawn W & S*
2 Adair Sarah				
3 Adair Betsy	531.40	Sarah Adair	L B Bell	
4 Adair William				
5 " Jalah				
6 " Norah	797.10	Wm Adair	L B Bell	
7 Adair Hugh M				*Pd 2055 –*
8 " Timothy M	531.40	H M Adair	L B Bell	*$546,013.52 – 9 unpaid –*
9 Adair Edward H	265.70	E H Adair	L B Bell	
10 Adair James W	265.70	Jas W Adair	L B Bell	
11 Adair William	265.70	William Adair	L B Bell	
12 Aversaw David	265.70	Geo. Ferguson	J.C. Starr	*pd Sept 22, 1894*
13 Adair Tandy W				
14 " Laura				
15 " Mertie	797.10	Laura Adair	L B Bell	
16 Adair Samuel				
17 " Martha				*Stepson of Samuel Adair*
18 Quinton Louis	797.10	Saml Adair	L B Bell	*3 years old Louis Quinton Sr Guard.*
19 Adams John Q	265.70	John Adams	L B Bell	
20 Akin Frank				
21 " Ann				
22 " Jesse				
23 " Lee	1062.80	Frank Akin	L B Bell	

1

Starr Roll 1894

We, the undersigned citizens of the Cherokee Nation, by right of Cherokee blood, do hereby acknowledge to have received of E. E. Starr, National Treasurer of the Cherokee Nation, the sums set opposite our names respectively, in full of our shares in the per capita distribution authorized by an Act of the National Council, dated ___MAY 3 1894___ 1894.

	Names of Head, and Members of Families	Amount	To Whom Paid	Witness to Payment	Remarks
24	Adair Peter				
25	" Charlotte				
26	" Betsy	773			
27	" Alsey	DEAD.			
28	" Louis				
29	" Edward				
30	" Nellie				
31	" Leaf				
32	" William P.				
33	" Hummingbird				
34	" Akie DEAD.	2922.70	Peter Adair	L B Bell	
35	Adair Joe				
36	" George	531.40	Joe Adair	L B Bell	
37	Adair John B.				
38	" Betty				
39	" John F.				
40	" Stand W.				
41	" William P.	1328.50	J B Adair	L B Bell	
42	Adair George W	265.70	Sarah E Adair Guardian	L B Bell	Said to live in Arkansas never saw the Cherokee Nation Orphan. John Hunt Guardian
43	Adair Samuel	265.70	Saml Adair	L B Bell	(age 14)
44	Adair Nelly				
45	Christie Nannie				
46	" Sallie				
47	" John	1062.80	Nelly Adair	L B Bell	
48	Adams Charlotte E	265.70	Charlotte Adams	L B Bell	
49	Adair Mary	265.70	Jo Lemaster	L B Bell	now Lemaster
50	Adair Foreman				
51	" Jennie				
52	" Love				order of Foreman Adair
53	" Jacob	1062.80	Charles Sanders	L B Bell	

2

Starr Roll 1894

We, the undersigned citizens of the Cherokee Nation, by right of Cherokee blood, do hereby acknowledge to have received of E. E. Starr, National Treasurer of the Cherokee Nation, the sums set opposite our names respectively, in full of our shares in the per capita distribution authorized by an Act of the National Council, dated _____ MAY 3 1894 _____ 1894.

Names of Head, and Members of Families	Amount	To Whom Paid	Witness to Payment	Remarks
54 Adair Candy				
55 " Thomas	531.40	Candy Adair	L B Bell	
56 Adair Sarah E	265.70	S E Adair	L B Bell	*Home said to be in Arkansas, and not a citizen of the Cherokee Nation*
57 Allison John L				
58 " Lee				
59 " Mildred	797.10	John L Allison	L B Bell	
60 Acorn Edward				
61 " Katy				
62 " John	797.10	Edward Acorn	L B Bell	
63 Acorn Eliza	265.70	Eliza Acorn	L B Bell	
64 Acorn Ezekiel	265.70	Ezekiel Acorn	L B Bell	
65 Adair Samuel Taylor				
66 " Cherokee				
67 " Qatie[sic] M.				
68 " Mary E.				
69 " George W.				
70 " Sam Wilson	1594.20	S.T. Adair	L B Bell	
71 Adair Loucinda	265.70	L M Adair	L B Bell	
72 Adair Sarah L	265.70	Sarah L Adair	L B Bell	
73 Adair Luther M.				
74 " Sarah L				
75 " William L				
76 " Mary				
77 " Mintie	1328.50	L M Adair	L B Bell	
78 Acorn Richard				
79 " Katy				
80 " Charley				
81 " Fields				
82 " Johnann				*Step-Daughter living with Richard Acorn*
83 Feather Chegha-us	1594.20	Ric^d Acorn	L B Bell	

3

Starr Roll 1894

We, the undersigned citizens of the Cherokee Nation, by right of Cherokee blood, do hereby acknowledge to have received of E. E. Starr, National Treasurer of the Cherokee Nation, the sums set opposite our names respectively, in full of our shares in the per capita distribution authorized by an Act of the National Council, dated ___MAY 3 1894___ 1894.

Names of Head, and Members of Families	Amount	To Whom Paid	Witness to Payment	Remarks
84 Adair Susan D				
85 " George S	531.40	Susan D Adair	L B Bell	
86 Allison Mildred T				
87 " Alex V.	DEAD.			
88 " Laura J.				
89 " Garfield E.				
90 " Narcena	1328.50	M.T. Allison	L B Bell	
91 Adair John W, Sr				
92 " John W				
93 " Eugine	797.10	John W Adair	L B Bell	
94 Allen Walter				
95 " Edward				
96 " Muntie				
97 " Caroline	DEAD.			
98 " Mary L	1328.50	Walter Allen	L B Bell	
99 Adair Lizzie	265.70	Lizzie Adair	L B Bell	
100 Allison Delano A	265.70	D A Allison	L B Bell	
101 Allison Ella N	265.70	Ella N Allison	L B Bell	
102 Alberty Blueford W				
103 " Clara K				
104 " John A.				
105 " Annie L.				
106 " Blueford W, Jr				
107 " Martha C.				
108 Adair Chrles[sic] L.				
109 " Maud				
110 " Norma B.	2391.30	B.W. Alberty	L B Bell	
111 Augerhole Alexander				
112 " Hattie B.				
113 " William W.				
114 " Lydia	1062.80	Alex Augerhole	L B Bell	

4

Starr Roll 1894

We, the undersigned citizens of the Cherokee Nation, by right of Cherokee blood, do hereby acknowledge to have received of E. E. Starr, National Treasurer of the Cherokee Nation, the sums set opposite our names respectively, in full of our shares in the per capita distribution authorized by an Act of the National Council, dated ____MAY 3 1894____ 1894.

	Names of Head, and Members of Families	Amount	To Whom Paid	Witness to Payment	Remarks
115	Augerhole Watt				
116	" Betsy				
117	Bird Scott				*Step children of*
118	Hewin Lizzie	1062.80	Watt Augerhole	L B Bell	*Watt Augerhole*
119	Buffington Ellis W.				
120	" Thomas C.				
121	" Otha F.	797.10	Ellis Buffington	Henry Eiffert	
122	Bateman Ninnie	DEAD.			
123	" Jasper N.				
124	" Lydia	797.10	George Furgueson[sic]	L B Bell	*check Furguson*
125	Batt Jack				
126	" Lucy				
127	" Samuel				
128	" Betty				
129	" Mose				
130	" Charles	1594.20	Jack Batt	L B Bell	
131	Batt John				
132	" Mary				
133	" Joseph	797.10	John Batt	L B Bell	
134	Brady Zeb V.				
135	" Addie E.				
136	" Zed A.				
137	" Feby B.	1062.80	Zeb V Brady	L B Bell	
138	Bigfeather Buck				
139	" Thomas	531.40	Buck Big Feather	L B Bell	
140	Bunch Jennie				
141	" George				
142	" Lizzie				
143	" Richard				
144	" Beckie				
145	" John	1594.20	Jennie Bunch	L B Bell	

Starr Roll 1894

We, the undersigned citizens of the Cherokee Nation, by right of Cherokee blood, do hereby acknowledge to have received of E. E. Starr, National Treasurer of the Cherokee Nation, the sums set opposite our names respectively, in full of our shares in the per capita distribution authorized by an Act of the National Council, dated ___MAY 3 1894___ 1894.

Names of Head, and Members of Families	Amount	To Whom Paid	Witness to Payment	Remarks
146 Bean Stick Olly	265.70	B.G. Fletcher	L B Bell	
147 " Ida	265.70	E W Buffington	J.P. Carter	*order*
148 Beanstick Becky	265.70	Beckey Beanstick	L B Bell	
149 Beanstick Aex[sic]				
149 1/2 " West.	531.40	Wutty Beanstick	L B Bell	
150 Beanstick Nannie	265.70	Nannie Beanstick	L B Bell	
151 Beanstick Mary	265.70	Mary Beanstick	L B Bell	
152 Batt Harry	265.70	Thos White guardan	L B Bell	*Tom White Guardian*
153 Batt Ellis				
154 " Akey				
155 " Susan				
156 " Jack				
157 " Sarah				
158 " So-watch-wee	1594.20	Ellis Batt	L B Bell	
159 Bigfoot Arch	~~order~~ 265.70	T.W. Triplet	L B Bell	*T.W.T. check*
160 Bigfeather Benjamin				
161 " Lucy				
162 " Betsy				
163 " John				
164 " Polly				
165 " Ben				
166 " Lydia				
167 " Money				
168 " David	2391.30	Ben Bigfeather	L B Bell	
169 Bigfeather Mitchel	265.70	Ben Bigfeather	L B Bell	
170 Bunch Alex				
171 " Eliza				
172 " Mary				
173 " Olly				
174 " Lizzie				

6

Starr Roll 1894

We, the undersigned citizens of the Cherokee Nation, by right of Cherokee blood, do hereby acknowledge to have received of E. E. Starr, National Treasurer of the Cherokee Nation, the sums set opposite our names respectively, in full of our shares in the per capita distribution authorized by an Act of the National Council, dated ____MAY 3 1894____ 1894.

	Names of Head, and Members of Families	Amount	To Whom Paid	Witness to Payment	Remarks
175	" Otter	1594.20	Alex Bunch	L B Bell	
176	Bowlin Annie	*order*			*Furguson Geo*
177	" Good Little Man	531.40	George Furgueson[sic]	L B Bell	*check*
178	Bigfeather Wash				
179	" Charlotte				
180	" Jennie				
181	" Rider	1062.80	Wash Bigfeather	L B Bell	
182	Beanstick Peggie	265.70	Peggy Beanstick	L B Bell	
183	Bunch Noah	265.70	Noah Bunch	L B Bell	
184	Batt Isaac	265.70	Christian Gulegar	L B Bell	*Gulegar Check*
185	Beaver Clem				*Creek*
	" ~~Sally~~				
186	" Chas	531.40	Clem Beaver	L B Bell	
187	Byers Nick				
188	" Ellen				
189	" Joe				
190	" Alfred	1062.80	Chas Bunch	L B Bell	
191	Bunch Charley				
192	" Nannie				
193	" James				
194	" Levi	1062.80	Chas Bunch	L B Bell	
195	Beaver William	265.70	E.S. Ellis	L B Bell	*Ellis check*
196	Bullet Nancy				
197	" Sarah				
198	" Leach	*8956*			
199	" Henry	1062.80	Nancy Bullett	L B Bell	
200	Bullett Sally	265.70	Walsh & Shutt	L B Bell	*Check W&S*
201	" Mack	265.70 *order*	R B Choate	L B Bell	*RB Choate*

7

Starr Roll 1894

We, the undersigned citizens of the Cherokee Nation, by right of Cherokee blood, do hereby acknowledge to have received of E. E. Starr, National Treasurer of the Cherokee Nation, the sums set opposite our names respectively, in full of our shares in the per capita distribution authorized by an Act of the National Council, dated _____MAY 3 1894_____ 1894.

Names of Head, and Members of Families	Amount	To Whom Paid	Witness to Payment	Remarks
202 Bearpaw Nancy				
203 Cochran Sam	531.40	Nancy Bearpaw	L B Bell	
204 Brown James				
205 " John				
206 " Cornelius				
207 " Benjamin	1062.80	Jas Brown	L B Bell	
208 Bearpaw Isaac	265.70	Isaac Bearpaw	L B Bell	
209 Batt Charles				
210 " Minnie				
211 " Gena				
212 " Frank	DEAD.			
213 " John DEAD.	1328.50	Charlie Batt	L B Bell	
214 Bowlin Martin				
215 " Annie				
216 " Fi-a-na				
217 " Jessie				
218 " Jennie				
219 " Hooley				
220 " William				
221 " Samuel				
222 " Dick				
223 " Columbus	2657.00	Martin Bowlin	L B Bell	
224 Bean Thomas	265.70	M L Paden	L B Bell	check
225 Beaver Jennie	265.70	Beaver	L B Bell	10 years old
226 Buzzard James				
227 " George	531.40	James Buzzard	L B Bell	
228 Bearpaw James	265.70	Jas Bearpaw	L B Bell	
229 Bull Sarah	265.70	Sarah Bull	L B Bell	
230 Bull Richard	265.70	Sarah Bull	L B Bell	

Starr Roll 1894

We, the undersigned citizens of the Cherokee Nation, by right of Cherokee blood, do hereby acknowledge to have received of E. E. Starr, National Treasurer of the Cherokee Nation, the sums set opposite our names respectively, in full of our shares in the per capita distribution authorized by an Act of the National Council, dated _____ MAY 3 1894 _____ 1894.

Names of Head, and Members of Families	Amount	To Whom Paid	Witness to Payment	Remarks
231 Bird John				
232 " Alcy				
233 " Jennie				
234 " Nellie	1062.80	John Bird	L B Bell	
235 Bunch Thomas				
236 " Ollie				
237 " Chu-kev-nunt				
238 " Levi				
239 " Lizzie				
240 " Tu-ni-yah	1594.20	Thos Bunch	L B Bell	
241 Brewer John				
242 " Thirza	531.40	John Brewer	L B Bell	
243 Buckner Mary				
244 " Joel M.				
245 " Sarah L.				
246 " Samuel H.	1062.80	Mary Buckner	L B Bell	
247 Buckner Martha A				
248 " Ivery C				
249 " Parthenia L	797.10	M A Buckner	L B Bell	
250 Bird Nan	265.70	Nan Bird by guardian		*Minors, Mrs. John*
251 Bird Cornelius	265.70	Tulsy guardian		*Tulsy Guardian*
252 Bowlin Nancy				
253 " Betsy	531.40	Nancy Bowlin	L B Bell	
254 Bendabout James				
255 " Lizzie	*order*			*Ellis Starr*
256 " Chi-ca-u	797.10	Starr & *(Illegible)*	L B Bell	*Check*
257 Bendabout Mose				
258 " Lucy				
259 " Blount				
260 " Lydia	1062.80	Mose Bendabout	L B Bell	

9

Starr Roll 1894

We, the undersigned citizens of the Cherokee Nation, by right of Cherokee blood, do hereby acknowledge to have received of E. E. Starr, National Treasurer of the Cherokee Nation, the sums set opposite our names respectively, in full of our shares in the per capita distribution authorized by an Act of the National Council, dated ___MAY 3 1894___ 1894.

	Names of Head, and Members of Families	Amount	To Whom Paid	Witness to Payment	Remarks
261	Bowlin Torker[sic]				
262	" Lizzie				
263	" Sargy	797.10	Tooker Bolin	L B Bell	
264	Bracket[sic] Daniel				
265	" Martha S	531.40	Danl Brackett	L B Bell	
266	" Emely L.	265.70	Emly[sic] L Bracket	L B Bell	
267	" Susan J	265.70	S J Brackett	L B Bell	
268	Broom Annie	265.70	Annie Broom	L B Bell	
269	Bowlin[sic] Annie				
270	" Mary				
271	" Tom	797.10	Annie Bowling	L B Bell	
272	Bowlin Charles				
273	" Sally				
274	" Charlotte				
275	" John	1062.80	Charles Bowlin	L B Bell	
276	Bowlin Wyly				
277	" Qua-te-na				
278	" Wolf				
279	" Sallie				
280	" Lizzie				
281	" Jackson				
282	" Jacob				
283	" Peggie	2125.60	Wyly Bowlin	L B Bell	
284	Bendabout Charles				
285	" Ti-a-na				
286	" Martha				
287	" Margaret	1062.80	Chas Bendabout	L B Bell	
288	Bracket William H	265.70	Geo Furgueson	L B Bell	Furguson check Furguson & Wilson
289	Bean Rachel A	265.70	R A Bean	L B Bell	
290	Bruner Theodore S.	265.70	Theadore Bruner	L B Bell	

10

Starr Roll 1894

We, the undersigned citizens of the Cherokee Nation, by right of Cherokee blood, do hereby acknowledge to have received of E. E. Starr, National Treasurer of the Cherokee Nation, the sums set opposite our names respectively, in full of our shares in the per capita distribution authorized by an Act of the National Council, dated _____ MAY 3 1894 _____ 1894.

Names of Head, and Members of Families	Amount	To Whom Paid	Witness to Payment	Remarks
291 Bruner Mary	265.70	Mary Bruner	L B Bell	
292 " Leathey A.	265.70	Lethe Bruner	L B Bell	
293 " John R.	265.70	John R Bruner	L B Bell	
294 " Claud	1062.80	~~Mary Bruner~~	L B Bell	
295 Bruner Isaac N				Lee Sanders
296 " Mays C				
297 " Larney H	797.10	Lee Sanders	L B Bell	order of Bruner
298 Bruner George S				
299 " Mary E	531.40	Geo S Bruner	L B Bell	
300 Bean Charles				
301 " Samuel				
302 " Pearl				
303 " Mack				
304 " Catherine	1328.50	Charles Bean	L B Bell	
305 Brown Lodusky A				
306 " Josephine				
307 " Saphronia E	797.10	L A Brown	L B Bell	
308 Bird Peter	265.70	Peter Bird	L B Bell	
309 Buffington Alex	265.70	George Furgueson	L B Bell	check Furguson
310 Bigby Margaret				on Minor Mrs. Bigby
311 Adair Lizzie	531.40	Jas Begley	L B Bell	order Guardian
312 Beaver Liddy	265.70	Lydia Beaver	L B Bell	
313 Bryson Jennie M.			order from	Minor children
314 " Mary J.			Alice Bryson	of
315 " William E.	797.10	JH Morris	L B Bell	Alice C. Bryson
316 Byers Everage	265.70	Joseph Hines	L B Bell	
317 Beanstick John	265.70	John Beanstick	L B Bell	

11

Starr Roll 1894

We, the undersigned citizens of the Cherokee Nation, by right of Cherokee blood, do hereby acknowledge to have received of E. E. Starr, National Treasurer of the Cherokee Nation, the sums set opposite our names respectively, in full of our shares in the per capita distribution authorized by an Act of the National Council, dated ____MAY 3 1894____ 1894.

	Names of Head, and Members of Families	Amount	To Whom Paid	Witness to Payment	Remarks
318	Bird				*100 yrs old*
319	" Allie	531.40	Allie Bird	L B Bell	
320	Byers Charley				
321	" Ann				
322	" Cary Ann				
323	" Ellen				
324	" James				
325	" Fannie				
326	" Ezekiel				
327	" Lizzie				
328	" Cornelia				
329	" Saphronia	2657.00	Charles Byers	L B Bell	
330	Beaver Mohawk				
331	" Washington				
332	" Mary				
333	" Lacy				
334	" Tarry				
335	" Annie				
336	" Arleach	1859.60	Mohawk Beaver	L B Bell	
337	Beaver Sarah				
338	" George				
339	" Otto				
340	" Charlotte				
341	" Charles	1328.50	Jas Beaver	L B Bell	
342	Beaver James	265.70	Jas Beaver	L B Bell	*This man belongs to family of Sarah Beaver*
343	Cloud Martha				
344	" George S.				
345	" William M.	797.10	J M Cloud	L B Bell	
346	Cloud Joseph H	265.70	J M Cloud	L B Bell	
347	Cloud Robert L				
348	" Lucy				
349	" Noah S.				
350	" Susan	1062.80	Robt L Cloud	L B Bell	

12

Starr Roll 1894

We, the undersigned citizens of the Cherokee Nation, by right of Cherokee blood, do hereby acknowledge to have received of E. E. Starr, National Treasurer of the Cherokee Nation, the sums set opposite our names respectively, in full of our shares in the per capita distribution authorized by an Act of the National Council, dated ___MAY 3 1894___ 1894.

	Names of Head, and Members of Families	Amount	To Whom Paid	Witness to Payment	Remarks
351	Coble Lou M				
352	" George R				
353	" Robert	797.10	Lou M Cable	L B Bell	
354	Cloud James L.				
355	" Sarah J.				
356	" Thomas				
357	" Fannie D.	DEAD.			
358	" James S.	1328.50	Jas L Cloud	L B Bell	
359	Cole Sut-a-wake				Known as Sutawake Beanstick
360	" Dicy				
361	" Charles				
362	" Sarah	1062.80	Sutawake Cole	L B Bell	
363	Chu-ca-late Rachel				
	" Mary	531.40	Rachel Chucalate	L B Bell	
364	Choate Eliza	265.70	Eliza Choate	L B Bell	
365	Choat[sic] Mary	265.70	Mary Choate	L B Bell	
366	Choat[sic] John	265.70	R B Choate	L B Bell	
367	Choat[sic] Richard B				
368	" Lydia	531.40	R B Choate	L B Bell	
369	Chuculate Emily	8268			
370	" Lydia	8268			
371	" Wash	797.10	Emily Chuculate	L B Bell	
372	Chuculate Wesley[sic]				
373	" Betty				
374	" Lydia				
375	" Fields				
376	" John				
377	" Shake				
378	" Blue				
379	" Che-nue-wa	2125.60	Westly Chuculate	L B Bell	
380	Christie Lucy	265.70	T W Triplet	L B Bell	Triplett check

13

Starr Roll 1894

We, the undersigned citizens of the Cherokee Nation, by right of Cherokee blood, do hereby acknowledge to have received of E. E. Starr, National Treasurer of the Cherokee Nation, the sums set opposite our names respectively, in full of our shares in the per capita distribution authorized by an Act of the National Council, dated ____MAY 3 1894____ 1894.

	Names of Head, and Members of Families	Amount	To Whom Paid	Witness to Payment	Remarks
381	Cumingdeer Isaac				
382	" Jennie				
383	" Ool-skunt-nee				*Fletcher*
384	" Tah-lou-tuske	1062.80	B J Fletcher	L B Bell	*check*
385	Cloud John E	2̶6̶3̶.̶7̶0̶	W̶a̶l̶s̶h̶ ̶&̶ ̶S̶h̶u̶t̶t̶ *John E Cloud*	L B Bell	*Walsh check*
386	Chuculate William *Walker*	265.70	Rachel Chuculate	L B Bell	*Enrolled with Rachel Chuculate*
387	Cochran Louis				
388	" Ti-a-na				
389	" Eva				
390	" William	*order*			*Sam Starr*
391	" Sunday				
392	" Mary				
393	" James				
394	" Water	2125.60	S J Starr	L B Bell	*check*
395	Cochran Columbus				
396	" Eva	883			
397	" James	797.10	Eva Cochran	L B Bell	
398	Cochran John			L B Bell	*W & Scheck*
399	" Ninnie	265.70	Ninnie Cochran	L B Bell	*C.L.Lynch*
400	Cochran Andrew				
401	" Eve				
402	" Nellie	797.10	Andrew Cochran	L B Bell	
403	Callahan Martha E				
404	" Dora I				
405	" Benjamin P				
406	" William R				
407	" James A.	1328.50	G B Callahan	L B Bell	
408	Clines William				
409	" Beckie	531.40	Wm Clines	L B Bell	

14

Starr Roll 1894

We, the undersigned citizens of the Cherokee Nation, by right of Cherokee blood, do hereby acknowledge to have received of E. E. Starr, National Treasurer of the Cherokee Nation, the sums set opposite our names respectively, in full of our shares in the per capita distribution authorized by an Act of the National Council, dated ___MAY 3 1894___ 1894.

Names of Head, and Members of Families	Amount	To Whom Paid	Witness to Payment	Remarks
410 Coon John	701			
411 " Darka	701			
412 " James				
413 " Zute				
414 " Walanute	701			
415 " Mary	1594.20	John Coon	L B Bell	
416 Canoe George				
417 " Sarah				
418 " Annie				
419 " Jennie				Fletcher
420 " Chu-cu-wee				
421 " Beaver				
422 " Otha	1859.90	*(Illegible)* Fletcher	L B Bell	check
423 Collins Thomas T				
424 " John W	531.40	T.T. Collins	L B Bell	
425 Cochran James				
426 " Betty				
427 " Tonny				
428 " Mary				
429 " Nelly				
430 " Jennie	1597.10[sic]	James Cochran	L B Bell	
431 Cochran John	265.70	John Cochran	L B Bell	
432 Crittenden Mary	265.70	Mary Crittenden	L B Bell	
433 Christie Buffalo				
434 " Akey				
435 " William				
436 " Jennie				
437 " Charles				
438 " Lilie				
439 " Jincy				
440 " George				
441 " Arch	2391.30	Buffaloe[sic] Christy	L B Bell	

15

Starr Roll 1894

We, the undersigned citizens of the Cherokee Nation, by right of Cherokee blood, do hereby acknowledge to have received of E. E. Starr, National Treasurer of the Cherokee Nation, the sums set opposite our names respectively, in full of our shares in the per capita distribution authorized by an Act of the National Council, dated ___MAY 3 1894___ 1894.

Names of Head, and Members of Families	Amount	To Whom Paid	Witness to Payment	Remarks
442 Chair Stout				
443 " Margaret				
444 " Narissie				
445 " Johnson				
446 " Ben				
447 " Levi				
448 " William J.	1859.90	Stout Chair	L B Bell	
449 Chair Samuel	265.70	Stout Chair	L B Bell	
450 Chulio Jack				
451 " Betty	*order*			*Payne*
452 " Ne-koo-to-ye				
453 " Edward				*order withdrn*
454 " Jennie	1328.50	Jack Chulio	L B Bell	*by Rogers*
455 Canoe Ellis	265.70	Ben Bigfeather *guardian*	L B Bell	*Minor. Charles Fogg Guardian*
456 Collins Ruth	265.70	Ruth Collins	L B Bell	
457 Chulio John	~~265~~.70 *order*	Geo Furguson	L B Bell	*Furguson check*
458 " Chu-cona	~~265~~.70 *order*	George Furguson	L B Bell	*" "*
459 " Betsy	~~265~~.70 *order*		L B Bell	*" "*
460 " Charlotte	265.70	E.S. Ellis	L B Bell	*Ellis check*
461 " Olly	~~265~~.70 *order*	George Furguson	L B Bell	*Furguson "*
462 Chambers George	265.70	Andrew Otterlifter *guardian*	L B Bell	*Minor Andrew orphan Otterlifter Guardian*
463 Cowart William L Sr.				
464 " Laura V.				
465 " James S.				
466 " Mary A.				
467 " William L Jr				
468 " Charles M.				
469 " Norma E.	1859.90	W.L. Cowart Jr	L B Bell	
470 Canoe Olly	265.70	Ollie Canoe	L B Bell	
471 Cochran George Sr				
472 " Betsy			L B Bell	

John Chucona Betsy & Olly
Chulio inmeakbak

16

Starr Roll 1894

We, the undersigned citizens of the Cherokee Nation, by right of Cherokee blood, do hereby acknowledge to have received of E. E. Starr, National Treasurer of the Cherokee Nation, the sums set opposite our names respectively, in full of our shares in the per capita distribution authorized by an Act of the National Council, dated ____MAY 3 1894____ 1894.

	Names of Head, and Members of Families	Amount	To Whom Paid	Witness to Payment	Remarks
473	" Sanders				
474	" Charley				
475	" Lucy	1328.50	Geo Cochran Jr	L B Bell	
476	Collins Robert E	265.70	Robt Collins	L B Bell	
477	Christie[sic] Katie				
478	" Lizzie				
479	" Jessie	797.10	Katie Christy	L B Bell	
480	Cochran Rufus				
481	" Olly				
482	" Emma				
483	" Sally				
484	" Josephine				
485	" John B	1594.60	Rufus Cochran	L B Bell	
486	Cochran George Jr	*order*			
487	" Stacy				
488	" Jack	797.10	JM Chandler & Son	J.C. Starr	*on order Sept 22, 94*
489	Christie[sic] Jackson				
490	" Nellie	531.40	Jackson Christy	L B Bell	
491	Christie[sic] Walker				
492	" Sallie	531.40	Walker Christy	L B Bell	
493	Christie Stand	265.70	*(Illegible)* Christy	L B Bell	
494	Christie George				
495	" Lucy				
496	" Katy				
497	" Bettie				
498	" Lacy				
499	" Ned				
500	" Susan	1059.90	Lucy Christy	L B Bell	
501	Cockran[sic] Russel	*order* 265.70	Walsh & Shutt	L B Bell	*W.&S. check*
502	Cloud William	265.70	Ellis Starr & E Buffington	J P Carter	*order Dec. 29 - 94*

17

Starr Roll 1894

We, the undersigned citizens of the Cherokee Nation, by right of Cherokee blood, do hereby acknowledge to have received of E. E. Starr, National Treasurer of the Cherokee Nation, the sums set opposite our names respectively, in full of our shares in the per capita distribution authorized by an Act of the National Council, dated ___MAY 3 1894___ 1894.

Names of Head, and Members of Families	Amount	To Whom Paid	Witness to Payment	Remarks
503 Christie James				
504 " Nancy				
505 " Tosker				
506 " Ailcy				
507 " Nelly				
508 " Watt				
509 " Sarah	1859.90	Nancy Christy	L B Bell	
510 Christie Stephen	265.70	Nancy Christy	L B Bell	
511 Christie Pheasant				
512 " Lucy				
513 " George	797.10	Pheasant Christy	L B Bell	
514 Christie Nancy	265.70	Pheasant Christy	L B Bell	
515 Coody Scott				T.W.T.
516 " Josie				
517 " Nellie				
518 " Riley	1062.80	T.W. Triplet	L B Bell	check
519 Christie William				
520 " Nellie				
521 " Watt				
522 " Eliza				
523 Blueduck John				Step-son of
524 Christie William	1594.20	William Christy	L B Bell	William Christie
525 Catcher Charles	265.70	Charley Catcher	L B Bell	
526 Campbell Wilson				
527 " Nancy				
528 " Maud	797.10	Wilson Campbell	L B Bell	
529 Christie Taylor				
530 " Jane				
531 " Fannie				
532 " Albert				
533 " Annie	1328.50	Taylor Christy	L B Bell	

18

Starr Roll 1894

We, the undersigned citizens of the Cherokee Nation, by right of Cherokee blood, do hereby acknowledge to have received of E. E. Starr, National Treasurer of the Cherokee Nation, the sums set opposite our names respectively, in full of our shares in the per capita distribution authorized by an Act of the National Council, dated ___MAY 3 1894___ 1894.

Names of Head, and Members of Families	Amount	To Whom Paid	Witness to Payment	Remarks
534 Christie Richard				
535 " Nancy	531.40	Richd Christy	L B Bell	
536 Carden Minnie				
537 " John				
538 " Etta				
539 " William				
540 " Ras	1328.50	John Gass	L B Bell	John Carden *order* Muskrat
541 Cloud Charles C.				
542 " Mary J.				
543 " John M.				
544 " Mattie B.				
545 " Joel B.				
546 " Caldonia				
547 " Pearl	1859.90	C C Cloud	L B Bell	
548 Chickalely[sic] Katy				
549 " Watt Killer	531.40	Katy Chickalealy	L B Bell	
550 Chuculate Consene				*Ellis*
551 " Nancy				Nancy Chuculate said to be a full blood Creek
552 " Jennie	797.10	E.E Ellis	L B Bell	Check
553 Daugherty Runabout				
554 " Lou				
555 " Walter	797.10	Runabout Daugherty	L B Bell	
556 Daugherty Sarah	265.70	Sarah Daugherty	L B Bell	
557 Daugherty[sic] Buck				
558 " Scott				
559 " Rachel	DEAD.			
560 " Callie				
561 " Cornelius	1328.50	Buck Dougherty	L B Bell	
562 Dannenberg T. Nat.				
563 " Ida				
564 " George R.				
565 " Byron				

Starr Roll 1894

We, the undersigned citizens of the Cherokee Nation, by right of Cherokee blood, do hereby acknowledge to have received of E. E. Starr, National Treasurer of the Cherokee Nation, the sums set opposite our names respectively, in full of our shares in the per capita distribution authorized by an Act of the National Council, dated ___MAY 3 1894___ 1894.

	Names of Head, and Members of Families	Amount	To Whom Paid	Witness to Payment	Remarks
566	" Jane E.	1328.50	TN Dannenberg	L B Bell	
567	Dannenberg[sic] John H.				
568	" Robert C.				
569	" Katy M.				
570	" Johnnie H.	1062.80	Anne Dannyberg[sic]	L B Bell	
571	Dannenberg[sic] Louis B.	265.70	Anne Dannyberg	L B Bell	
572	Down Water				
573	" Tia-na	531.40	Tiana Waterdown	L B Bell	
574	Doublehead Peter				
575	" Ah-na-wake				
576	" Aky				
577	" John				
578	" Nancy				
579	Canoe Peter	1594.20	Peter Doublehead	L B Bell	*minor in care of Peter Doublehead*
580	Doublehead Blackbird				
581	" Ansey				
582	" Addie				
583	" Aannie[sic]				
584	" Nancy				
585	" Jennie				
586	" Beckie				
587	" James	2125.60	Blackbird Doublehead	L B Bell	
588	Daugherty[sic] Moses[sic]				
589	" Linda				
590	" Soap				
591	" Wattie				
592	" John				
593	" Polly				
594	" George	1859.90	Mose Dougherty	L B Bell	
595	Dick William				
596	" Tu-ker	531.40	John Ratt guardian	L B Bell	*minors*
597	Dannenberg William	265.70	M L Paden	L B Bell	*Paden Check*

20

Starr Roll 1894

We, the undersigned citizens of the Cherokee Nation, by right of Cherokee blood, do hereby acknowledge to have received of E. E. Starr, National Treasurer of the Cherokee Nation, the sums set opposite our names respectively, in full of our shares in the per capita distribution authorized by an Act of the National Council, dated ____MAY 3 1894____ 1894.

Names of Head, and Members of Families	Amount	To Whom Paid	Witness to Payment	Remarks
598 Duck Ollie	265.70	Ollie Duck	L B Bell	
599 Duncan Lizzie				
600 Bird Jennie				*Same Mother, but*
601 Cochran Maggie				*different Fathers*
602 " Roach	1062.80	Lizzie Duncan	L B Bell	
603 Daniel Jennie				
604 Bird James				*Same Mother but*
605 Cornelius	797.10	Jennie Daniel	L B Bell	*different Fathers*
606 Downing Stand	265.70	Stand Downing	L B Bell	
607 Deerinwater[sic] George				
608 " Loucinda				
609 " Richard				
610 " Susie				
611 " Polly				
612 " Charley				
613 " Sarah				
614 " Thomas				
615 " John	2391.30	Geo Deerinthewater	L B Bell	
616 Deerinwater[sic] Lucy	265.70	Lucy Deerinthewater	L B Bell	
617 Doublehead Charlotte	265.70	Peter Doublehead	L B Bell	*Peter Doublehead Guardian*
618 Deerinwater[sic] John				
619 " Eliza				
620 " Charlie				
621 Rooster Polly				*Step children of*
622 " Sally	1328.50	John Deerinthewater	L B Bell	*John Deerinwater*
623 Daugherty Silk				
624 " Polly				
625 " Ella	797.10	Silk Daugherty	L B Bell	
626 Duck Lucy	265.70	Lucy Duck	L B Bell	

21

Starr Roll 1894

We, the undersigned citizens of the Cherokee Nation, by right of Cherokee blood, do hereby acknowledge to have received of E. E. Starr, National Treasurer of the Cherokee Nation, the sums set opposite our names respectively, in full of our shares in the per capita distribution authorized by an Act of the National Council, dated ___MAY 3 1894___ 1894.

Names of Head, and Members of Families	Amount	To Whom Paid	Witness to Payment	Remarks
627 Dollar David				
628 " Ceiley				
629 " Sally	797.10	Davie Dollar	L B Bell	
630 Dannenberg Louis L				
631 " William	531.40	Lewis L Danenberg[sic]	L B Bell	
632 David George	265.70	M.E. Folsom *Guardian*	L B Bell	*M.E. Folsom Guardian*
633 Daugherty Robert	265.70	Robert Daugherty	L B Bell	
634 Duck Blue	265.70	Martin Hopper	L B Bell	*check on order of (Illegible) in N.S. Penetentiary*
635 Duncan Taylor				
636 " Lydia				
637 " Joseph				
638 " John				
639 " Lynda				
640 " Nathaniel				
641 " Herbert				
642 " Sally				
643 " Emma				
644 " Jennie	2657.00	Taylor Duncan	L B Bell	
645 Duncan Martha	265.70	Martha Duncan	L B Bell	
646 Eagle William				
647 " Beckie				
648 " Ezekiel				
649 " John				
650 " Polly				
651 " George	1594.20	Wm Eagle	L B Bell	
652 Ely Thomas				
653 " Lydia				
654 " Henry				
655 " Eva				
656 " George	1328.50	Thomas Ely	L B Bell	
657 Eagle Nancy	265.70	Edward Acorn	L B Bell	

Starr Roll 1894

We, the undersigned citizens of the Cherokee Nation, by right of Cherokee blood, do hereby acknowledge to have received of E. E. Starr, National Treasurer of the Cherokee Nation, the sums set opposite our names respectively, in full of our shares in the per capita distribution authorized by an Act of the National Council, dated ___MAY 3 1894___ 1894.

Names of Head, and Members of Families	Amount	To Whom Paid	Witness to Payment	Remarks
658 Ely Buck				
659 " Ella				
660 " Taylor				
661 " Lenny				
662 " May				
663 " William	1594.20	Ely Buck	L B Bell	
664 Ely Alcy	265.70	Ollie Wane[sic]	L B Bell	Olla Wayne Guardian
665 Eagle Nancy	265.70	Ellis Starr	S.W. Mayfield	order
666 Fletcher John F.				
667 " Jennie				
668 " Mary				
669 " Nora	1062.80	JT Fletcher	L B Bell	
670 Fletcher Charlotte E				
671 " James L				
672 " Ruth L.				
673 " Robert N.				
674 " Annie	1328.50	Charlotte E Fletcher	L B Bell	
675 Furguson Allie E				
676 " John W.	531.40	Waller Furguson	L B Bell	
677 Fogg John				
678 " Lizzie				
679 " White				
680 " Nancy				
681 " Lucy				
682 Diver Ezekiel	1594.20	John Fogg	L B Bell	orphan John Fogg Guardian
683 Feather Jesse				
684 " Jennie				
685 " James	797.10	Jesse Feather	L B Bell	
686 Feather William DEAD.	265.70	Jesse Feather	L B Bell	
687 Feather Linda				
" Mack	531.40	Linda Feather	L B Bell	

23

Starr Roll 1894

We, the undersigned citizens of the Cherokee Nation, by right of Cherokee blood, do hereby acknowledge to have received of E. E. Starr, National Treasurer of the Cherokee Nation, the sums set opposite our names respectively, in full of our shares in the per capita distribution authorized by an Act of the National Council, dated ___MAY 3 1894___ 1894.

Names of Head, and Members of Families	Amount	To Whom Paid	Witness to Payment	Remarks
688 Feather Nancy				
689 " Pain				
690 " Sar-take	797.10	Nancy Feather	L B Bell	
691 Feather Sarah	265.70	Sarah Feather	L B Bell	
692 French Naked				
693 " Charlotte				
694 " Tiana				
695 " Loucinda	1062.80	Naked French	L B Bell	
696 Feather Sellout				
697 " Susan				
698 " Sally				
699 " Josia	8247			
700 " Polly	1328.50	Sellout Feather	L B Bell	
701 Feather David	265.70	Sellout Feather	L B Bell	
702 Fogg William	8240			
703 " Sarah	709 order			Furguson
704 " Nelson				
705 " Sam	1062.80	George Furguson	L B Bell	check
706 Fogg Charles				
707 " Nancy				
708 " Ely				
709 " Lidia				
710 " David	1328.50	Nancy Fogg	L B Bell	
711 Fletcher Benj G				
712 " Mary				
713 " Mag				
714 " Sarah				
715 " John B				
716 " Lorenzo				
717 " Dora				
718 " Della				
719 " Jennette				
720 " Eve	2657.00	B.G. Fletcher	L B Bell	Check

24

Starr Roll 1894

We, the undersigned citizens of the Cherokee Nation, by right of Cherokee blood, do hereby acknowledge to have received of E. E. Starr, National Treasurer of the Cherokee Nation, the sums set opposite our names respectively, in full of our shares in the per capita distribution authorized by an Act of the National Council, dated ____MAY 3 1894____ 1894.

Names of Head, and Members of Families	Amount	To Whom Paid	Witness to Payment	Remarks
721 Feather Scale[sic]				
722 " Jennie				
723 " Joshua				
724 " Beckie				
725 " George	1328.50	Scales Feather	L B Bell	
726 Feather White R.				
727 " Lula				
728 " Lee			*Lulu*	*Father dead living*
729 Gibney George	1062.80	Cynthia Feather or	L B Bell	*with Step Father*
730 Fogg Tuker	265.70	Joanna Rowe *guardian*	L B Bell	*Minor Mrs Rowe Guardian*
731 Falling Sally				
732 " Robert	531.40	Sally Falling	L B Bell	
733 Folsom Mary E	*order* 265.70	M L Paden	L B Bell	*ML Paden check*
734 Frog Thompson				
735 " Lucy				
736 " Mary				
737 " Redbird				
738 " Lizzie	1328.50	Thompson Frog	L B Bell	
739 Fogg Betsy	265.70	Eintinnel (*Sellout Feather*) *guardian*	L B Bell	
740 Fivekiller Joseph				
741 " Cleavland				
742 " Callie				
743 " Spencer	1062.80	Joseph Fivekiller	L B Bell	
744 Foster Peter				
745 " Betsy				
746 " Jack	DEAD.			
747 " Mary	1062.80	Peter Foster	L B Bell	
748 Frizley[sic] George	265.70	George Frisly	L B Bell	
749 Flute Mark	*order*			*withdrawn*
750 " Lizzie				*RB Choate*

Starr Roll 1894

We, the undersigned citizens of the Cherokee Nation, by right of Cherokee blood, do hereby acknowledge to have received of E. E. Starr, National Treasurer of the Cherokee Nation, the sums set opposite our names respectively, in full of our shares in the per capita distribution authorized by an Act of the National Council, dated ___MAY 3 1894___ 1894.

Names of Head, and Members of Families	Amount	To Whom Paid	Witness to Payment	Remarks
751 " Jessie			L B Bell	
" Rhoda	1062.80	Mark Flute		
752 Frogg Sellout				
753 " Peggie	*order*			*Ellis*
754 " Rider	797.10	E.S. Ellis	L B Bell	*Check*
755 Fisher Loucretia[sic]				
756 " Mattie				
757 " Bessie B	797.10	Lucretia Fisher	L B Bell	
758 Furguson Annie				
759 " Eda	531.40	Anne Furguson	L B Bell	
760 Freeman Nancy E.				
761 " William P.				
762 " Mary L.				
763 " Jennie				
764 " John B.				
765 " Charles K.	1594.20	N.E. Freeman	L B Bell	
766 Fishhawk George				
767 " Lizzie				
768 " Timothy				
769 " Rachel	1062.80	Geo Fishhawk	L B Bell	
770 Gonzailas John A.	265.70	Walter Six Killer *guardian*	L B Bell	*orphan W. Six Killer Guardian*
771 Gettingdown Jessie				*Ellis*
772 " Jennie	531.40	E.S. Ellis	L B Bell	*Check*
773 Gettingdown Charles				
774 " Lucy	531.40	Charles Gettingdown	L B Bell	
775 Gonzailas Caleb	265.70	Thos Horn *guardian*	L B Bell	*Minor Tom Horn Guardian*
776 Glass Lizzie	DEAD.			
777 " Lucy	724			
778 " Mary	797.10	Lizzie Glass	L B Bell	

26

Starr Roll 1894

We, the undersigned citizens of the Cherokee Nation, by right of Cherokee blood, do hereby acknowledge to have received of E. E. Starr, National Treasurer of the Cherokee Nation, the sums set opposite our names respectively, in full of our shares in the per capita distribution authorized by an Act of the National Council, dated _____ MAY 3 1894 _____ 1894.

Names of Head, and Members of Families or (Glass)	Amount	To Whom Paid	Witness to Payment	Remarks
779 Goodrich Julia				
780 " Lydia	531.40	Wm Glass	L B Bell	*father*
781 Glass Louisa		8123		
782 " Bettie				
783 " Mary				
784 " Annie	1062.80	Louisa Glass	L B Bell	
785 Glass Annie	265.70	Annie Glass	L B Bell	
786 " Lucy DEAD.	265.70	Lucy Glass D7859	L B Bell	
787 Gonzailas[sic] Spencer	265.70	Spencer Gonzales	L B Bell	
788 Glass Rufus	265.70	John Deerinthewater	*husband of Lizzie Deer-water* L B Bell	*Minor Lizzie Deerinwater Mother*
789 Glass William				
790 " Mary				
791 " Nancy				
792 " Stephen				
793 " Sallie				
794 " Lizzie	1594.20	Wm Glass	L B Bell	
795 Glass Joshua				
796 " Anna	531.40	Joshua Glass	L B Bell	
797 Guthery[sic] Martha J				
798 " Oscar				
799 " Jesse				
800 " Lorenzo L.	1062.80	C P Guthrie	L B Bell	
801 Gonzailas Levi				
802 " Mary	531.40	Levi Gonzales	L B Bell	
803 Glass John	265.70	John Glass	L B Bell	
804 Goodrich John	265.70	John Goodrich	L B Bell	
805 Goback Lydia	265.70	Lydia Goback	L B Bell	
806 Glass Thomas	265.70	Thompson Frogg *guardian*	L B Bell	*Step-son of Thompson Frog*

27

Starr Roll 1894

We, the undersigned citizens of the Cherokee Nation, by right of Cherokee blood, do hereby acknowledge to have received of E. E. Starr, National Treasurer of the Cherokee Nation, the sums set opposite our names respectively, in full of our shares in the per capita distribution authorized by an Act of the National Council, dated ___MAY 3 1894___ 1894.

	Names of Head, and Members of Families	Amount	To Whom Paid	Witness to Payment	Remarks
807	Glory Martha				
808	" Charles				
809	" Henry	797.10	Martha Glory	L B Bell	
810	Goss Jane B.				
811	" George O.				
812	" Noah O.	797.10	John Goss	L B Bell	
813	Goff[sic] William				
814	" Mary L.				
815	" John V.				
816	" Pearl				
817	" Ruth				
818	" Ella S.				
819	" Kinney	849.90[sic]	William Gott	L B Bell	
820	Groundhog Annie	265.70	Annie Groundhog	L B Bell	
821	Guthrie Calvin				
822	" Oscar				
823	" Margaret				
824	" Lawrence	1062.80	Calvin Guthrie	L B Bell	
825	Glass Caroline				
826	" Ready	*order*			Fletcher
827	" Betty				
828	" Cole	1062.80	B.G. Fletcher	L B Bell	Check
829	Guthery[sic] Walter D	265.70	Walter Guthrie	L B Bell	
830	" Elizabeth				
831	Tweedle Florence M	531.40	Elizabeth Guthrie	L B Bell	minor child of Walter D. Guthery
832	Glory Richard				
833	" William P.	531.40	Richd Glory	L B Bell	
834	Hughes Gracie A.				
835	" Samuel L.				
836	" Laura E.				
837	" Lizzie A.				
838	" Louis C.				

Starr Roll 1894

We, the undersigned citizens of the Cherokee Nation, by right of Cherokee blood, do hereby acknowledge to have received of E. E. Starr, National Treasurer of the Cherokee Nation, the sums set opposite our names respectively, in full of our shares in the per capita distribution authorized by an Act of the National Council, dated ____MAY 3 1894____ 1894.

	Names of Head, and Members of Families	Amount	To Whom Paid	Witness to Payment	Remarks
839	" George H.				
840	" James H				
841	" Jane	2125.60	S.C. Hughes	L B Bell	
842	Holland Noah S.				
843	" Julia A.	DEAD.			
844	" Georgia A.				
845	" Florence L.				
846	" Laura M.				
847	" Isaac J.				
848	" Mary B.	1859.90	Noah S Holland	L B Bell	
849	Holland John A.				
850	" Ada	531.40	John A Holland	L B Bell	
851	Heaven Alexander				
852	" Aggie				
853	" William	*order*			*Fletcher*
854	" James				
855	" Stephen	1328.50	B G Fletcher	L B Bell	*Check*
856	Holt Charles	265.70	Charles Holt	Henry Eiffert	
857	Humanstriker Jennie	265.70	Jennie Humanstriker	L B Bell	
858	Holland Mary E.	265.70	Mary Holland	L B Bell	
859	" Lillie B.	265.70	I H Zebra	L B Bell	*husband of Lilly B Holland*
860	" Ida	265.70	James Halford	L B Bell	*husband of Ida Holland*
861	" William H.	265.70	Mary Holland	L B Bell	
862	Holland Dolphus	265.70	J.D. Harlan	L B Bell	
863	Hooper Ailsey				
864	" Turkey				
865	" John	797.10	Ailsey Hooper	L B Bell	
866	Hughes Robert	265.70	Robt Hughes	L B Bell	
867	Hannah Julia				
868	" Lee H.				

Starr Roll 1894

We, the undersigned citizens of the Cherokee Nation, by right of Cherokee blood, do hereby acknowledge to have received of E. E. Starr, National Treasurer of the Cherokee Nation, the sums set opposite our names respectively, in full of our shares in the per capita distribution authorized by an Act of the National Council, dated ___MAY 3 1894___ 1894.

	Names of Head, and Members of Families	Amount	To Whom Paid	Witness to Payment	Remarks
869	" William T				
870	" Stella M.	1062.80	John W Hannah	L B Bell	
871	Hugh Charles	635.70 265.70	Charles Hughes	L B Bell	
872	Harrison Celey				
873	" Claud				
874	" Benjamin				
875	" Jessie				
876	" Otto				
877	More Lovely	1594.20	Cecelia Harrison	L B Bell	Son of Celey Harrison
878	Hunt Lucy	265.70	WE Johnson Adm	L B Bell	on order Dead
879	Hewin John				
880	" Peggie				
881	" Susan				
882	" Dobson	order 8432			Fletcher
883	" Loucinda	8432			
884	" Lou. A.	1594.20	B.G. Fletcher	L B Bell	check
885	Holland Lydia				
886	" Isabella W.				
887	" Benjamin H.				
888	" Flora S.	1062.80	Lydia Holland	L B Bell	
889	Hardbarger John				
890	" Lila				
891	" Louis				
892	" Johnson	1062.80	John Hardbarger	L B Bell	
893	Henson Jennie				
894	" Drucilla				
895	" John M.				
896	" Thomas	order			Fletcher
897	" Sallie				
898	" Jackey	DEAD.			
899	" Johnie				
900	" Charlotte	2125.60	B.G. Fletcher	L B Bell	check

Starr Roll 1894

We, the undersigned citizens of the Cherokee Nation, by right of Cherokee blood, do hereby acknowledge to have received of E. E. Starr, National Treasurer of the Cherokee Nation, the sums set opposite our names respectively, in full of our shares in the per capita distribution authorized by an Act of the National Council, dated _____ MAY 3 1894 _____ 1894.

	Names of Head, and Members of Families	Amount	To Whom Paid	Witness to Payment	Remarks
901	Hand William				
902	" Lilly				
903	" Thomas	797.10	Wm Hand	L B Bell	
904	Hooper Di-ha-lane				
905	" Lucy				
906	" Jack				
907	" Mary				
908	" James				
909	" Bud				
910	" Louis	1859.90	Di ha lane Hooper	L B Bell	
911	Hooper John	265.70	Di ha lane Hooper	L B Bell	
912	Holmes James				
913	" Ailcy				
914	" Allen				
915	" Drum				
916	" Mary				
917	" Bar				
918	" Sowin	1859.90	J B Lynch	L B Bell	*on order*
919	Hopper Martin				
920	" Lucy				
921	" Olley				
922	" Peggie				
923	Rat William	1328.50	Martin Hopper	L B Bell	*Living with Martin Hopper*
924	Housebug John				
925	" Lizzie				
926	" Ruth				
927	" Bettie				
928	" Johnson				
929	" Samuel	1594.20	John Housebug	L B Bell	
930	Hummingbird Thompson				
931	" Daniel				
932	" James	797.10	Thompson Hummingbird	L B Bell	

31

Starr Roll 1894

We, the undersigned citizens of the Cherokee Nation, by right of Cherokee blood, do hereby acknowledge to have received of E. E. Starr, National Treasurer of the Cherokee Nation, the sums set opposite our names respectively, in full of our shares in the per capita distribution authorized by an Act of the National Council, dated ___MAY 3 1894___ 1894.

Names of Head, and Members of Families	Amount	To Whom Paid	Witness to Payment	Remarks
933 Horn Thomas				
934 " Minerva				
935 " Clyde				
936 " John	1062.80	Thos Horn	L B Bell	
937 Hannah[sic] Mary				
938 " William P.				
939 " Lillie B.				
940 " Mary E.				
941 " John				
942 " Doney				
943 " Hettie	1659.90[sic]	A N Hanna	L B Bell	
944 Hunter Lizzie				*minor child of*
945 Fogg John	531.40	Lizzie Hunter	L B Bell	*Lizzie Hunter*
946 Harp Sarah J				
947 " Ellis				
948 " Maggie				
949 " Leroy				
950 " Annie				
951 " Ruth				
952 " Floyd	1859.90	S.J. Harp	L B Bell	
953 Humanstriker Saky				
954 " Lizzie	531.40	Wm Humanstriker	L B Bell	
955 Humanstriker George				
956 " Mary				
957 " Katie	797.10	Geo Humanstriker	L B Bell	
958 Hines Cynthia				
959 " Rocksy				
960 " Joseph				
961 " Mary B.				
962 Neighbors Isaac				*Children of*
963 Lowdermilk Sonewall[sic]	1062.80	Joseph Hines	L B Bell	*Cynthia Hines*
964 Humminbird[sic] Annie	265.70	Annie Hummingbird	L B Bell	

We, the undersigned citizens of the Cherokee Nation, by right of Cherokee blood, do hereby acknowledge to have received of E. E. Starr, National Treasurer of the Cherokee Nation, the sums set opposite our names respectively, in full of our shares in the per capita distribution authorized by an Act of the National Council, dated _____MAY 3 1894_____ 1894.

Names of Head, and Members of Families	Amount	To Whom Paid	Witness to Payment	Remarks
965 Housebug Henry				
966 " Sarah				
967 " Ellen				
968 Samuel	1062.80	Blue Housebug	L B Bell	*on order*
969 Holland Lizzie				
970 " Mary				
971 " Lou				
972 " Benjamin W.				
973 " Henry L.	1328.50	A.E. Holland	L B Bell	
974 Hooper Young S.	265.70	Y S Hooper	L B Bell	
975 Hooper Waste DEAD.	265.70	*D1732 by Nate Adair* J B Welch DEAD Henry Eiffert		
976 Howard George A.				
977 " Cicero				
978 " Louis	797.10	G A Howard	L B Bell	
979 Holland Alfred B.				
980 " Felix N.				
981 " Thomas E.				
982 " Maggie A.				
983 " John A.				
984 " Mary C.				
985 " William P. DEAD.	1859.50	A B Holland	L B Bell	
986 Humanstriker William	265.70	Wᵐ Humanstriker	L B Bell	
987 Holsom Rachel	265.70	R B Choate	L B Bell	*on order*
988 Ice William	*order* 265.70	E S Ellis	L B Bell	*check*
989 Ice Louis	*order* 265.70	R B Choate	L B Bell	*check* R.B. Choate
990 Justus John Sr.				*B.G.F.*
991 " Betsy				
992 " Molly	*order*			
993 " Olly	1062.80	B G Fletcher	L B Bell	*check*

Starr Roll 1894

We, the undersigned citizens of the Cherokee Nation, by right of Cherokee blood, do hereby acknowledge to have received of E. E. Starr, National Treasurer of the Cherokee Nation, the sums set opposite our names respectively, in full of our shares in the per capita distribution authorized by an Act of the National Council, dated ___MAY 3 1894___ 1894.

Names of Head, and Members of Families	Amount	To Whom Paid	Witness to Payment	Remarks
994 Johnson Cora E.	265.70	John Johnson	L B Bell	
995 Johnson Thomas				
996 " Maud				
997 " Winnie V.				
998 " Lillie E.	1062.80	Maud Johnson	L B Bell	
999 Johnson Alsy A				
1000 " Julia A.				
1001 " James N.	797.10	Ailsy Johnson	L B Bell	
1002 Johnson George W.				
1003 " Cherokee C.				
1004 " Alla L				
1005 " Bula M.				
1006 " Bessie	1328.50	Geo Johnson	L B Bell	
1007 Jones Mary	265.70	Mary Jones	L B Bell	
1008 John Long	265.70	Lucinda Paden *guardian*	L B Bell	100 yrs old. *Loucinda Paden Guardian* *Dorinda Johnson is a daughte*
1009 Johnson Dorinda	265.70	B.G. Fletcher	J.P. Carter	*George H. Johnson. Mother a wi* *woman living in Coo Dist. and* *married to one Lee.* by orde
1010 Jess Susan	265.70	Susan Jess	L B Bell	
1011 Johnson William	265.70	Candy Adair *guardian*	L B Bell	*minor Candy* *Adair Guardian*
1012 Jones Reader				
1013 " Lizzie				
1014 " Samuel				
1015 " William				
1016 " Cobb				
1017 " John				
1018 " Maggie				
1019 " Elmira				
1020 " Jennie	2391.30	Reader Jones	L B Bell	
1021 Jones Johnson	265.70	Reader Jones *guardian*	L B Bell	

34

Starr Roll 1894

We, the undersigned citizens of the Cherokee Nation, by right of Cherokee blood, do hereby acknowledge to have received of E. E. Starr, National Treasurer of the Cherokee Nation, the sums set opposite our names respectively, in full of our shares in the per capita distribution authorized by an Act of the National Council, dated ____MAY 3 1894____ 1894.

	Names of Head, and Members of Families	Amount	To Whom Paid	Witness to Payment	Remarks
1022	Johnson George H.				
1023	" Elenor	531.40	G H Johnson	L B Bell	
1024	Justus[sic] John Jr.	265.70	Betsey Justice	L B Bell	*mother of John Justice*
1025	Justus Arch				
1026	" Lydia	*order*			*Ellis*
1027	" Watt				
1028	" Alsey	1062.80	E.C. Ellis	L B Bell	*check*
1029	Johnson William E.				
1030	" Lucy				
1031	" Thomas E.				
1032	" John A.				
1033	" Mary D.				
1034	" George A.				
1035	" Mays				
1036	" Cicero				
1037	" Lucy	2391.30	W E Johnson	L B Bell	
1038	Johnson Whitetobacco	265.70	BG Fletcher	Henry Eiffert	*Stepson of David Sanders*
1039	Jones Jennie				
1040	" Joseph	531.40	Jennie Jones	L B Bell	
1041	Jonah Ezekiel	265.70	Ezekiel Jonah	L B Bell	
1042	Jones La-what-tee	265.70	Sulteesky Ezekiel *or Sam* *guardian* L B Bell		*orphan Sulteskee Sam, Guardian*
1043	Johnson Martha A.				
1044	" Joseph R.				
1045	" William O.				
1046	" James B.				
1047	" Minnie L.				
1048	" John H.				
1049	" Margaret E.				
1050	" Jesse				
1051	" Annie B.				
1052	" Lucy M.	2657.00	Sam[l] L Johnson	L B Bell	

35

Starr Roll 1894

We, the undersigned citizens of the Cherokee Nation, by right of Cherokee blood, do hereby acknowledge to have received of E. E. Starr, National Treasurer of the Cherokee Nation, the sums set opposite our names respectively, in full of our shares in the per capita distribution authorized by an Act of the National Council, dated ___MAY 3 1894___ 1894.

	Names of Head, and Members of Families	Amount	To Whom Paid	Witness to Payment	Remarks
1053	Killer Sarah				
1054	" Annie				
1055	" Katie	797.10	Sarah Killer	L B Bell	
1056	Killer Rollin	265.70	Rollin Killer	L B Bell	
1057	Keys Williamson R.				
1058	" Richard M.				
1059	" Maderson T.				
1060	" George A.				
1061	" Lorenzo D.				
1062	" Clara A.				
1063	" Walter C.	1859.90	W R Keys	L B Bell	
1064	Killer Alice				*child of Alice*
1065	Gonzailes Ella	531.40	Alice Killer	L B Bell	*Killer*
1066	Killer Lila	265.70	Lila Killer	L B Bell	
1067	Ketcher Charles				
1068	" Ann				
1069	" Lewis				
1070	" Rebecka				
1071	" John				
1072	" Betsey				
1073	" George				
1074	" Mary	2125.60	Charles Ketcher	L B Bell	
1075	Keith Kattie[sic]				
1076	" Annie				
1077	" James				
1078	" Johnson				
1079	" Soldier				
1080	McKee Eddie	1594.20	Katie Keith	L B Bell	*Infant child of Annie Keith*
1081	Keith Sarah				*Infant of Sarah Keith*
1082	Christie Stand	531.40	Sarah Keith	L B Bell	

Starr Roll 1894

We, the undersigned citizens of the Cherokee Nation, by right of Cherokee blood, do hereby acknowledge to have received of E. E. Starr, National Treasurer of the Cherokee Nation, the sums set opposite our names respectively, in full of our shares in the per capita distribution authorized by an Act of the National Council, dated ___MAY 3 1894___ 1894.

	Names of Head, and Members of Families	Amount	To Whom Paid	Witness to Payment	Remarks
1083	Kelley Sarah A.				
1084	" Sarah S.				
1085	" George W.				
1086	" Nota				
1087	" Mays				
1088	" Addie	1594.20	J N Kelly	L B Bell	
1089	Killiniger[sic] Petter[sic]				
1090	" Jennie				
1091	" Beckie				
1092	" Sarah				J B Lynch
1093	" Thomas				
1094	" Akey	1594.20	John B Lynch	L B Bell	check

****

(The letter below was inserted in the logbook before the page containing Thompson Leech #1095 and was originally handwritten and is typed as given.)

Flint C.N.I.T.

August 1st, 1894

Hon E. E. Starr   Dear Sir

I Let George Furgerson have my order or claim to draw my Strip money and I found it out he was cheating me and Sr I with draw that order & draw the money my sewlf and I will pay George what I owe him.

So you will Return the order to me

Thompson Leach

****

		Amount	To Whom Paid	Witness to Payment	Remarks
1095	Leech[sic] Thompson	265.70	Thompson Leach	L B Bell	Furguson
1096	" Ar-na-wake	265.70	Thompson Leach	L B Bell	
1097	" Henry	265.70	Thompson Leach	L B Bell	Furguson
1098	" Willie	265.70	Thompson Leach	L B Bell	
1099	" Watt	265.70	Thompson Leach	L B Bell	

1100	Lynch Cicero L.
1101	" Nancy E.
1102	" Charlotte E.

Starr Roll 1894

We, the undersigned citizens of the Cherokee Nation, by right of Cherokee blood, do hereby acknowledge to have received of E. E. Starr, National Treasurer of the Cherokee Nation, the sums set opposite our names respectively, in full of our shares in the per capita distribution authorized by an Act of the National Council, dated ___MAY 3 1894___ 1894.

Names of Head, and Members of Families	Amount	To Whom Paid	Witness to Payment	Remarks
1103 " Thomas S.				
1104 " Mary B.	DEAD.			
1105 " Joseph N.	1594.20	Nancy Lynch	L B Bell	
1106 Long Bird				
1107 " Jennie				
1108 " Ned				
1109 " Martha				*Ellis*
1110 " Mollie				
1111 " Samuel				
1112 " Sallie				
1113 " Annie	2125.60	E.S. Ellis	L B Bell	*check*
1114 Long Jack	265.70	Jack Long	L B Bell	
				Smith Long was sent to Detroit I am under the
1115 Long Smith	265.70	E S Ellis	L B Bell *check*	*impression he is dead or there is something wrong about it.*
1116 Lee Mary M				
1117 " Leila M.				
1118 " Snowden L.				
1119 " Ambrose E.				
1120 " James Allen	1328.50	Westly[sic] Lee	L B Bell	
1121 Lemaster Joseph	265.70	Jo Lemaster	L B Bell	
1122 Liver John				
1123 " Lydia				
1124 " Benjamin				
1125 " Lula				
1126 " Lizzie				
1127 " John	1594.20	John Liver	L B Bell	
1128 Locust Margaret				
1129 " Nancy				
1130 " William	797.10	Margaret Locust	L B Bell	
1131 Locust Nawhoo				
1132 " Ida				
1133 " Joseph				
1134 " Kah-whe				

Starr Roll 1894

We, the undersigned citizens of the Cherokee Nation, by right of Cherokee blood, do hereby acknowledge to have received of E. E. Starr, National Treasurer of the Cherokee Nation, the sums set opposite our names respectively, in full of our shares in the per capita distribution authorized by an Act of the National Council, dated ____MAY 3 1894____ 1894.

Names of Head, and Members of Families	Amount	To Whom Paid	Witness to Payment	Remarks
1135 Glass Peggie	1328.50	Ida Locust	L B Bell	
1136 Locust Jess	9272 265.70	Ida Locust	L B Bell	
1137 Lassley Samuel	265.70	Silk Daugherty guadan[sic]	L B Bell	minor Silk Daugherty Guardian
1138 Long Joseph	265.70	Alex Long guadan[sic]	L B Bell	minor Alex Long Guardian
1139 Littlejohn Ada S.	265.70	N B Littlejohn	L B Bell	
1140 Lynch John	265.70	J B Lynch	L B Bell	
1141 Lynch Josie B	265.70	Josie B Lynch	L B Bell	
1142 Leach Mary				
1143 " Tooker	order			E.C. Thompson check
1144 " Richard	797.10	E C Thompson	L B Bell	
1145 Lemaster Narcissas				
1146 " Edward				
1147 " William				
1148 " Curtis				
1149 " Lizzie				
1150 " May				
1151 " Nellie	1859.90	John Lemaster	L B Bell	
1152 Locust Sand				
1153 " Susan				C Gulager check
1154 " Henry	797.10	Christian Gulager	L B Bell	
1155 Locust Joseph				
1156 " Susan	531.40	John Scott guadan[sic]	L B Bell	
1157 Littlejohn Lida	265.70	Jas Bigby	L B Bell	on order from Mrs Margaret Bigby
1158 Liver Chulio				
1159 " Eliza				
1160 " Bettie				
1161 " Jennie				
1162 " John				

Starr Roll 1894

We, the undersigned citizens of the Cherokee Nation, by right of Cherokee blood, do hereby acknowledge to have received of E. E. Starr, National Treasurer of the Cherokee Nation, the sums set opposite our names respectively, in full of our shares in the per capita distribution authorized by an Act of the National Council, dated ___MAY 3 1894___ 1894.

	Names of Head, and Members of Families	Amount	To Whom Paid	Witness to Payment	Remarks
1163	" Taylor				
1164	" Katie				
1165	" Emma				
1166	" Mary	2391.30	Chulio Liver	L B Bell	
1167	Liver Jackson	265.70	Chulio Liver	L B Bell	
1168	Liver Darka	265.70	Chulio Liver	L B Bell	
1169	Liver Thomas				
1170	" Eliza				
1171	" Cheke-a	797.10	Tho⁵ Liver	L B Bell	
1172	Liver George	order 265.70	E S Ellis	L B Bell	*Ellis check*
1173	Lee Tu-ny	265.70	Ollie Beanstick adm	L B Bell	
1174	Liver Charlotte				*Infant child of*
1175	Goodrich Jacob	531.40	Charlotte Liver	L B Bell	*Charlotte Liver*
1176	Littlejohn Narcena				
1177	" May				
1178	" Lela				
1179	" Felix E.	1062.80	N B Littlejohn	L B Bell	
1180	Miller Nancy				
1181	" John H.				
1182	" Joseph M.				
1183	" Nancy	1062.80	Nancy Miller	L B Bell	
1184	Muskrat Dorcas[sic]	265.70	Darcus Muskrat	L B Bell	*(old) Living with family of Taylor Duncan*
1185	McLemore Samuel	265.70	Samuel McLemore	J P Carter	*Nov 7/94*
1186	Mankiller Jacob				
1187	" Susan				
1188	" Crabgrass				
1189	" Chu-con-a-lus-ka				
1190	" Lucy	1328.50	Jake Mankiller	L B Bell	

40

Starr Roll 1894

We, the undersigned citizens of the Cherokee Nation, by right of Cherokee blood, do hereby acknowledge to have received of E. E. Starr, National Treasurer of the Cherokee Nation, the sums set opposite our names respectively, in full of our shares in the per capita distribution authorized by an Act of the National Council, dated ___ MAY 3 1894 ___ 1894.

Names of Head, and Members of Families	Amount	To Whom Paid	Witness to Payment	Remarks
1191 Mankiller Ely				
1192 " Nannie				
1193 " Jananna				
1194 " George				
1195 " Ailcy	1328.50	Nannie Mankiller	L B Bell	
1196 McKee William J.	265.70	Adda E McKee	L B Bell	
1197 " Adda E.	265.70	Adda E McKee	L B Bell	
1198 " Joe Rasmus	265.70	Adda E McKee	L B Bell	
1199 " Alfred C.	265.70	Adda E McKee	L B Bell	
1200 " George D	265.70	Adda E McKee	L B Bell	
1201 " Johnie T	265.70	Adda E McKee	L B Bell	
1202 " Pearl	265.70	Adda E McKee	L B Bell	
1203 " Cadett	265.70	Adda E McKee	L B Bell	
1204 " Sequoyah	265.70	Phoebe Marrs M. M. Fouts in guardianship	L B Bell	
1205 " Thomas V.	2657.00	Adda E McKee	L B Bell	
1206 McKee William R.	265.70	W^m R McKee	L B Bell	
1207 McKee Florence S	265.70	Florence McKee	L B Bell	
1208 Muskrat Nancy				
1209 " William				
1210 " Charles	797.10	Nancy Muskrat	L B Bell	
1211 Moore Fanny				
1212 " William A.				
1213 " Charles T.				
1214 " Mary N.				
1215 " Albert S.				
1216 " Lizzie				
1217 " Edwin C.				
1218 " Callie A.				
1219 " (Illegible) C.	2391.30	Smith Moore	L B Bell	
1220 Moore Mary E.				
1221 " Walter T.				
1222 " Alice M.				
1223 " Charles E.				
1224 " Jessie J.				

41

Starr Roll 1894

We, the undersigned citizens of the Cherokee Nation, by right of Cherokee blood, do hereby acknowledge to have received of E. E. Starr, National Treasurer of the Cherokee Nation, the sums set opposite our names respectively, in full of our shares in the per capita distribution authorized by an Act of the National Council, dated _____ MAY 3 1894 _____ 1894.

	Names of Head, and Members of Families	Amount	To Whom Paid	Witness to Payment	Remarks
1225	" Dora	1594.20	Charles Moore	L B Bell	
1226	McLemore French				
1227	" Julia				
1228	" Thomas				
1229	" Sarah				
1230	" Lugy				
1231	" Winchester				
1232	" Robert				
1233	" Lizzie				
1234	" John	2391.30	Julia McLemore	L B Bell	
1235	Muskrat Chickaleele[sic]				
1236	" Peggie				
1237	" Joseph				
1238	" Henry				
1239	" Richard				
1240	" Mark	1594.20	Chickaleelee Muskrat	L B Bell	
1241	Miller John W.				
1242	" Louvina				
1243	" Ida M.				
1244	" William H				
1245	" Joseph				
1246	" Nate B.				
1247	" Frank	1859.90	John W Miller	L B Bell	
1248	Miller Cornelius				
1249	" John				
1250	" Nora B	*order*			Sam Starr check
1251	" George W.	1062.80	S.J. Starr	L B Bell	
1252	Muskrat Maggie	265.70	J M Chandler & Son	L B Bell	J.M.C. & S. check
1253	McLemore Mary	265.70	Mary McLemore	L B Bell	
1254	Morris John				
1255	" Annie				
1256	" Sally				
1257	" George				

Starr Roll 1894

We, the undersigned citizens of the Cherokee Nation, by right of Cherokee blood, do hereby acknowledge to have received of E. E. Starr, National Treasurer of the Cherokee Nation, the sums set opposite our names respectively, in full of our shares in the per capita distribution authorized by an Act of the National Council, dated _____ MAY 3 1894 _____ 1894.

	Names of Head, and Members of Families	Amount	To Whom Paid	Witness to Payment	Remarks
1258	" Rufus				
1259	" Joseph	1594.20	Annie Morris	L B Bell	
1260	Mankiller William				
1261	" Nancy				
1262	" Lizzie				
1263	" Lucy				
1264	" Cynthia				
1265	" Bessie	1594.20	Wm Mankiller	L B Bell	
1266	Mink Nancy	265.70	Nancy Mink	L B Bell	
1267	McLemore George				
1268	" Lizzie				
1269	" John	797.10	Lizzie McLemore	L B Bell	
1270	Morris Joseph H.				
1271	" Mark D.				
1272	" Minnie E.				
1273	" Willie A.	1062.80	J H Morris	L B Bell	
1274	Morris Wilson E.				
1275	" Polly				
1276	" Lee				
1277	" Oasie E.				
1278	" Pearl M.				
1279	" John A.				
1280	" Jessie E.	1859.90	W E Morris	L B Bell	
1281	Morris Mary A	265.70	M A Morris	L B Bell	
1282	Muskrat Jincy	265.70	David Muskrat Adm	L B Bell	
1283	McLemore William				
1284	" Eliza Arby				
1285	" Mary				
1286	" Annie				
1287	" Thomas				
1288	" Levi				
1289	" Wut				

Starr Roll 1894

We, the undersigned citizens of the Cherokee Nation, by right of Cherokee blood, do hereby acknowledge to have received of E. E. Starr, National Treasurer of the Cherokee Nation, the sums set opposite our names respectively, in full of our shares in the per capita distribution authorized by an Act of the National Council, dated ___MAY 3 1894___ 1894.

	Names of Head, and Members of Families	Amount	To Whom Paid	Witness to Payment	Remarks
1290	" Richard	2125.60	Arby McLemore	L B Bell	
1291	Marrs Benjamin ⎤				
1292	" Annie ⎦ *dead*				
1293	" David	7465			
1294	" Richard	7465			
1295	" Katy	7465			
1296	" Sarah	7465			
1297	" Lizzie *Dead*	1859.90	Benj Marrs	L B Bell	
1298	Marrs Charles	265.70	Benj Marrs	L B Bell	*father*
1299	Muskrat David				
1300	" Polly				
1301	" Lizzie	797.10	Polly Muskrat	L B Bell	
1302	Muskrat John	265.70	Polly Muskrat	L B Bell	*minor*
1303	Morris Lou C.	265.70	L C Morris	L B Bell	
1304	Morris Gideon F	265.70	G F Morris	L B Bell	
1305	Miller Alfred	265.70	Lucinda Ross	L B Bell	
1306	Murphy Katy				
1307	" Jennie				
1308	" Katy	930			
1309	" Lydia				
1310	" John				
1311	" Lugi				
1312	" William				
1313	" Emma *a2⁸*	2125.60	Katy Murphy	L B Bell	
1314	Mink Sarah				
1315	" Charles				
1316	" Ellen				
1317	" William				
1318	" Silk				
1319	" Mary	1594.20	Sarah Mink	L B Bell	

44

Starr Roll 1894

We, the undersigned citizens of the Cherokee Nation, by right of Cherokee blood, do hereby acknowledge to have received of E. E. Starr, National Treasurer of the Cherokee Nation, the sums set opposite our names respectively, in full of our shares in the per capita distribution authorized by an Act of the National Council, dated ____MAY 3 1894____ 1894.

Names of Head, and Members of Families	Amount	To Whom Paid	Witness to Payment	Remarks
1320 Mink Candy				
1321 " Charlotte				
1322 " George				
1323 " Martha				
1324 " Eva				
1325 " Lizzie				
1326 " Josie	1859.90	Candy Mink	L B Bell	
1327 Mankiller Arch				
1328 " Eliza	531.40	Arch Mankiller	L B Bell	
1329 Mankiller Annie				
1330 Bendabout Katy	531.40	Annie Mankiller	L B Bell	*Daughter of Mose Bendabout. Care of Annie Mankiller.*
1331 Nofire Jessee[sic]				
1332 " Jane				
1333 " Annie				
1334 " Allen				
1335 " Andy				
1336 " James				
1337 " Nancy	1859.90	Jess Nofire	L B Bell	
1338 Nofire John	265.70	Jess Nofire	L B Bell	
1339 Nofire Charles				
1340 " Lizzie				
1341 " Mollie				
1342 " Jack	1062.80	Lizzie Nofire	L B Bell	
1343 Noisywater Alia				
1344 " Chowin				
1345 " Ailcy	797.10	Alia Noisywater	L B Bell	
1346 Ned John	265.70	Ben Bigfeather	L B Bell	
1347 Noisywater John	265.70	John Noisywater	L B Bell	
1348 Nakedhead John	265.70	Ida Locust	L B Bell	

Starr Roll 1894

We, the undersigned citizens of the Cherokee Nation, by right of Cherokee blood, do hereby acknowledge to have received of E. E. Starr, National Treasurer of the Cherokee Nation, the sums set opposite our names respectively, in full of our shares in the per capita distribution authorized by an Act of the National Council, dated ___MAY 3 1894___ 1894.

	Names of Head, and Members of Families	Amount	To Whom Paid	Witness to Payment	Remarks
1349	Ned Polly				*Payne*
1350	" Scott	*order*			*withdrawn*
1351	" Annie				
1352	" William	1062.80	Polly Ned	L B Bell	
1353	Nakedhead Bear				
1354	" Lizzie				
1355	" Thomas				
1356	Hewin Levi				*Step children of*
1357	Sevenstarr Jennie	1328.50	Bear Nakedhead	L B Bell	*Bear Nakedhead*
1358	Nakedhead Flea				
1359	" Linda				
1360	" Ar-qua-take				
1361	Miller Rufus	1062.80	Flea Nakedhead	L B Bell	
1362	Nakedhead				*Son of James Nakedhead*
1363	" Jack	531.40	Nakedhead	L B Bell	*Tahlequah Dist.*
1364	Otterlifter Andrew				
1365	" Susan	531.40	Andrew Otterlifter	L B Bell	
1366	Osage Sarah	265.70	Charley Thrower	S.W. Mayfield	*Admist.*
1367	" Alcy	265.70	Alcy Osage	L B Bell	
1368	" Lucy	265.70	Charley Thrower	S W Mayfield	*Guardian*
1369	Cuculate[sic] Wesley	265.70	Alcy Osage	L B Bell	
1370	Owl Nancy				
1371	" Sarah				
1372	" Louis				
1373	" Charlotte				
1374	" Charles	1328.50	Nancy Owl	L B Bell	
1375	Pritchet Thomas	487			*Minor children*
1376	" Ice	487			*Johnson Simmons*
1377	Skiff Ollie				*Guardian of these*
1378	Simmons Henry	1062.80	Johnson Simmons	L B Bell	*four children*
1379	Poorbear Charles				
1380	" Nelly				

46

Starr Roll 1894

We, the undersigned citizens of the Cherokee Nation, by right of Cherokee blood, do hereby acknowledge to have received of E. E. Starr, National Treasurer of the Cherokee Nation, the sums set opposite our names respectively, in full of our shares in the per capita distribution authorized by an Act of the National Council, dated ____MAY 3 1894____ 1894.

Names of Head, and Members of Families	Amount	To Whom Paid	Witness to Payment	Remarks
1381 Mose Sally	797.10	Charles *(Illegible)*	L B Bell	
1382 Pigeon Annie				
1383 " Nelly	531.40	Annie Pigeon	L B Bell	
1384 Pheasant Lizzie				
1385 " Eve				
1386 " Mollie	797.10	Lizzie Pheasant	L B Bell	
1387 Price Joseph				
1388 " Nancy M.				
1389 " Ophelia B.	797.10	Joseph Price	L B Bell	
1390 Patterson William	265.70	Wm Patterson	L B Bell	
1391 Pritchet Lucy				
1392 " Lydia	531.40	Lucy Pritchet	L B Bell	
1393 Price Joel L.	265.70	J.L Price	L B Bell	
1394 Philips Hattie A.				
1395 Mankiller Thomas H.				
1396 " Beecher	797.10	Harriet Philips	L B Bell	
1397 Paden Andrew T.				
1398 " Martha J.				
1399 " Zackria				
1400 " George				
1401 " Edward				
1402 " Margaret	1594.20	A.T. Paden	L B Bell	
1403 Painter Nancy R.				
1404 " Lelia				
1405 " Susan				
1406 " George				
1407 " Thomas	1328.50	John P Painter	L B Bell	
1408 Paden Mary L	265.70	Mary L Paden	Henry Eiffert	check sent to *(Illegible)* Sep 26/94
1409 Price James H.	265.70	J H Price	L B Bell	

47

Starr Roll 1894

We, the undersigned citizens of the Cherokee Nation, by right of Cherokee blood, do hereby acknowledge to have received of E. E. Starr, National Treasurer of the Cherokee Nation, the sums set opposite our names respectively, in full of our shares in the per capita distribution authorized by an Act of the National Council, dated ___MAY 3 1894___ 1894.

Names of Head, and Members of Families	Amount	To Whom Paid	Witness to Payment	Remarks
1410 Pritchet[sic] Thomas				
1411 " Jennie				
1412 " Che-squa-ne-kaulu			L B Bell	
1413 " Eliza	1062.80	Tho⁵ Pritchett		
1414 Puppy Sally				
1415 Hogg Martha				*Children of*
1416 Nakedhead Oscar	2⁵			*Sally Puppy*
1417 West Ned				" "
1418 " Sally	1328.50	Sally Puppy	L B Bell	" "
1419 Proctor George	365.70	B.G. Fletcher	L B Bell	*B.G.F. check*
1420 " Ellen	order			*E C T*
1421 " John H.	531.40	E C Thompson	L B Bell	*E C T check*
1422 Palone Mary				
1423 " Patsy	531.40	Mary Palone	L B Bell	
1424 Proctor Nelson				
1425 " Lydia				
1426 " Tana DEAD.				
1427 " Charles				
1428 " Walter				
1429 " Lucy DEAD.	1594.20	Nelson Proctor	L B Bell	
1430 Proctor Lucy				*minor in care of*
1431 Starr Joseph	531.40	Lucy Proctor	L B Bell	*Lucy Proctor*
1432 Paden Thomas J.				
1433 " Martha J.				
1434 " Thomas A.				
1435 " Dathula				
1436 " Susan				
1437 " Vann				
1438 " Nannie				
1439 " Austin	2125.60	Z.J. Paden	L B Bell	
1440 Patterson Lenard				
1441 " John A.				
1442 " Charles W.				

48

Starr Roll 1894

We, the undersigned citizens of the Cherokee Nation, by right of Cherokee blood, do hereby acknowledge to have received of E. E. Starr, National Treasurer of the Cherokee Nation, the sums set opposite our names respectively, in full of our shares in the per capita distribution authorized by an Act of the National Council, dated ____MAY 3 1894____ 1894.

	Names of Head, and Members of Families	Amount	To Whom Paid	Witness to Payment	Remarks
1443	" Joseph A.	1062.80	Charles Patterson	L B Bell	*Father*
1444	Philips[sic] Robert A	265.70	Charles Phillips	Emmet Starr	
1445	Philips Lesley M.				*minors & children of*
1446	" James	531.40	Charles Phillips	Emmet Starr	*Charles Philips*
1447	Proctor Crawler				
1448	" Nancy				
1449	" Joseph				
1450	" Levi				
1451	" Susan	1328.50	Crawler Proctor	L B Bell	
1452	Petitt[sic] Nancy	265.70	Nancy Pettette	L B Bell	
1453	Paden Benjamin F.				
1454	" Loucinda				
1455	" Jennie M.				
1456	" Margaret				
1457	" Loucinda				
1458	" Benjamin Jr	1594.20	Lucinda Paden	L B Bell	
1459	Paden John H.				
1460	" John E.				
1461	" George	797.10	*(Illegible)* T. Paden	L B Bell	
1462	Pritchet[sic] William				
1463	" Mary				
1464	" Ellen	797.10	Wm Pritchett	L B Bell	
1465	Poorbear Hunter				
1466	" Akey	531.40	Hunter Poorbear	L B Bell	
1467	Quinton George				
1468	" Lydia	531.40	Geo Quinton	L B Bell	
1469	Quinton Mack				
1470	" Emily				
1471	" Lula	797.10	Mack Quinton	L B Bell	

Starr Roll 1894

We, the undersigned citizens of the Cherokee Nation, by right of Cherokee blood, do hereby acknowledge to have received of E. E. Starr, National Treasurer of the Cherokee Nation, the sums set opposite our names respectively, in full of our shares in the per capita distribution authorized by an Act of the National Council, dated ___MAY 3 1894___ 1894.

Names of Head, and Members of Families	Amount	To Whom Paid	Witness to Payment	Remarks
1472 Quinton Louis				
1473 " Leathe				
1474 " Frank				
1475 " Corena DEAD.				
1476 " James				
1477 " Johnson				
1478 " Louis Jr.	1859.90	Lewis Quinton	L B Bell	
1479 Quinton Nola	265.70	Nola Quinton	L B Bell	
1480 Quinton David	265.70	George Furguson	L B Bell	Furguson check
1481 Ross Olly	265.70	Olly Ross	L B Bell	
1482 Ross Cely	265.70	Cecelia Ross	L B Bell	
1483 Rooster James	order 265.70	R B Choate	L B Bell	check Choate
1484 Rowe Lydia				minor enrolled
1485 Bunch Bettie	531.40	Lydia Rowe	L B Bell	with Lydia Rowe
1486 Ross Samuel	265.70	Saml Ross	L B Bell	
1487 Russell William				
1488 " Lucy				
1489 " James				
1490 " George				
1491 " Lee	1328.50	Lucy Russell	L B Bell	
1492 Russell May	265.70	May Russell	L B Bell	
1493 Ratt Sally				
1494 " Takey	order			
1495 " James				Choate
1496 " Jennie				
1497 " Mary	1328.50	R B Choate	L B Bell	check
1498 Rooster Peggie				
1499 " Jennie	531.40	Peggie Rooster	L B Bell	

50

Starr Roll 1894

We, the undersigned citizens of the Cherokee Nation, by right of Cherokee blood, do hereby acknowledge to have received of E. E. Starr, National Treasurer of the Cherokee Nation, the sums set opposite our names respectively, in full of our shares in the per capita distribution authorized by an Act of the National Council, dated ___MAY 3 1894___ 1894.

Names of Head, and Members of Families	Amount	To Whom Paid	Witness to Payment	Remarks
1500 Ross John	265.70	John Ross	L B Bell	
1501 Ross Cely	646			
1502 " Emma	DEAD.			
1503 " Lila	797.10	Celia Ross	L B Bell	
1504 Ross Cinda	DEAD.			
1505 " Nellie	646			
1506 " Sally	797.10 646	Cinda Ross	L B Bell	
1507 Rattler Mary	7538			
1508 Bunch Eli	531.40 7538	Mary Rattler	L B Bell	
1509 Rowe Joanna	8262			
1510 " or Fogg Bird				
1511 " Sarah	797.10	Joanna Rowe		
1512 Rooster Lucy				
1513 " Annie	531.40	R B Choate	L B Bell	Choate check
1514 " Mary	265.70	E.C. Thompson	L B Bell	E.C. Thompson check
1515 Ragsdale Isaac				
1516 " Johnsy[sic] A.				
1517 " George H.				
1518 " Ella J.				
1519 " Susan N.				
1520 " Mary V.				
1521 " Charles O.				
1522 " John A.				
1523 " Richard	2391.30	Isaac Ragsdale	L B Bell	
1524 Ross Loucinda				
1525 " Penelopa[sic]				
1526 " William				
1527 " Albert	1062.80	Lucinda Ross	L B Bell	
1528 Ross Rufus	265.70	Rufus Ross	L B Bell	
1529 Ross Jack	265.70	Lucinda Ross	L B Bell	

51

Starr Roll 1894

We, the undersigned citizens of the Cherokee Nation, by right of Cherokee blood, do hereby acknowledge to have received of E. E. Starr, National Treasurer of the Cherokee Nation, the sums set opposite our names respectively, in full of our shares in the per capita distribution authorized by an Act of the National Council, dated ____MAY 3 1894____ 1894.

	Names of Head, and Members of Families	Amount	To Whom Paid	Witness to Payment	Remarks
1530	Ratt John				
1531	" Sarah	*order*			Furguson & Fletcher
1532	" Eddie				
1533	" Ella	1062.80	George Furgueson	L B Bell	check
1534	Ratt Nellie	265.70	Nellie Ratt	L B Bell	
1535	" James	331.40	Nellie Ratt	L B Bell	
1536	Rattler Allen				
1537	" Wut				
1538	" Jefferson				
1539	" Samuel				
1540	" Lydia				
1541	Hawk Peggie				Peggie Richards
1542	" Richard				Bettie Joseph & James
1543	Sharp Bettie	8163			children of
1544	Flinn Joseph				Mrs. Wut Rattler
1545	" James	2657.00	Allen Rattler	L B Bell	
1546	Rattler William	*order* 265.70	Allen Rattler	L B Bell	minor Furguson
1547	Ross Louis	265.20	E S Ellis	L B Bell	Ellis check
1548	Rabbit Arch	*order* 265.70	J M Chandler & Son	L B Bell	Chandler check
1549	Rattler William	*order* 265.70	Wm Rattler	L B Bell	Furguson
1550	Ratt James	265.70	John E Gunter	L B Bell	check 193.70 John E Gunter cash 72.00
1551	" Lyla	265.70	Ellis Starr	L B Bell	Ellis Starr
1552	Sanders Samuel L.	265.70	Saml Sanders	L B Bell	
1553	Sanders Charles L.	265.70	C L Sanders	L B Bell	
1554	Scott Huckleberry	265.70	Huckleberry Scott	L B Bell	
1555	Starr Caleb E.				
1556	" Malzarene	DEAD.			
1557	" George A.				
1558	" Nat. F.				

Starr Roll 1894

We, the undersigned citizens of the Cherokee Nation, by right of Cherokee blood, do hereby acknowledge to have received of E. E. Starr, National Treasurer of the Cherokee Nation, the sums set opposite our names respectively, in full of our shares in the per capita distribution authorized by an Act of the National Council, dated _____ MAY 3 1894 _____ 1894.

	Names of Head, and Members of Families	Amount	To Whom Paid	Witness to Payment	Remarks
1559	" Samuel				
1560	" Katie	DEAD.			
1561	" Charles				
1562	" Louvina				
1563	" Frank				
1564	" Hooley				
1565	" Nancy	2923.70	Caleb E Starr	L B Bell	Check
1566	Stepp Daskey				
1567	" Carnio				
1568	" Batt	797.10	Charles Gettingdown	guardian L B Bell	
1569	Scott Charles				
1570	" Nancy				
1571	" Dora				
1572	" Ned				
1573	" Charles Jr.				
1574	Gritts William	1594.20	Charles Scott	L B Bell	minor
1575	Swimmer Lydia	265.70	Lydia Swimmer	L B Bell	
1576	Swimmer Annie				
1577	" Callie	947			
1578	" Lily	797.10	Annie Swimmer	L B Bell	
1579	Swimmer William				
1580	" Susan				
1581	" Lydia				
1582	" Nancy				
1583	" Olley				
1584	" Levi				
1585	" Akey	1859.90	Wm Swimmer	L B Bell	
1586	Scott Polly				
1587	" Daniel				
1588	" Peggie	797.10	Polly Scott	L B Bell	
1589	Scott French				
1590	" Caroline				
1591	" Jennie				

Starr Roll 1894

We, the undersigned citizens of the Cherokee Nation, by right of Cherokee blood, do hereby acknowledge to have received of E. E. Starr, National Treasurer of the Cherokee Nation, the sums set opposite our names respectively, in full of our shares in the per capita distribution authorized by an Act of the National Council, dated ____MAY 3 1894____ 1894.

	Names of Head, and Members of Families	Amount	To Whom Paid	Witness to Payment	Remarks
1592	" Nancy	1062.80	Caroline Scott	L B Bell	
1593	Stepp Polly				
1594	" Charley				
1595	" Lizzie				
1596	" Annie				
1597	" Charlie Jr.				
1598	" Jennie				
1599	" Annaleese	1859.90	Charley Stepp	L B Bell	
1600	Sanders George				
1601	" Nellie	531.40	Hooly Sanders	L B Bell	
1602	Scott John				
1603	" Norah	531.40	John Scott	L B Bell	
1604	Smith Charles				
1605	" Eliza				
1606	" George				
1607	" Ely				
1608	" Adaline				
1609	" Nellie				
1610	" Henry				
1611	Foster Mary				Step children of
1612	Leach Samuel	628			Charles Smith
1613	Hopper Katy	2657.00	Charles Smith	L B Bell	
1614	Smith Loucinda	265.70	Charles Smith	L B Bell	
1615	Smith Daniel	265.70	Chas Smith	Henry Eiffert	
1616	Sawnee Columbus				
1617	" Jennie				
1618	" John				
1619	" Peter				
1620	" Kate	1328.50	Jennie Sawnee	L B Bell	
1621	Still Richard				
1622	" Tonny	order			Payne
1623	" Lizzie	797.10	Gabriel Tozen	L B Bell	check

54

Starr Roll 1894

We, the undersigned citizens of the Cherokee Nation, by right of Cherokee blood, do hereby acknowledge to have received of E. E. Starr, National Treasurer of the Cherokee Nation, the sums set opposite our names respectively, in full of our shares in the per capita distribution authorized by an Act of the National Council, dated _____ MAY 3 1894 _____ 1894.

	Names of Head, and Members of Families	Amount	To Whom Paid	Witness to Payment	Remarks
1624	Sawnee Ceily				
1625	" Samuel				
1626	" William	8253			
1627	" Johnanna				
1628	" Moses				
1629	" Annie				
1630	" Ninnie	1859.90	Ceily Sawnee	L B Bell	
1631	Sawnee Betsy				
1632	" Nasissa[sic]				
1633	" Sallie				
1634	" Robert				
1635	" Slopinglong	1328.50	Betsy Sawnee	L B Bell	
1636	Sawnee Nancy	265.70	Nancy Sawnee	L B Bell	
1637	Sunshine Peter				
1638	" Olley[sic]				
1639	" Jack				
1640	" Mary	1062.80	Olly Sunshine	L B Bell	
1641	Send Sawnee				
1642	" Sally	531.40	Sawney Send	L B Bell	
1643	Stand Sally				
1644	" Maggie	531.40	Sally Stand	L B Bell	
1645	Sanders Thomas J.				
1646	" Lizzie				
1647	" Thomas				
1648	" James				
1649	" Mary				
1650	" Monroe				
1651	" Lydia				
1652	" Lula	2125.60	Tho[s] Sanders	L B Bell	
1653	Starr James				
1654	" Sopha				
1655	" Jack				
1656	" Tob				

Starr Roll 1894

We, the undersigned citizens of the Cherokee Nation, by right of Cherokee blood, do hereby acknowledge to have received of E. E. Starr, National Treasurer of the Cherokee Nation, the sums set opposite our names respectively, in full of our shares in the per capita distribution authorized by an Act of the National Council, dated ___MAY 3 1894___ 1894.

	Names of Head, and Members of Families	Amount	To Whom Paid	Witness to Payment	Remarks
1657	" Hettie				
1658	" Katy				
1659	" Mary				
1660	" Charley				
1661	" John B.	2391.30	Jas Starr	L B Bell	
1662	Sawnee Alexander	265.70	Sawney	L B Bell	on order
1663	Starr Leroy	265.70	Leroy Starr	L B Bell	
1664	Smith William	265.70	Wm Smith	L B Bell	
1665	Sevenstarrs[sic] Adam				
1666	" Cynthia				
1667	" Larkin				
1668	" Ella				
1669	" Nancy				
1670	" Jennie	1594.20	Adam Sevenstarr	L B Bell	
1671	Sevenstarr Thomas	265.70	Thos Sevenstarr	L B Bell	
1672	Soap Thomas				
1673	" Betsy				
1674	" Johnson	order			
1675	" Sulasteska				order
1676	" Columbus	1328.50	J M Chandler	Henry Eiffert	Oct 3-1894
1677	Starr Fannie				
1678	Taylor Nancy				Same Mother, but
1679	Hampton Bettie				different Fathers all
1680	Rogers Callie	1062.80	Fannie Starr	L B Bell	living with Mother
1681	Soap Nick				
1682	" Nellie				
1683	" Johnson				
1684	" William				
1685	" Carlus				(old) Mother of
1686	Soap Jennie	1594.20	Nick Soap	L B Bell	Nick Soap
1687	Sanders Lizzie	267.70	Lizzie Sanders	L B Bell	

Starr Roll 1894

We, the undersigned citizens of the Cherokee Nation, by right of Cherokee blood, do hereby acknowledge to have received of E. E. Starr, National Treasurer of the Cherokee Nation, the sums set opposite our names respectively, in full of our shares in the per capita distribution authorized by an Act of the National Council, dated ___MAY 3 1894___ 1894.

	Names of Head, and Members of Families	Amount	To Whom Paid	Witness to Payment	Remarks
1688	Sanders Jane	265.70	Jane Sanders	L B Bell	
1689	Sanders Alsey[sic]	265.70	Ailsy Sanders	L B Bell	
1690	Swimmer Lizzie				
1691	" Nancy				
1692	" Richard				
1693	" Levi				Chandler
1694	" Akey				
1695	" Nar-na				
1696	" Julia	1859.90	J M Chandler & Son	L B Bell	check
1697	Sam Ezekiel				orphan, raised by
1698	Daugherty Ti-a-na	79531.40	Ezekiel Sam	L B Bell	Ezekiel Sam
1699	Scott John				
1700	" Emaline				
1701	" Lilly				
1702	" Coming				
1703	" Minnie				
1704	" William	1594.20	Emeline Scott	L B Bell	
1705	Simmons Johnson				
1706	" Nancy	531.40	Johnson Simmons	L B Bell	
1707	Sanders Nancy				
1708	" Hickory	531.40	Nancy Swan	L B Bell	
1709	Seabolt Lucy				orphans
1710	" Ceily				Jack Christie
1711	" Joseph	797.10	Jackson Christie Guardian	L B Bell	Guardian
1712	Sam Sulteeska				
1713	" Cindy				
1714	" Nancy				
1715	" Levi				
1716	" Jonah	1328.50	Sutleesky Sam	L B Bell	
1717	Soap Jennie	265.70	Jennie Soap	L B Bell	

Starr Roll 1894

We, the undersigned citizens of the Cherokee Nation, by right of Cherokee blood, do hereby acknowledge to have received of E. E. Starr, National Treasurer of the Cherokee Nation, the sums set opposite our names respectively, in full of our shares in the per capita distribution authorized by an Act of the National Council, dated _____ MAY 3 1894 _____ 1894.

Names of Head, and Members of Families	Amount	To Whom Paid	Witness to Payment	Remarks
1718 Starr Ellis				
1719 " Martha				
1720 " Daisy				
1721 " Dora A.				
1722 " Florence				
1723 " Charles C				
1724 " Jesse James DEAD.				
1725 " Susan J. DEAD.	2125.60	Ellis Starr	L B Bell	
1726 Starr Mary L.	265.70	Ellis Starr	L B Bell	
1727 Sanders Rachel	265.70	Rachel Sanders	L B Bell	
1728 Sanders Na-ky	265.70	Nakey Sanders	L B Bell	
1729 Skitt Bird				
1730 " Martha				
1731 " Samuel				*Furguson*
1732 " Nancy	1062.80	George Furguson	L B Bell	*check*
1733 Sawney Jack				
1734 " Susan A				
1735 " John				
1736 " Lydia	1062.80	Jack Sawnee	L B Bell	
1737 Sixkiller Samuel				
1738 " Nancy				
1739 " Arch				
1740 " Lynch				
1741 " George				
1742 " Emma				
1743 " Edward				
1744 " Dely	2125.60	Sam¹ Sixkiller	L B Bell	
1745 Sixkiller Gafford	265.70	Sam Sixkiller	L B Bell	
1746 Sanders Lyla	265.70	Jno B. Lynch	L B Bell	
1747 Skitt Ben				
1748 " Jennie			L B Bell	*J.B. Lynch*

Starr Roll 1894

We, the undersigned citizens of the Cherokee Nation, by right of Cherokee blood, do hereby acknowledge to have received of E. E. Starr, National Treasurer of the Cherokee Nation, the sums set opposite our names respectively, in full of our shares in the per capita distribution authorized by an Act of the National Council, dated ____MAY 3 1894____ 1894.

	Names of Head, and Members of Families	Amount	To Whom Paid	Witness to Payment	Remarks
1749	" Alsie				
1750	" Mattie	1026.80	Ben Skitt	L B Bell	
1751	Skitt Annie	order 265.70	Ellis Starr	L B Bell	check Ellis Starr
1752	Still Mary				
1753	" Samuel				
1754	" Mary				
1755	" Margaret				
1756	" Johnanna	1328.50	Sarah Smith guardian	L B Bell	
1757	Smith Rosa	265.70	Sarah Smith	L B Bell	
1758	Skitt John				
1759	" Betsy				
1760	" John Jr.				
1761	Ratt Mary	1062.80	John Skitt	L B Bell	Orphan
1762	Skitt Arch	265.70	John Skitt	L B Bell	
1763	Shell Jennie				
1764	" John	DEAD.			
1765	" Richard	797.10	Jennie Shell	L B Bell	
1766	Shell Samuel	265.70	Jennie Shell	L B Bell	
1767	Seabolt Benjamin	265.70	Jennie Shell guardian	L B Bell	
1768	Scott George				
1769	" Ellen				(old) George Scott
1770	" Hu-yah-na	797.10	Ellen Scott	L B Bell	Guardian
1771	Skuntey Cornelius	order 265.70	George Furgueson	L B Bell	Furguson Check
1772	Skitt Bird	265.70	Bird Sckit[sic]	L B Bell	
1773	Scraper Field				
1774	" Can-ta-ca-na				
1775	" Edward				
1776	" Richard				

Starr Roll 1894

We, the undersigned citizens of the Cherokee Nation, by right of Cherokee blood, do hereby acknowledge to have received of E. E. Starr, National Treasurer of the Cherokee Nation, the sums set opposite our names respectively, in full of our shares in the per capita distribution authorized by an Act of the National Council, dated ___MAY 3 1894___ 1894.

	Names of Head, and Members of Families	Amount	To Whom Paid	Witness to Payment	Remarks
1777	" Susan				
1778	" James				
1779	" Jessee[sic]				
1780	" Charles	2125.60	Fields Scraper	L B Bell	
1781	Scott George				
1782	" Loucinda	531.40	Lucinda Scott	L B Bell	orphan George Scott Guardian
1783	Na-e-so	265.70	Sellout Feather *guardian*		
1784	Stealer Thomas				
1785	" Betsy	531.40	Thos Stealer	L B Bell	
1786	Smith Sarah	265.70	Sarah Smith	L B Bell	
1787	Starr Samuel J.				
1788	" Sarah R.				
1789	" George E.				
1790	" Martin C.				
1791	" Lenora DEAD.	1328.50	S J Starr	L B Bell	
1792	Sanders Isaac				
1793	" Isabelle				
1794	" David				
1795	" Susan				
1796	" Charles				
1797	" Eliza	1594.20	Isaac Sanders D2871	L B Bell	
1798	Sixkiller Walter				
1799	" Julia				
1800	" Charlotte				
1801	" Andrew				
1802	" Martha				
1803	" Henry				
1804	" Narcissie				
1805	" Frank A.	2125.60	Walter Sixkiller	L B Bell	
1806	Sanders David				
1807	" Ne-coo-tar-za				
1808	" Sally				
1809	" Washington				

Starr Roll 1894

We, the undersigned citizens of the Cherokee Nation, by right of Cherokee blood, do hereby acknowledge to have received of E. E. Starr, National Treasurer of the Cherokee Nation, the sums set opposite our names respectively, in full of our shares in the per capita distribution authorized by an Act of the National Council, dated ____MAY 3 1894____ 1894.

	Names of Head, and Members of Families	Amount	To Whom Paid	Witness to Payment	Remarks
1810	" Claborn				J B Lynch
1811	" Ca-lun-se-za-ha	order			
1812	" Robbin				
1813	" Benjamin				
1814	" John H.				
1815	" Pigeon	2657.00	David Sanders	L B Bell	with Lynches consent
1816	Sanders Hooley[sic]				
1817	" Mary				
1818	" Walter				
1819	" Moses				
1820	" Nancy	1328.50	Hooly Sanders	L B Bell	
1821	Sanders John	265.70	Hooly Sanders	L B Bell	
1822	Sixkiller John B.	265.70	Jennie Bunch	L B Bell	Enrolled with Jennie Bunch family
1823	Tulsy[sic] Lizzie	265.70	Lizzie Tulsey	L B Bell	
1824	Tehee Polly				
1825	" Charles				
1826	" Lizzie				
1827	" Johnson				
1828	" Sally	1328.50	Polly Tehee	L B Bell	
1829	Taylor William				
1830	" Ailcy[sic]				
1831	" Jennie				
1832	" John	1062.80	Ailsy Taylor	L B Bell	
1833	Tidwell Minor L.				
1834	" Ada M.				
1835	" Robert G.	797.10	M L Tidwell	L B Bell	
1836	Tidwell Pleasant H.				
1837	" Eliza L.				
1838	" James P.	797.10	P H Tidwell	L B Bell	
1839	Townsend Jesse H	265.70	Charles Cloud guardian	L B Bell	

Starr Roll 1894

We, the undersigned citizens of the Cherokee Nation, by right of Cherokee blood, do hereby acknowledge to have received of E. E. Starr, National Treasurer of the Cherokee Nation, the sums set opposite our names respectively, in full of our shares in the per capita distribution authorized by an Act of the National Council, dated ___MAY 3 1894___ 1894.

Names of Head, and Members of Families	Amount	To Whom Paid	Witness to Payment	Remarks
1840 Taylor Peggie	265.70	Peggy Taylor	L B Bell	
1841 Tehee Nelson	265.70			Minor. Son of Charles Tehee. Tahlequah Dist
1842 Tassell Sarah	265.70	Sarah Tassell	L B Bell	
1843 Taylor Richard L.				
1844 " Maggie E.				
1845 " Nancy C.				
1846 " Annie E.				
1847 " Amelia				
1848 " Susan B.				
1849 " Richard L. Jr				
1850 " Benjamin W.	2125.60	Ric'd Taylor	L B Bell	
1851 Thompson Jesse D.				
1852 " Robert H.				
1853 " William F.				
1854 " Andy	1062.80	Jess Thompson	L B Bell	
1855 Thrower Charles	order 265.70	R B Choate	L B Bell	R.B. Choate check
1856 Tehee Sarah	265.70	Nohool[sic] Locust	J P Carter	order Nov 13-94
1857 Tankesley Ella	265.70	Charlotte Adamsdn	L B Bell	Minor Charlotte Adams Guardian
1858 Tehee[sic] Jesse				
1859 " Jennie				
1860 " Nancy				
1861 " Yose				
1862 " William				
1863 " Charley	1594.20	Jesse Teehee	L B Bell	
1864 Tootle Rachel			See Protest	
1865 " Mary Lee	order			Ellis
1866 " Harriet				
1867 " Charles	1062.80	E.S. Ellis		
1868 Thomas James M	265.70	Menerva Thomas	L B Bell	check

Starr Roll 1894

We, the undersigned citizens of the Cherokee Nation, by right of Cherokee blood, do hereby acknowledge to have received of E. E. Starr, National Treasurer of the Cherokee Nation, the sums set opposite our names respectively, in full of our shares in the per capita distribution authorized by an Act of the National Council, dated ___MAY 3 1894___ 1894.

Names of Head, and Members of Families	Amount	To Whom Paid	Witness to Payment	Remarks
1869 Thomas Manerva				
1870 " George E				
1871 " Lucius F.				
1872 " Mordica[sic]	1062.80	D2875 Menerva Thomas	L B Bell	
1873 Taylor William				
1874 " Sarah				
1875 " William Jr.				
1876 " Jackson	1062.80	William Taylor	L B Bell	
1877 Tucker Marcus L.				
1878 " Amanda E.				
1879 " Louellen				
1880 " Lillian				
1881 " Nelvelle E				
1882 " Luer C.				
1883 " Felix A.	1859.20	M L Tucker	L B Bell	
1884 Tindle Annie				
1885 " Julia				
1886 " Wallie				
1887 " Henry C.				
1888 " Alex	1328.50	Annie Tindle	L B Bell	
1889 Vann Loucinda	265.70	George Welch guardian	L B Bell	old. George Welch Guardian
1890 Vann George	265.70	Lydia Quinton	Henry Eiffert	Guardian Sept 20 94
1891 Vann Jesse				
1892 " Chic-can-na-len				
1893 " Jack	order			Ellis Starr
1894 " Lotta				
1895 " Josiah	1328.50	Ellis Starr	L B Bell	check
1896 Vann Charles	265.70	Charles Vann	L B Bell	
1897 Vann Ellis	265.70	Ellis Vann	L B Bell	
1898 " Nancy	265.70	Nancy Vann	L B Bell	

Starr Roll 1894

We, the undersigned citizens of the Cherokee Nation, by right of Cherokee blood, do hereby acknowledge to have received of E. E. Starr, National Treasurer of the Cherokee Nation, the sums set opposite our names respectively, in full of our shares in the per capita distribution authorized by an Act of the National Council, dated ____MAY 3 1894____ 1894.

Names of Head, and Members of Families	Amount	To Whom Paid	Witness to Payment	Remarks
1899 Vann Alesey[sic]				Ellis – Starr
1900 " Nancy	order			
1901 " Jesse		Ailsy Vann	L B Bell	
1902 " Scott	1062.80	Ellis Starr	L B Bell	check
1903 Vann Kinny[sic]	265.70	Kinny Vann	L B Bell	
1904 Vann Akey				
1905 " Jackson				
1906 " Annie D.				
1907 " Johnanna	1062.80	Akey Vann	Akey Vann	
1908 Vann Nancy	265.70	Akey Vann	Akey Vann	
1909 Vann Vic				Ellis
1910 " Dick	531.40 order	E.S. Ellis	L B Bell	Check
1911 Vann Martha				
1912 " William				Martha Vann
1913 Skitt Margaret	797.10 order	Martha Vann	L B Bell	Guardian
1914 Vann Wolf				Ferguson[sic]
1915 " Sarah	order			
1916 " Lily				
1917 " John	1062.80	George Furgueson	L B Bell	check
1918 Vann Bay	265.70	E Starr & E Buffington	J P Carter	Pd order Dec 29-94
1919 Vann Heavy				
1920 " Nancy	531.40	Heavy Vann	L B Bell	
1921 Vann Allen	265.70 order	R B Choate	L B Bell	Check Choate
1922 Vann Dirtthrower				
1923 " Mary				
1924 " Katy				
1925 " Andrew				
1926 " Bearpaw				
1927 " James				
1928 " White	1859.90	J.M. Chandler By J S Stapler	J.S. Stapler	Order

Starr Roll 1894

We, the undersigned citizens of the Cherokee Nation, by right of Cherokee blood, do hereby acknowledge to have received of E. E. Starr, National Treasurer of the Cherokee Nation, the sums set opposite our names respectively, in full of our shares in the per capita distribution authorized by an Act of the National Council, dated ___MAY 3 1894___ 1894.

Names of Head, and Members of Families	Amount	To Whom Paid	Witness to Payment	Remarks
1929 Vann Mack	265.70	Henry Housburg[sic]	S.W. Mayfield	Paid on order
1930 Vann Noname[sic]				
1931 " Sina	531.40	Noname Vann	L B Bell	
1932 Walker William H.				
1933 " Lucy J.				
1934 " Robert W.				
1935 " Frank L.	1062.80	George Howard	L B Bell	on order
1936 Walker William				
1937 " Mary				
1938 " Ely				
1939 " Charlotte				
1940 " Peggie	1328.50	Wm Walker	L B Bell	
1941 Wicket Susan	265.70	Susanna Wicket	L B Bell	
1942 Wolf Thomas				
1943 " Jackson				
1944 " Peggie				
1945 " Lydia				
1946 " Dick	1328.50	Thomas Wolf	Henry Eiffert	Sept 13/94
1947 Waters Vina E.				
1948 " Gertrude A.				
1949 " Eva M.				
1950 " Florence W.	1062.80	Geo A Waters	L B Bell	
1951 Welch John E.				
1952 " Mack	5667			
1953 " Charles				
1954 " Richard L.				
1955 " Jesse	1328.50	John E Welch	L B Bell	
1956 Welch John D.	265.70	John E Welch	L B Bell	
1957 Welch George T	265.70	John E Welch	L B Bell	
1958 Walkingstick Nancy	265.70	Jas Adair	L B Bell	

65

Starr Roll 1894

We, the undersigned citizens of the Cherokee Nation, by right of Cherokee blood, do hereby acknowledge to have received of E. E. Starr, National Treasurer of the Cherokee Nation, the sums set opposite our names respectively, in full of our shares in the per capita distribution authorized by an Act of the National Council, dated ___MAY 3 1894___ 1894.

	Names of Head, and Members of Families	Amount	To Whom Paid	Witness to Payment	Remarks
1959	Ward Samuel				
1960	" Sabra C.				
1961	" Samuel H.				
1962	" Charles Y.	1062.80	Saml Ward	L B Bell	
1963	Ward George W	265.70	Saml Ward	L B Bell	
1964	Ward Martin				
1965	" Sally	531.40	Martin Ward	L B Bell	
1966	Whitmire Ethel				
1967	" Maud	531.40	Ethel Whitmire	L B Bell	
1968	Wright Elizabeth				
1969	" William C.				
1970	" Tennie				
1971	" George				
1972	" Nettie				
1973	" Mart	1594.20	Frank Wright	L B Bell	
1974	Wicket Maria				
1975	Sawnee Eve	531.40	Maria Wicket	L B Bell	Father refused to register with Mrs. Wicket
1976	Walker Lydia	265.70	J.M.Chandler & Son	L B Bell check	Nancy Daugherty Guardian for these orps
1977	" Juan	265.70	Nancy Daugherty	T.W. Triplet	
1978	Wicket Charles				
1979	" Emily	531.40	Charles Wicket	L B Bell	
1980	Waterdown Leach				
1981	" Nellie				
1982	" Jennie				
1983	" Tiana				
1984	" Annie				
1985	" Joe				
1986	" Richard	1859.60	Leach Waterdown	L B Bell	
1987	Waterdown Lynch	265.70	Leach Waterdown	L B Bell	

Starr Roll 1894

We, the undersigned citizens of the Cherokee Nation, by right of Cherokee blood, do hereby acknowledge to have received of E. E. Starr, National Treasurer of the Cherokee Nation, the sums set opposite our names respectively, in full of our shares in the per capita distribution authorized by an Act of the National Council, dated _____MAY 3 1894_____ 1894.

	Names of Head, and Members of Families	Amount	To Whom Paid	Witness to Payment	Remarks
1988	Walkingstick Wilson				
1989	" Nancy				
1990	" Johnie				
1991	" Ada	1062.80	Wilson Walkingstick	L B Bell	
1992	Weavel Chowin				
1993	" Oo-ti-ye				
1994	" William	797.10	Chowin Weavel	L B Bell	
1995	Wright Caleb P.				
1996	" Benjamin G.	531.40	Caleb Wright	L B Bell	
1997	Walkabout Nancy				The right name of
1998	" Samuel	*order*			Chandler this family is
1999	" Annie				"Daugherty"
2000	" Jennie	1062.80	JM Chandler & Son	L B Bell	check
2001	Walkingstick Jennie	265.70	Nancy Adair Adms	L B Bell	
2002	" Stephen	265.70	Charley Bolt *gardn*	L B Bell	
2003	Canoe Mary	265.70 *329*	Ben Bigfeather *guardian*	L B Bell	*orphan Jennie Walkingstick Guardian*
2004	Welch Alfred G				
2005	" Elmira				
2006	" Mary				
2007	" Robert				
2008	" Joseph	1328.50	A G Welch	L B Bell	
2009	Weavel Miller				T.W.T.
2010	" Kut-e-cloy	*order*	8161		
2011	" Nancy				
2012	" Betsy	1062.80	T.W. Triplett	L B Bell	check
2013	Weavel Betsy				*minors Betsy Weavel*
2014	Hewin Spade				*Guardian*
2015	" Sarah	797.10	Betsy Weavel	L B Bell	*for Hewin children*
2016	Wane Olley				
2017	" Beckie				
2018	" John				
2019	" Ice				

Starr Roll 1894

We, the undersigned citizens of the Cherokee Nation, by right of Cherokee blood, do hereby acknowledge to have received of E. E. Starr, National Treasurer of the Cherokee Nation, the sums set opposite our names respectively, in full of our shares in the per capita distribution authorized by an Act of the National Council, dated _____ MAY 3 1894 _____ 1894.

	Names of Head, and Members of Families	Amount	To Whom Paid	Witness to Payment	Remarks
2020	" William	1328.50	Ollie Wane	L B Bell	
2021	Weavel John	265.70	E S Ellis	L B Bell	E.S. Elis check
2022	" Katy	265.70	John Weavel	L B Bell	
2023	White James				
2024	" Jennie				Ellis Starr
2025	" Tom	order			
2026	" Sundy	1062.80	Ellis Starr	L B Bell	check
2027	Weavel Samuel	265.70	George Furguson	L B Bell	Furguson check
2028	Wolf Katy 521	265.70	Jack Batt	L B Bell	Living with Jack Batt
2029	Willis Florence A				
2030	" Nora				
2031	" Robert H.	797.10	J P Willis	L B Bell	
2032	West Allice				
2033	" Sarah K.				
2034	" James M^c	797.10	S.J. West	L B Bell	
2035	Wolf Katy				
2036	" Jennie				
2037	" Fannie	797.10	Katy Wolf	L B Bell	
2038	Weavel Lucy				
2039	" Writer				
2040	" Louis				
2041	" Richard	1062.80	Lucy Weavel	L B Bell	
2042	White Thomas				
2043	" Akey	531.40	Thos White	L B Bell	
2044	Weavel Mary	265.70	Mary Weavel	L B Bell	
2045	Welch George W.				
2046	" Jackoline				
2047	" John B.				
2048	" Hooley	1062.80	G W Welch	L B Bell	

Starr Roll 1894

We, the undersigned citizens of the Cherokee Nation, by right of Cherokee blood, do hereby acknowledge to have received of E. E. Starr, National Treasurer of the Cherokee Nation, the sums set opposite our names respectively, in full of our shares in the per capita distribution authorized by an Act of the National Council, dated ___MAY 3 1894___ 1894.

Names of Head, and Members of Families	Amount	To Whom Paid	Witness to Payment	Remarks
2049 Wrinkle John	265.70	G W Welch	L B Bell	(old) George Welch Guardian
2050 Young William				
2051 " Hester				
2052 " Thomas				
2053 " Ely				
2054 " Houston				
2055 " John	1594.20	Wm Young	L B Bell	
2056 Young Minnie	265.70	Minnie Young	L B Bell	
2057 Young Charles				
2058 " Bettie				
2059 " Roach				
2060 " Callie				
2061 " Silas	1328.50	Charles Young	L B Bell	

Tahlequah, Ind. Ter., *May 19th,* 189 *4.*

I, *C. J. Harris, Principal Chief of the Cherokee Nation, and*

I, *E. E. Starr, Treasurer of said Nation,*

do hereby certify that the foregoing enrollment of persons resident in Flint District, in this nation, is a correct transcript from the original census of said district, as ordered by the Act of the National Council, approved May 15th, 1893, and that the number, so ascertained, to participate in the per-capita distribution of the $6,640,000. provided by the Act of the National Council, approved May 3, 1894, is two thousand and sixty-four, [2064].

Attest.

Seal of the Cherokee Nation.

C. J. Harris
Principal Chief.

E. E. Starr
Treasurer.

****

Going Snake *(District)*

Starr Roll 1894

We, the undersigned citizens of the Cherokee Nation, by right of Cherokee blood, do hereby acknowledge to have received of E. E. Starr, National Treasurer of the Cherokee Nation, the sums set opposite our names respectively, in full of our shares in the per capita distribution authorized by an Act of the National Council, dated ____MAY 3 1894____ 1894.

Names of Head, and Members of Families	Amount $ cts	To Whom Paid	Witness to Payment	Remarks
1 Alberty, Lizzie				
2 " Jesse W.				
3 " Rob't. L.	797.10	Lizzie Alberty	L B Bell	
4 Alberty, Jacob				
5 " Ella				
6 " Myrtle				
7 " Fred	1062.60	Jacob Alberty	L B Bell	
8 Alberty, Tho⁵ B.				
9 " Julia A.				
10 " Albert C.	797.10	T B Alberty	L B Bell	
11 Alberty, Nancy				
12 " Ellis C.				
13 " Jesse V.				
14 " Wᵐ W.				
15 " Moses				
16 " Peter S.	1594.20	Nancy Alberty	L B Bell	
17 Alberty, Ellis R.				
18 " Callie				
19 " Rob't. G.	797.10	E R Alberty	L B Bell	
20 Alberty, John W.				
21 " Wᵐ R.				
22 " Ada				
23 " Ida				
24 " Minnie				
25 " Elbridge[sic] B	1594.20	JW Alberty	L B Bell	
26 Alberty, Mattie	265.70	JW Alberty	L B Bell	
27 Adair, Katie	6695			Lacy Wolfe
28 " Lucy				
29 " John	797.10	Lucy Wolfe Guardian	L B Bell	Guardian
30 Adair, Jesse	265.70	Jesse Adair	L B Bell	

71

Starr Roll 1894

We, the undersigned citizens of the Cherokee Nation, by right of Cherokee blood, do hereby acknowledge to have received of E. E. Starr, National Treasurer of the Cherokee Nation, the sums set opposite our names respectively, in full of our shares in the per capita distribution authorized by an Act of the National Council, dated ___MAY 3 1894___ 1894.

Names of Head, and Members of Families	Amount $ cts	To Whom Paid	Witness to Payment	Remarks
31 Akin, Andrew T				
32 Jennie				
33 " Ellis A.				
34 " Modie				
35 " Watie T.				
36 " Willie O.				
37 " Thomas	1859.90	Andrew T Akin	L B Bell	
38 Alberty, Jesse C.				
39 " Gibson W.	531.40	Jesse C Alberty	L B Bell	
40 Alberty, John A.	265.70	E M Alberty	L B Bell	
41 Alberty, Elizabeth	265.70	E M Alberty	L B Bell	
42 Alberty, Ellis M				
43 " Martha				
44 " Spencer L.				
45 " W$^{\underline{m}}$ H.				
46 " Lula				
47 " Watie M.	1594.20	E M Alberty	L B Bell	
48 Alberty, John				
49 " Emily				
50 " Katie				
51 " Mattie				
52 " La Fayette				
53 " Mollie	1594.20	John Alberty	L B Bell	
54 Adair, Penelope	265.70	Sam H Adair	L B Bell	*order*
55 Adair, Sam'l. H				
56 " Sarah S.				
57 " Florence W.				
58 " Venia F				
59 " Gula R				
60 " John T	1594.20	Sam H Adair	L B Bell	
61 Adair, Virgil B				
62 " Madison B.				

Starr Roll 1894

We, the undersigned citizens of the Cherokee Nation, by right of Cherokee blood, do hereby acknowledge to have received of E. E. Starr, National Treasurer of the Cherokee Nation, the sums set opposite our names respectively, in full of our shares in the per capita distribution authorized by an Act of the National Council, dated ___MAY 3 1894___ 1894.

	Names of Head, and Members of Families	Amount $ cts	To Whom Paid	Witness to Payment	Remarks
63	" Francis C.				
64	" Ezekiel E.				
65	" Julius K	1328.50	John T Adair	L B Bell	on order
66	Adair, John T.	265.70	John T. Adair	L B Bell	
67	Allison, W^m A	DEAD.			
68	" Eddie	826			
69	" Laura B	826			
70	" Paden	1062.80	E.W. Buffington	G W Benge	on order
71	Alberty, Ned	order 265.70	J.T Evans	L B Bell	check on order
72	Alberty, Catharine	order			
73	" Delilah	order 531.40	S.J. Starr	L B Bell	check on order
74	Akin, Isabel	851			
75	Addington, Cicero				
76	Akin, Caroline				
77	" Tennessee	1062.80	Isabell Akin	L B Bell	
78	Alberty, Andrew J				
79	" Elnora				
80	" Theodosia				
81	" William				
82	" Ada May				
83	" Bishop M.				
84	" Samuel	1859.90	A J Alberty	L B Bell	
85	Andrews, Mary	265.70	Wm Matoy	Henry Eiffert	
86	Alberty, Arch				
87	" Joseph				
88	" William				
89	" Bertha				
90	" Jesse	1328.50	Arch Alberty	L B Bell	
91	Adair, Wm P.				
92	" Arthur				
93	" Annie	797.10	Wm P. Adair	L B Bell	

73

Starr Roll 1894

We, the undersigned citizens of the Cherokee Nation, by right of Cherokee blood, do hereby acknowledge to have received of E. E. Starr, National Treasurer of the Cherokee Nation, the sums set opposite our names respectively, in full of our shares in the per capita distribution authorized by an Act of the National Council, dated ___MAY 3 1894___ 1894.

Names of Head, and Members of Families	Amount $ cts	To Whom Paid	Witness to Payment	Remarks
94 Alberty, John G.				
95 " Grover L.	531.40	John G Alberty	L B Bell	
96 Acorn, Sarah	265.70	Jasper Newton	L B Bell	order October 1 1894
97 Allen, Nancy A.	265.70	C H Allen	L B Bell	C.H. Allen
98 " Henry	265.70	Henry Allen	L B Bell	Guardian
99 " Michael	265.70	C H Allen	L B Bell	for
100 " Oscar	265.70	C H Allen	L B Bell	Alice Round
101 Round, Alice	265.70	C H Allen	L B Bell	
102 Allen, Lewis	265.70	Lewis Allen	L B Bell	
103 Ames, Julian				
104 " Geo. L.				
105 " Leonard	797.10	J R Johnson	L B Bell	
106 Alberty, Joseph V[sic].				Zoe C. Akin
107 " Nannie L.				is the
108 " Clara L.				daughter of
109 " Tota A				Nannie L.
110 " Julia				Alberty
111 Akin, Zoe C.	1594.20	J W Alberty	L B Bell	
112 Beck, Aaron				Josephine
113 " Josephine				Beck, mother
114 " Tony				of Mattie
115 " Susie				Bell
116 Bell, Mattie	1328.50	Aaron Beck	L B Bell	
117 Bean, John	ENROLLMENT REFUSED. R 30			
118 " Henrietta	ENROLLMENT REFUSED. R 30			
119 " Jack Stan	265.70	Jack Stan Bean	L B Bell	
120 " Nat				
121 " Casper	ENROLLMENT REFUSED. R 30			on order to
122 " Grover ENROLLMENT	1328.50	R M Dannenberg	L B Bell	R M Dannenberg
	REFUSED.			
123 Baggett, Pearl E.				
124 " Julia A.				
125 " P. Elaine	797.10	Thoˢ J Brackett	L B Bell	

Starr Roll 1894

We, the undersigned citizens of the Cherokee Nation, by right of Cherokee blood, do hereby acknowledge to have received of E. E. Starr, National Treasurer of the Cherokee Nation, the sums set opposite our names respectively, in full of our shares in the per capita distribution authorized by an Act of the National Council, dated _____MAY 3 1894_____ 1894.

	Names of Head, and Members of Families	Amount $ cts	To Whom Paid	Witness to Payment	Remarks
126	Bright, Marion	265.70	Marion Bright	L B Bell	
127	Blackwood, Isaac	265.70	Isaac Blackwood	L B Bell	
128	Barton, Mary L.				
129	" Edwin H.	531.40	Mary L Barton	L B Bell	
130	Bushyhead, Lizzie	265.70	Lizzie Bushyhead	Henry Eiffert	
131	Bean, Nancy J.				
132	Catcher, Emma				
133	Walkingstick, Cecil				*Children of*
134	" Sam'l				*Nancy J. Bean*
135	" Calvin	1328.50	Nancy J. Bean	L B Bell	
136	Buffington, Louisa	265.70	Jno D Buffington	L B Bell	
137	Bean, Jack M				
138	" Nannie E.				
139	" Sarah Z				
140	" Ruth				
141	" Venie				
142	" Jennie				
143	" Dan	1859.90	J.R. Garrett	L B Bell	*check on order*
144	Brackett, Benj.				
145	" Dan'l. Rob't.				
146	" W͟m T.				
147	" Louisa E				
148	" Martha J				
149	" Amelia E.	1594.20	Ben Brackett	L B Bell	
150	Brackett, Caldonia S.	265.70	Caldonia S Brackett	L B Bell	
151	Blackwood, Emma				
152	" Mary				
153	" Lydia				
154	" W͟m				
155	" Cora				
156	" Leander				

75

Starr Roll 1894

We, the undersigned citizens of the Cherokee Nation, by right of Cherokee blood, do hereby acknowledge to have received of E. E. Starr, National Treasurer of the Cherokee Nation, the sums set opposite our names respectively, in full of our shares in the per capita distribution authorized by an Act of the National Council, dated ___MAY 3 1894___ 1894.

	Names of Head, and Members of Families	Amount $ cts	To Whom Paid	Witness to Payment	Remarks
157	" Burr				
158	" John H	2125.60	J W Blackwood	L B Bell	
159	Bark, Walker	265.70	R M Wolf	Henry Eiffert	order
160	Brown, Marshal[sic]				
161	" Mary M.				
162	" Bascom				
163	" Elizabeth				
164	" Eliza				
165	" Nannie				
166	" Martha				
167	" Wᵐ G.				
168	" Sarah	2391.30	Marshall Brown	L B Bell	
169	Brown, Ollie	265.70	John W Brown	L B Bell	Father on order
170	Brown, Ida	265.70	John W Brown	L B Bell	Father on order
171	Brown, Jaˢ S.	265.70	Jas S Brown	L B Bell	
172	Bright, Sam'l				
173	" Beersheba				
174	" Charles	797.10	L.L. Duckworth	L B Bell	order
175	Bright, Lethe	265.70	L L Duckworth	L B Bell	order
176	Buffington, Jno. D.				
177	" Fannie				
178	" Stella				
179	" Etta				
180	" Grover I.				
181	" Vade				
182	" Jay D.				
183	" Wᵐ G.	2125.60	J D Buffington	L B Bell	
184	Brown, John				
185	" Michael				
186	" Josie				
187	" Myra				

76

Starr Roll 1894

We, the undersigned citizens of the Cherokee Nation, by right of Cherokee blood, do hereby acknowledge to have received of E. E. Starr, National Treasurer of the Cherokee Nation, the sums set opposite our names respectively, in full of our shares in the per capita distribution authorized by an Act of the National Council, dated _____ MAY 3 1894 _____ 1894.

	Names of Head, and Members of Families	Amount $ cts	To Whom Paid	Witness to Payment	Remarks
188	" Richard				
189	" Florence				
190	" Rob't.				
191	" Demerit	2125.60	John W. Brown	L B Bell	
192	Bearpaw, Susan				
193	" Jennette	531.40	Susan Bearpaw	L B Bell	
194	Belle[sic], Stephen				
195	" Jennie		Stephen Bell	L B Bell	
196	" Susie	797.10	~~Susan Bearpaw~~	~~L B Bell~~	
197	Bark, David	265.70	David Bark	L B Bell	
198	Brown, Frank G.				
199	" Geo. C.				
200	" Maggie	Order			
201	" Tennessee B.				
202	" Fannie A.	1328.50	B J Rhea	L B Bell	check on order
203	Brown, Eliza	265.70	Jas Brown	L B Bell	on order
204	Brown, Polly	265.70	Jas Brown	L B Bell	on order
205	Brown, Florence	265.70	Jas Brown	L B Bell	on order
206	Bird, Lewis				
207	" Betsy				
208	" Jesse				
209	" Lucy				
210	" Anna				
211	" Henry				
212	Bear. George	1859.90	Lewis Bird	L B Bell	
213	Bean, Polly	265.70	Rufus Downing	L B Bell	on order
214	Bell, Sam'l				Sam Bell Guardian for Jennie Glass
215	Glass, Jennie	531.40	Stephen Bell	L B Bell	

77

Starr Roll 1894

We, the undersigned citizens of the Cherokee Nation, by right of Cherokee blood, do hereby acknowledge to have received of E. E. Starr, National Treasurer of the Cherokee Nation, the sums set opposite our names respectively, in full of our shares in the per capita distribution authorized by an Act of the National Council, dated ____MAY 3 1894____ 1894.

Names of Head, and Members of Families	Amount $ cts	To Whom Paid	Witness to Payment	Remarks
216 Brewer, Mollie				
217 Wright, Jesse	531.40	J M Stovo	L B Bell	Infant
218 Bright, W<u>m</u>				
219 " Sallie				
220 " John H.				
221 " Tho<u>s</u> R.	1062.80	L L Duckworth	L B Bell	order
222 Brown, Palmyra				
223 " Margaret R.				
224 " Myrtle	797.10	Andrew R Brown	L B Bell	
225 Bell, Jack	order			
226 " Lizzie	531.40	Stephen Bell	L B Bell	
227 Baley, George	265.70	Geo Baley	L B Bell	
228 Blackwood, Hooley				
229 " Polly				
230 " Mary				
231 " Bob	1062.80	Hoolie Blackwood	L B Bell	
232 Bean, Jack, Sr.				
233 " Susie				
234 Wolfe, Wattie				
	797.10	Jack Bean Sr	L B Bell	minor
235 Brown, James	265.70	Thomas Sheffield	Henry Eiffert	Step Father of Boy Sept 22 1894
236 Blackwood, Lucy	265.70	Lucy Blackwood	L B Bell	
237 Blackwood, Sally	265.70	Lucy Blackwood	L B Bell	
238 Blackbird, Wilson				
239 " Nannie				
240 " Jesse	797.10	Wilson Blackbird	L B Bell	
241 Blackbird, Betsie	265.70	Betsy Blackbird	L B Bell	
242 Brantly, Lizzie				
243 " Charlotte				

Starr Roll 1894

We, the undersigned citizens of the Cherokee Nation, by right of Cherokee blood, do hereby acknowledge to have received of E. E. Starr, National Treasurer of the Cherokee Nation, the sums set opposite our names respectively, in full of our shares in the per capita distribution authorized by an Act of the National Council, dated ____MAY 3 1894____ 1894.

	Names of Head, and Members of Families	Amount $ cts	To Whom Paid	Witness to Payment	Remarks
244	" Mary A				
245	" Dick	1062.80	Elizabeth Brantly	L B Bell	
246	Bull-frog, Teana[sic]	265.70	Tianna Bullfrog	L B Bell	
247	Bigby, Thoˢ W.				
248	" Chaˢ T.				
249	" Thoˢ B.				
250	" David E.				
251	" Ed'w. C.				
252	" Sam'l. A.				
253	" Sarah C.				
254	" Minnie C.	2125.60	Thos W. Bigby	L B Bell	
255	Bean, Joseph M	265.70	R J Garntt[sic]	L B Bell	*Check order*
256	Bean, Lydia	265.70	Nancy J Bean	L B Bell	*on order*
257	Bradford, Bettie				
258	" John	531.40	Martin Bradford	L B Bell	
259	Baley, Polly				
260	" Jane				
261	" Charles				
262	" Stephen	1062.80	Polly Baley	L B Bell	
263	Blackwood, Lewis				
264	" Jennie				
265	" Martin				
266	" Lydia				
267	" Nancy				
268	" Jane	1594.20	Lewis Blackwood	L B Bell	
269	Bean, Ruth	265.70	John Bell Paden	L B Bell	
270	Bear, Lewis				
271	" Nancy				
272	" Simon				
273	" Oscar				
274	" Polly	1328.50	G.W. Benge	G.W. Benge	*on order*

Starr Roll 1894

We, the undersigned citizens of the Cherokee Nation, by right of Cherokee blood, do hereby acknowledge to have received of E. E. Starr, National Treasurer of the Cherokee Nation, the sums set opposite our names respectively, in full of our shares in the per capita distribution authorized by an Act of the National Council, dated ___MAY 3 1894___ 1894.

Names of Head, and Members of Families	Amount $ cts	To Whom Paid	Witness to Payment	Remarks
275 Bigby, Ja^s L.				*Jas L. Bigby*
276 " Nancy C.				*Guardian for*
277 Payne, Victoria	797.10	Jas L Bigby	L B Bell	*Victoria Payne*
278 Bigby, Malinda J	265.70	T B Greer	L B Bell	*Check on order*
279 Bigby, David T				
280 " Nancy J.				
281 " Wm T.				
282 " Sam'l. A				
283 " John B.				
284 " Arthur E.				
285 " Henry C. D.				
286 " Abraham L				
287 " Martha J.				
288 " Walter A.	2657.00	D.T. Bigby	L B Bell	
289 Bean, Mark				
290 " Jno. W.	531.40	Mark Bean	J.C. Starr	
291 Bigby, Walter D.	265.70	Thos W Bigby	L B Bell	*Check ½ Sept 25, 94 62451*
292 Bull-frog, Ned				*Ned Bull-frog*
293 " Nancy	*order*			*Guardian for*
294 Poorboy Ka skun neh	797.10	R.J. Alfrey & Ned Bullfrog	L B Bell	*Poor-boy Ka sk --*
295 Blackfox, Ellis	265.70	Ellis Blackfox	L B Bell	
296 Blue, Sam'l.				
297 " Isaac	531.40	Saml Blue	L B Bell	
298 Bearpaw, Annie				
299 " Willie				
300 " Joe Chu-wee	797.10	Annie Bearpaw	L B Bell	*Infant*
301 Beck, Richard	433			
302 " Ida	531.40	Ric^d Beck	L B Bell	
303 Bird, Susie	265.70	*(Illegible)*	L B Bell	*on order*

80

Starr Roll 1894

We, the undersigned citizens of the Cherokee Nation, by right of Cherokee blood, do hereby acknowledge to have received of E. E. Starr, National Treasurer of the Cherokee Nation, the sums set opposite our names respectively, in full of our shares in the per capita distribution authorized by an Act of the National Council, dated ___ MAY 3 1894 ___ 1894.

	Names of Head, and Members of Families	Amount $ cts	To Whom Paid	Witness to Payment	Remarks
304	Blackwood, Cora A.				
305	" Henry F.	531.40	CH. Allen	L B Bell	on order
306	Blackfox, James				
307	" Darkie				
308	" Susan				
309	" Ben'j				
310	" David				
311	" Wilson	1594.20	James Blackfox	L B Bell	
312	Barnett, Margaret				
313	" Jesse				
314	" Geo				
315	" Ben'j.				
316	" John	1328.50	James Barnett	L B Bell	
317	Bearpaw, Dick				
318	" Celia				
319	" Willeah				
320	" Cornelius	1062.80	Celia Bearpaw	L B Bell	
321	Bearpaw, Dan'l.				
322	" Lucy				
323	" Sarah	797.10	G W Mitchell	L B Bell	check to G.W. Mitchell
324	Blackfox, Ned				
325	" Anna				
326	" Jennie	797.10	Ned Blackfox	L B Bell	
327	Blackfox, Eli				
328	" Nancy	order Filed 531.40	Saml Russell	L B Bell	order to Sam Russell
329	Bean, Thompson	265.70	Thompson Bean	L B Bell	
330	Blair, Arthur	265.70	W.M. Gullager	S.W. Mayfield	Paid on order Unpaid July 2-1895
331	Beamer, Aleck				
332	" Lucinda				
333	" Lydia				
334	" Orra				

Starr Roll 1894

We, the undersigned citizens of the Cherokee Nation, by right of Cherokee blood, do hereby acknowledge to have received of E. E. Starr, National Treasurer of the Cherokee Nation, the sums set opposite our names respectively, in full of our shares in the per capita distribution authorized by an Act of the National Council, dated ___MAY 3 1894___ 1894.

	Names of Head, and Members of Families	Amount $ cts	To Whom Paid	Witness to Payment	Remarks
335	" W$\underline{m}$				
336	" Rosa	1594.2	Epps Thompson	L B Bell	*on order*
337	Barnett, Ja^s W.				
338	" Alman				
339	" Rob't. E.	797.10	Jas W Barnett	L B Bell	
340	Beck, John	265.70	John Beck	L B Bell	
341	Beck, Julia				
342	" Willona				
343	" Mary E.	797.10	John Beck	L B Bell	*check to Julia Beck*
344	Bell, Mary S				*Laura O. Harless*
345	" Geo. W.	531.40	Arthur Harless	L B Bell	*minor children*
346	Barnett, Julia A.	265.70	Jesse Barnett	L B Bell	
347	Broad, Seneca	265.70	Seneca Broad	L B Bell	
348	Blackfox, David				
349	" Nellie	531.40	David Blackfox	L B Bell	
350	Bell, Titton	265.70	Arthur Harless	L B Bell	*Harless family*
351	Crittenden, Sam'l.	265.70	Saml Crittenden	L B Bell	
352	Clyne, Tim	265.70	Tim Clyne	L B Bell	
353	Crittenden, Stephen				
354	" Walter	531.40	Stephen Crittenden	L B Bell	
355	Crittenden, W$\underline{m}$	265.70	Wm Crittenden	L B Bell	
356	Crittenden, Geo. W.				
357	" Nancy				
358	" Sookie				
359	" John				
360	" Rebecca				
361	" Jesse Sidney	1594.20	Geo W Crittenden	L B Bell	

82

Starr Roll 1894

We, the undersigned citizens of the Cherokee Nation, by right of Cherokee blood, do hereby acknowledge to have received of E. E. Starr, National Treasurer of the Cherokee Nation, the sums set opposite our names respectively, in full of our shares in the per capita distribution authorized by an Act of the National Council, dated ___MAY 3 1894___ 1894.

	Names of Head, and Members of Families	Amount $ cts	To Whom Paid	Witness to Payment	Remarks
362	Crittenden, Joe	265.70	Jo[sic] Crittenden	L B Bell	
363	Cordray[sic], Mary E.				
364	" Henry A				
365	" James T.				
366	" Edward C.				
367	" Eutha M.				
368	" Nannie B.	1594.20	Mary E Cordry	L B Bell	
369	Crittenden, Vinnie R.	265.70	Vinnie R Crittenden	L B Bell	
370	Carnes, Jeff D.	386			
371	" Henry A.	386			
372	" John J.	386			
373	" Dempsey A.	386			
374	" Eddie	1328.50	Jeff Carnes	L B Bell	
375	Carnes, Andrew J.	432			
376	" Joseph E	432			
377	" Maude J.	797.10 432	A J Carnes	L B Bell	
378	Chu-wee, Wᵐ	265.70	Wᵐ Chuwee	L B Bell	
379	Crittenden, Henry C.				
380	" Mary				
381	" Chaˢ S.				
382	" Wᵐ H.				
383	" Cicero				
384	" Pearl				
385	" Thomas	1859.90	H C Crittenden	Henry Eiffert	
386	Condreay, Alley				
387	" Maude				
388	" Edward				
389	" Charles				
390	" Hattie				
391	" Mary	1594.20	Martha Condreay	L B Bell	
392	Crittenden, John R.				
393	" Alice				

Starr Roll 1894

We, the undersigned citizens of the Cherokee Nation, by right of Cherokee blood, do hereby acknowledge to have received of E. E. Starr, National Treasurer of the Cherokee Nation, the sums set opposite our names respectively, in full of our shares in the per capita distribution authorized by an Act of the National Council, dated ___MAY 3 1894___ 1894.

	Names of Head, and Members of Families	Amount $ cts	To Whom Paid	Witness to Payment	Remarks
394	" George				
395	" Henry				
396	" Martin	1328.50	Saml Crittenden	L B Bell	
397	Crittenden, Mary	265.70	Geo Crittenden	Henry Eiffert	order Sept 10
398	Costen, Margaret M				
399	" Bessie				
400	" Cassie				
401	" Edna				
402	" Rob't R				
403	" Sam'l. H				
404	" W^m T	1859.90	W W Costen	L B Bell	
405	Cox, Sallie M				
406	" Frankie M.	531.70	C.M. Cox	L B Bell	
407	Conley, Sophia	265.70	Sophia Conley	L B Bell	
408	Chu-wee, Walter				
409	" Lucinda				
410	" Sallie	797.10	Walter Chuwee	L B Bell	
411	Collins, Nancy				
412	" Theodosia	531.40	Nancy Collins	Robt B Ross	P^d by check Oct 22, 97
413	Chance, Maggie				
414	" James				
415	" Myrtle				
416	" Edaman	1062.80	Tillman Chance	L B Bell	
417	Crittenden, Moses[sic]				
418	" Nancy A				
419	" Eliza J				
420	" Dora B.				
421	" Margaret R.				
422	" Isaac M.	1594.20	Mose Crittenden	L B Bell	
423	Crittenden, Hugh				
424	" Lelia				

Starr Roll 1894

We, the undersigned citizens of the Cherokee Nation, by right of Cherokee blood, do hereby acknowledge to have received of E. E. Starr, National Treasurer of the Cherokee Nation, the sums set opposite our names respectively, in full of our shares in the per capita distribution authorized by an Act of the National Council, dated ___MAY 3 1894___ 1894.

	Names of Head, and Members of Families	Amount $ cts	To Whom Paid	Witness to Payment	Remarks
425	" Annie E				
426	" Hengh[sic] Jr	1062.80	Hugh Crittenden	L B Bell	
427	Chu-wee, James	265.70	James Chuwee	L B Bell	
428	Crowder, Polly				
429	" Nelson				
430	" W̲ᵐ P.	797.10	Polly Crowder	L B Bell	
431	Crowder, Cha̲ˢ	265.70 265.79̶0̶	P̶o̶l̶l̶y̶ Crowder John Pierce	L B Bell	on order
432	Crowder, Margaret	5̶3̶1̶.̶4̶0̶	P̶o̶l̶l̶y̶ ̶C̶r̶o̶w̶d̶e̶r̶	L B Bell	on order of Divorced Margaret Crowder
433	Catcher, George				
434	" Martha				
435	" Lee				
436	" Henry				
437	" Willie	1328.50	Geo Catcher	L B Bell	
438	Crittenden, Ben'j.				Benj. Crittenden
439	" Emily				Guardian for
440	" Lewis				Rob't. Bushyhead
441	Bushyhead, Rob't.	1062.80	Benj Crittenden	L B Bell	
442	Choo-wee[sic], John				
443	" Nancy				
444	" Mary				
445	" W̲ᵐ				
445½	" Bettie	1328.50	Nancy Chuwee	L B Bell	Administrator
446	Corntassel[sic], Aaron				
447	" Nancy	531.40	Aaron Corntassell	L B Bell	
448	Catcher, Rich				
449	" Susie	531.40	Rich Catcher	L B Bell	
450	Crittenden, Israel				
451	" Melvina	531.40	Israel Crittenden	L B Bell	
452	Catcher, John, Sr.				
453	" Margaret				

85

Starr Roll 1894

We, the undersigned citizens of the Cherokee Nation, by right of Cherokee blood, do hereby acknowledge to have received of E. E. Starr, National Treasurer of the Cherokee Nation, the sums set opposite our names respectively, in full of our shares in the per capita distribution authorized by an Act of the National Council, dated ___MAY 3 1894___ 1894.

	Names of Head, and Members of Families	Amount $ cts	To Whom Paid	Witness to Payment	Remarks
454	" Moses	1303			
455	" John Jr.				
456	" Sarah I.	9441			
457	" James				
458	" George	1859.90	John Catcher Sr	L B Bell	
459	Crittenden, Peggy				
460	" Isaac				
461	" Jack				
462	" Felix				
463	" John	DEAD.	D2895		
464	" James				
465	" Mary	1859.90	Peggy Crittenden	L B Bell	
466	Corntassel, Lewis	order Filed			
467	" Betsy	531.40	H.C. Crittenden	L B Bell	check on order
468	Chicken	265.70	Lydia Taylor Adm	L B Bell	administrator
469	Christie[sic], Jennie Z.				
470	" James				
471	" Emma	797.10	Jennie Christy	L B Bell	
472	Christie[sic], Geo. W.				
473	" Ada				
474	" Mary	797.10	Jennie Christy	L B Bell	order
475	Christie, Arch				
476	" Katie	531.40	Arch Christie	L B Bell	
477	Christie, Sallie				
478	" Lizzie				
479	" Mary	797.10	Sallie Christie	L B Bell	
480	Christie[sic], Nancy				
481	" Charlie				
482	" Nancy, Jr.	797.10	Nancy Christy	L B Bell	claims one share
483	Chandler, Fannie E.				
484	" Ja⁵ A.				

Starr Roll 1894

We, the undersigned citizens of the Cherokee Nation, by right of Cherokee blood, do hereby acknowledge to have received of E. E. Starr, National Treasurer of the Cherokee Nation, the sums set opposite our names respectively, in full of our shares in the per capita distribution authorized by an Act of the National Council, dated ___MAY 3 1894___ 1894.

	Names of Head, and Members of Families	Amount $ cts	To Whom Paid	Witness to Payment	Remarks
485	" Rebecca C.				
486	" Oliver R.				
487	" Jennette B.				
488	" John W.				
489	" Ben'j. E.	1859.90	Ben T Chandler	L B Bell	
490	Corntassel[sic], Thoˢ				
491	" Lizzie				
492	" John				
493	" Jinnanna				
494	" Jinne	1328.50	Thomas Corntassell	L B Bell	
495	Corntassel, Adam				
496	" Lucretia				
497	" Ben'j.				
498	" Ezekial	1062.80	Adam Corntassel	L B Bell	Check
499	Corntassel, Johnson	265.70	Johnson Corntassel	L B Bell	
500	Coon, Wolf				
501	" Sarah				
502	" Dick				
503	" Annie				
504	" Rabbit				
505	" Mary	1594.20	Wolf Coon	L B Bell	
506	Clyne, Sallie E	265.70	John Clyne	L B Bell	
507	Chicken, Linnie	265.70	Linnie Chicken	L B Bell	
508	Chicken, Betsy	265.70	Betsy Chicken	L B Bell	
509	Chu-wee, Alex				
510	" Lucy	531.40	Alex Chuwee	L B Bell	
511	Chu-wee, Nancy				
512	" Nannie	531.40	Nancy Chuwee	L B Bell	
513	Chu-wee, Frame				
514	" Sarah			L B Bell	

87

Starr Roll 1894

We, the undersigned citizens of the Cherokee Nation, by right of Cherokee blood, do hereby acknowledge to have received of E. E. Starr, National Treasurer of the Cherokee Nation, the sums set opposite our names respectively, in full of our shares in the per capita distribution authorized by an Act of the National Council, dated ____MAY 3 1894____ 1894.

	Names of Head, and Members of Families	Amount $ cts	To Whom Paid	Witness to Payment	Remarks
515	" Nancy				
516	" Charles				
517	" Susan				
518	" W$^{\underline{m}}$				
519	" Nannie	1859.90	Frame Chuwee	L B Bell	
520	Chu-wee, Cornelius	265.70	Cornelius Chuwee	L B Bell	
521	Christie, Go-back	265.70	Goback Christy	L B Bell	
522	Cornsilk, John				
523	" Jennie	8263			
524	" Stephen				
525	" Sarah				
526	" Jane				
527	" Alex				
528	" Jack				
529	" Delilah				
530	" Jennie				
531	" Catherine	2657.00	Jennie Cornsilk	L B Bell	
532	Catcher, Anderson				
533	" Rachel				
534	" Alsie	DEAD.			
535	" Tho$^{\underline{s}}$ J.				
536	" Atta V.				
537	" Nancy				
538	" Rob't. E.				
539	" Linie	2125.60	Anderson Catcher	L B Bell	
540	Catcher, Ellis				
541	" Lucy				
542	" Nancy J				
543	" Richard				
544	" Ezekiel				
545	" Sallie				
546	" Eli	1859.90	Ellis Catcher	L B Bell	
547	Coon, Linnie	265.70	Linnie Coon	L B Bell	

Starr Roll 1894

We, the undersigned citizens of the Cherokee Nation, by right of Cherokee blood, do hereby acknowledge to have received of E. E. Starr, National Treasurer of the Cherokee Nation, the sums set opposite our names respectively, in full of our shares in the per capita distribution authorized by an Act of the National Council, dated ___MAY 3 1894___ 1894.

Names of Head, and Members of Families	Amount $ cts	To Whom Paid	Witness to Payment	Remarks
548 Catcher, Jefferson				
549 " Ben'j.				
550 " John				
551 " Joseph	1062.80	Jefferson Catcher	L B Bell	
552 Catcher, Jennie	265.70	George Catcher	L B Bell	
553 Clyne, Ella B.	265.70	John Clyne	L B Bell	
554 Catcher, Cornelius	265.70	Cornelius Catcher	L B Bell	
555 Cochran, Sam'l.	265.70	Nellie Hogher ^mother	L B Bell	Check
556 Clyne, Ed				
557 " Emma B				
558 " John				
559 " Lunney	1062.80	Ed Clyne	L B Bell	
560 Clyne, John				
561 " Jane	531.40	John Clyne	L B Bell	
562 Catcher, John				
563 " Susie				
564 " Lettie				
565 " Rebecca	1062.80	John Catcher	L B Bell	
566 Catcher, Rachel	265.40[sic]	Rachel Catcher	L B Bell	
567 Chicken, Nannie				
568 " Nancy	531.40	Nannie Chicken ^8650	L B Bell	
569 Crittenden, Sanders C				
570 " Susan C.				
571 " James E.				
572 " Wm H.				
573 " Mary Alice				
574 " Ora Anna	1594.20	Sanders Crittenden	L B Bell	
575 Charles, Lazarus	order	E.S. Ellis ^p. 1825	J.C. Starr	E.S. Ellis Pd on order Sept 22, 1894
576 " Jennie	531.40			

89

Starr Roll 1894

We, the undersigned citizens of the Cherokee Nation, by right of Cherokee blood, do hereby acknowledge to have received of E. E. Starr, National Treasurer of the Cherokee Nation, the sums set opposite our names respectively, in full of our shares in the per capita distribution authorized by an Act of the National Council, dated ___MAY 3 1894___ 1894.

Names of Head, and Members of Families	Amount $ cts	To Whom Paid	Witness to Payment	Remarks
577 Crittenden, Wm P.	265.70	W^m P Crittenden	L B Bell	
578 Crittenden, James				
579 " Riley				
580 " Ella	797.10	Jas Crittenden	L B Bell	
581 Charlie, Thompson				
582 " Ann	*order*			
583 " Johnson				
584 " Polly				
585 " Jennie				
586 " Rose Thompson	1594.20	H C Crittenden	L B Bell	*check on order*
587 Catcher, George	754			
588 " Charlotte				
589 " Elizabeth				
590 " Mary	754			
591 " Nancy	754			
592 " Georgian	754			
593 " Joanna	1859.90	Geo Catcher	L B Bell	
594 Crittenden, Ada	265.70	Jas Crittenden	L B Bell	*James Crittenden family continued.*
595 Crittenden, Curle	265.70	Curle Crittenden	L B Bell	
596 Cannon, Edwin				
597 " Chas L.				
598 " Ira				
599 " Dublin				
600 " Claude				
601 " Maude				
602 " And[sic]				
603 " Cand[sic]	2125.60	Irby Cannon	L B Bell	
604 Crittenden, Sam'l				
605 " Annie				
606 " James				
607 " Joseph				
608 " Walter	1328.50	Saml Crittenden	L B Bell	

We, the undersigned citizens of the Cherokee Nation, by right of Cherokee blood, do hereby acknowledge to have received of E. E. Starr, National Treasurer of the Cherokee Nation, the sums set opposite our names respectively, in full of our shares in the per capita distribution authorized by an Act of the National Council, dated ___MAY 3 1894___ 1894.

	Names of Head, and Members of Families	Amount $ cts	To Whom Paid	Witness to Payment	Remarks
609	Carick[sic], Lydia		*Investigate* –		
610	" Susie				
611	" Rob't.				
612	" Carrie	1062.80	Carric Lydia	L B Bell	
613	Chuwee, Sarah				
614	" Sallie	531.40	Sarah Chuwee	L B Bell	
615	Cole, John	265.70	John⁹⁰³⁸Cole	L B Bell	
616	Cheney, Eliza				
617	" Coleman	531.40	Eliza Cheney	L B Bell	
618	Crittenden, Christopher C				
619	" Nancy J.				
620	" W^{m}				
621	" Joel				
622	" Kitty Ann				
623	" Leroy				
624	" Sallie				
625	" Thos M.				
626	" C. C.	2391.30	C C Crittenden	L B Bell	
627	Crittenden, Cornelius				
628	" Jennie				
629	" Charles				
630	" Allie				
631	" Martin				
632	" Lusie[sic]	1594.20	Cornelius Crittenden	L B Bell	
633	Cannon, Elizabeth				
634	" Ollie V	531.40	Irby Cannon	L B Bell	
635	Carnes, Anna F.	265.70	Anna F Carnes	L B Bell	
636	Carnes, Sarah A	265.70 ⁴²⁵	Sarah A Carnes	L B Bell	
637	Crittenden, James				*Continued on page 7 of Book B.*
638	" Moses				
639	" Bruce	797.10	Jas Crittenden	L B Bell	

Starr Roll 1894

We, the undersigned citizens of the Cherokee Nation, by right of Cherokee blood, do hereby acknowledge to have received of E. E. Starr, National Treasurer of the Cherokee Nation, the sums set opposite our names respectively, in full of our shares in the per capita distribution authorized by an Act of the National Council, dated ___MAY 3 1894___ 1894.

Names of Head, and Members of Families	Amount $ cts	To Whom Paid	Witness to Payment	Remarks
640 Carnes, Jno. W.	424			
641 " Dianna	531.40 425	Jno W Carnes	L B Bell	
642 Carnes, Geo. W.				
643 " Henry L.				
644 " Geo. B.				
645 " Ida T				
646 " Eliza C.				
647 " Lenora				
648 " Walter Oscar	1859.90	Geo W Carnes	L B Bell	
649 Coffee, David		Investigate –		
650 " Mary	531.40	Mary Coffee	L B Bell	
651 Crittenden, Jesse	265.70	Jesse Crittenden	L B Bell	
652 Cannon, John	265.70	Irby Cannon	L B Bell	on order
653 Cannon, Wᵐ L.				
654 " Alice				
655 " Grover	797.10	Irby Cannon	L B Bell	on order
656 Cannon, Oscar				
657 " Bertha	531.40	Oscar Cannon	L B Bell	
658 Catcher, Green				
659 " Lizzie				
660 Downing, Jesse	797.10	Lizzie Catcher	L B Bell	Minor
661 Carnes, Elizabeth	265.70 425	E P Carnes	L B Bell	
662 Downing, Ned				
663 " Betsy				
664 " Thoˢ				
665 " Clem				
666 " Lucy				
667 " Joshua				
668 " Dick				
669 " Alex				

Starr Roll 1894

We, the undersigned citizens of the Cherokee Nation, by right of Cherokee blood, do hereby acknowledge to have received of E. E. Starr, National Treasurer of the Cherokee Nation, the sums set opposite our names respectively, in full of our shares in the per capita distribution authorized by an Act of the National Council, dated _____MAY 3 1894_____ 1894.

	Names of Head, and Members of Families	Amount $ cts	To Whom Paid	Witness to Payment	Remarks
670	Murphy, Lydia				
671	" Sallie				
672	" George				
673	" Lizzie	3188.40	Ned Downing	L B Bell	$3000, check
674	Deer in water, Sallie	265.70	Sallie Deerinwater	L B Bell	
675	Dannenberg, W^{m}	265.70	R.M. Dannenberg	G W Benge	on order
676	Dick, Taylor	265.70	Robt (Illegible) Adm	L B Bell	Admis
677	Downing, George				
678	" David M.				
679	" Timmie J.				
680	" Kate				
681	" Louie				
682	" Effie O				
683	" W^{m} A, Jr	1859.90	Geo Downing	L B Bell	
684	Downing, Wm A. Sr				
685	" Eliza J.				
686	" Geo. G.				
687	" Carrie S				
688	" Sam'l. S.				
689	" Nannie M.				
690	" Elodie				
691	" Ella V.	2125.60	W^m A Downing	L B Bell	
692	Doherty[sic], Chas E.				
693	" Essie M				
694	" Maude				
695	" Callie D.				
696	" Homer				
697	" Hillard				
698	" Lora				
699	" Lizzie	2125.60	Chas E Dougherty	L B Bell	
700	Doherty[sic], Susan	265.70	Chas E Dougherty	L B Bell	
701	Duncan, Wm W.	265.70	Sallie E Duncan	L B Bell	Sallie E Duncan Mother

Starr Roll 1894

We, the undersigned citizens of the Cherokee Nation, by right of Cherokee blood, do hereby acknowledge to have received of E. E. Starr, National Treasurer of the Cherokee Nation, the sums set opposite our names respectively, in full of our shares in the per capita distribution authorized by an Act of the National Council, dated ___MAY 3 1894___ 1894.

	Names of Head, and Members of Families	Amount $ cts	To Whom Paid	Witness to Payment	Remarks
702	Duncan, Felix G	DEAD.			
703	" Lizzie	711			
704	" Clinton	711			
705	" Mary L.	711			
706	" Clee D.	711			
707	" Lola J.	1594.20	Lizzie Duncan	L B Bell	
708	Duncan, Nancy A	265.70	F.G. Duncan Adm	L B Bell	
709	Dragger, Lincoln				
710	" Martha				
711	" Mary				
712	" Annie				
713	Watt, Susie	1328.50	Lincoln Dragger	L B Bell	minor
714	Downing, Rufus	265.70	Rufus Downing	L B Bell	
715	Divine, Thoˢ N.				
716	" Chaˢ W.				
717	" James	order Filed			
718	" Joel M.				
719	" Wᵐ R				
720	" Jackson B.	1594.20	B J Chandler	L B Bell	check to BJ Chandler
721	Downing, Carrie				
722	" Wm H				
723	" Kate				
		797.10	Carrie Downing	L B Bell	
724	Dudley, Mollie E.				
725	" Fannie B				
726	" Jessie F	797.10	Jas A Dudley	L B Bell	
727	Dannenberg, Christine A	265.70	R M Dannyberg[sic]	L B Bell	
728	Dannenberg, Ruth	265.70	R M Dannenberg	G W Benge	on order
729	Deal, Adelaide				
730	" John				
731	Joseph Jasper				
732	" Elizabeth				

94

Starr Roll 1894

We, the undersigned citizens of the Cherokee Nation, by right of Cherokee blood, do hereby acknowledge to have received of E. E. Starr, National Treasurer of the Cherokee Nation, the sums set opposite our names respectively, in full of our shares in the per capita distribution authorized by an Act of the National Council, dated ___MAY 3 1894___ 1894.

	Names of Head, and Members of Families	Amount $ cts	To Whom Paid	Witness to Payment	Remarks
733	" Marion L.	1328.50	Adelaide Deal	L B Bell	
734	Deal, Charles	2*order filed* 0	E W Buffington	L B Bell	*check on order*
735	Dannenberg, White S.	265.70	R M Denningbug[sic]	L B Bell	
736	Dudley, Alfred C.	*order*			
737	" Henry D	*Filed*			
738	" Joseph	797.10	George Furguson	L B Bell	*check on order*
739	Downing, W^m				
740	" Nancy Jane				
741	" Jemima	797.10	Nancy Downing	L B Bell	
742	Downing, Jennie	265.70	Jennie Downing	L B Bell	
743	Double-head, Nancy	265.70	Nancy Doublehead	L B Bell	
744	Downing, Henry	*order filed*			*to go to J.B.P.*
745	" Conne	5~~3~~1.40	S R Walkingstick	L B Bell	*check on order*
746	Dick, George	265.70	L B Bell	Henry Eiffert	*check on order*
747	Downing, Margaret	265.70	Margaret Downing	L B Bell	
748	Dial, Mattie	265.70	Martin Dial	L B Bell	*Martin Dial*
749	Duckworth, Lavin A				
750	" Frank M.				
751	" Lula				
752	" Vade				
753	" Effie				
754	" Nancy				
755	" Gunter				
756	" Fannie	2391.30	L.L. Duckworth	L B Bell	
757	" Rob't.				
758	Dry, Simon				
759	" Mattie				
760	" Birkie				

Starr Roll 1894

We, the undersigned citizens of the Cherokee Nation, by right of Cherokee blood, do hereby acknowledge to have received of E. E. Starr, National Treasurer of the Cherokee Nation, the sums set opposite our names respectively, in full of our shares in the per capita distribution authorized by an Act of the National Council, dated ___MAY 3 1894___ 1894.

	Names of Head, and Members of Families	Amount $ cts	To Whom Paid	Witness to Payment	Remarks
761	" Agnis				
762	" John	1328.50	Simon Dry	L B Bell	
763	Dry, Thos				
764	" Lydia				
765	" Susie	797.10	Thos Dry	L B Bell	
766	Dry, Sam'l.	~~265.70~~ ~~797.10~~	Saml Dry	L B Bell	
767	Dry, John				
768	" Jennie				
769	" Isaac	797.10	John Dry	L B Bell	
770	Dry, Nancy	265.70	Nancy Dry	L B Bell	
771	Easky, Cale	order Filed			
772	" Patsy				
773	" Joe				
774	" Andy	1062.80	Walsh & Shutt	L B Bell	check on order
775	England, Link				
776	" Betsy				42 years
777	" Betsy				12 "
778	" Jackson				
779	" Mattie				
780	" Permelia				
781	" Charlotte				
782	Walkingstick, Malinda				Minor children of
783	" Lydia	2391.30	Betsy England	L B Bell	Betsy England
784	England, Jennie				
785	" Charles	531.40	Jennie England	L B Bell	
786	England, Mary	265.70	John Rogers	L B Bell	on order
787	Ellis, Francis	265.70	JW Alberty	L B Bell	on order
788	Ellis, Mary	265.70	JW Alberty	L B Bell	
789	Eldrige[sic], Clara L	265.70	Clara L Eldridge	L B Bell	see Cooweescoowee

Starr Roll 1894

We, the undersigned citizens of the Cherokee Nation, by right of Cherokee blood, do hereby acknowledge to have received of E. E. Starr, National Treasurer of the Cherokee Nation, the sums set opposite our names respectively, in full of our shares in the per capita distribution authorized by an Act of the National Council, dated ____MAY 3 1894____ 1894.

Names of Head, and Members of Families	Amount $ cts	To Whom Paid	Witness to Payment	Remarks
790 England, Geo	265.70	Geo England	L B Bell	
791 England, Esau				
792 " Geo	531.40	G.W. Mayes	G.W. Benge	*on order*
793 Eaton, Rebecca	265.70	Geo Crittenden	Henry Eiffert	*order Sept 10 94*
794 Easky, Lula	~~265.70~~	William M. Gulager	N.W. Wright	*Paid Sept 1896* *unpaid 96*
795 England, Mary	265.70	Mary England	L B Bell	
796 Early, Martha A.				*Robt. Early*
797 " Dora				*Guardian*
798 " John W.				*for Elly Welch*
799 " Mary A.				
800 " Mattie J.				
801 Welch, Elly L.	1594.20	Robt Early	L B Bell	
802 Easky, Andrew	DEAD.			
803 " Mary				
804 Harlin, James	797.10	Andrew Easky	L B Bell	*minor*
805 Easky, Joseph M.				
806 " Maggie				
807 " Mamie				
808 " Eli				
809 " Lula	1328.50	Jo M Easkey	L B Bell	
810 England, Ollie				
811 " W$^{\underline{m}}$				
812 " Malinda				
813 " Killa				
814 " Columbus	1328.50	Ollie England	L B Bell	
815 England, Levi	265.70	Ollie England ^{Adm}	L B Bell	*administrator*
816 Ela-guy, John				
817 " David				
818 " George				
819 " Frank	1062.80	David Blackfox	L B Bell	*guardian*

Starr Roll 1894

We, the undersigned citizens of the Cherokee Nation, by right of Cherokee blood, do hereby acknowledge to have received of E. E. Starr, National Treasurer of the Cherokee Nation, the sums set opposite our names respectively, in full of our shares in the per capita distribution authorized by an Act of the National Council, dated ___MAY 3 1894___ 1894.

Names of Head, and Members of Families	Amount $ cts	To Whom Paid	Witness to Payment	Remarks
820 Forbes, Rob't. F	9447			
821 " Ora	531.40	Eve Folson[sic]	L B Bell	on order
822 Forbes, W<u>m</u> M.	265.70	Eve Folsom	L B Bell	on order
823 Forbes, Agnes E.	265.70	J.W Folsom	L B Bell	on order
824 Forbes, Francis E.				
825 " Cora				
826 " Pearlie	797.10	Frances Forbes	L B Bell	
827 Folsom[sic], Jo<u>s</u> W.	265.70	Joe W. Fulsom	L B Bell	
828 Fodder, Peggy	265.70	Peggy Fodder	L B Bell	
829 Fields, Rich'd.	265.70	Rich'd Fields	L B Bell	
830 Fouts, Harriet				
831 " Mary	531.40	E W Buffington	G W Benge	on order
832 Fields, Thompson				
833 " Linnie	531.40	Thompson Fields	L B Bell	
834 Fodder, Crabgrass	265.70	Crabgrass Fodder	L B Bell	
835 Fodder, John	8761			
836 " Susie	8761 8761			
837 " Mattie	8804 8804			
838 " Lunnie	1062.80	Susie Fodder	L B Bell	
839 Foreman, Tho<u>s</u>	265.70	Peggy *(Illegible)*	L B Bell	
840 Fodder, Bettie	265.70	Bettie Fodder	L B Bell	
841 Foreman, Elias G.				
842 " Mary				
843 " Elizabeth				
844 " W<u>m</u> P.				
845 Sanders, Mary B.	1328.50	Mary Foreman	L B Bell	

Starr Roll 1894

We, the undersigned citizens of the Cherokee Nation, by right of Cherokee blood, do hereby acknowledge to have received of E. E. Starr, National Treasurer of the Cherokee Nation, the sums set opposite our names respectively, in full of our shares in the per capita distribution authorized by an Act of the National Council, dated _____ MAY 3 1894 _____ 1894.

Names of Head, and Members of Families	Amount $ cts	To Whom Paid	Witness to Payment	Remarks
846 Frog, Jaˢ B.				Bull-frog
847 " Lizzie B.				
848 " Still B.				
849 " Wilson B.	1062.80	Jas B Frog	L B Bell	
850 Folsom, Malving[sic]				
851 " Levi, Jr.				
852 " Tandy W.				
853 " Roxean[sic]				
854 " Wᵐ S.	1328.50	Levi Folsom	L B Bell	
855 Forbes, Nancy E.				
856 " Susan L.	531.40	N E Forbes	L B Bell	
857 Forbes, Nancy L.	265.70	Nancy L Forbes	L B Bell	
858 Four-killer, Takey	265.70	Takey Fourkiller	L B Bell	
859 " Sarah				
860 " Sam'l				
861 " Willie	797.10	Sarah Fourkiller	L B Bell	
862 Fodder, John				
863 " Katie	531.40	John Fodder	L B Bell	
864 Foreman, Edward				
865 " Thoˢ H.				
866 " Jaˢ E				
867 " Claude C.	1062.80	Edward Foreman	L B Bell	
868 Foreman, Charlie				
869 " Thomas				
870 " Myrtle	797.10	Charles Foreman	L B Bell	
871 Foreman, Edward				
872 " Willie				
873 " Elmore				
874 " Dennis				
875 " Orlando	1328.50	Edward Foreman	L B Bell	

Starr Roll 1894

We, the undersigned citizens of the Cherokee Nation, by right of Cherokee blood, do hereby acknowledge to have received of E. E. Starr, National Treasurer of the Cherokee Nation, the sums set opposite our names respectively, in full of our shares in the per capita distribution authorized by an Act of the National Council, dated ___MAY 3 1894___ 1894.

	Names of Head, and Members of Families	Amount $ cts	To Whom Paid	Witness to Payment	Remarks
876	Fox, John B.				
877	" Martha B.	$31.40	James A Furgeson	L B Bell	*check on order*
878	Foreman, Lydia				
879	" Aggie				
880	" Susie				
881	" Alice	1062.80	Lydia Foreman	L B Bell	
882	Fields, John				
883	" Nannie				
884	" Florence	797.10⁴⁶⁶	John Fields	L B Bell	
885	Fouts, Maggie V.				
886	" Jacob R				
887	" Rich' L.				
888	" Mildred *(?)*	1062.80	E.W. Buffington	G.W. Benge	*on order*
889	Freeman, George	265.70	Celia Parnell	L B Bell	
890	Foreman, Sam'l				
891	" Lizzie				
892	" Cooweescoowee	797.10	Saml Foreman	L B Bell	
893	Fallin, Nancy	256.70	Nancy Fallin	L B Bell	
894	Fallin, Aggie				
895	Wilkerson, Eliza	531.40	Aggie Fallen[sic]	L B Bell	*minor child*
896	Four-killer, Tommie				
897	" Caleb				
898	" Spade	797.10	Tommie Fourkiller	L B Bell	
899	Fixen, Blackbird				
900	" Alsie	531.40	Blackbird Fixen	L B Bell	
901	Foreman, Alice				
902	Bell, Lizzie				*minor*
903	" Hoolie	797.10	Alice Foreman	L B Bell	*children*

Starr Roll 1894

We, the undersigned citizens of the Cherokee Nation, by right of Cherokee blood, do hereby acknowledge to have received of E. E. Starr, National Treasurer of the Cherokee Nation, the sums set opposite our names respectively, in full of our shares in the per capita distribution authorized by an Act of the National Council, dated ___ MAY 3 1894 ___ 1894.

	Names of Head, and Members of Families	Amount $ cts	To Whom Paid	Witness to Payment	Remarks
904	Four killer, Fish-hawk	order	order		
905	" Neppy				
906	" Cicero				
907	" Richard				
908	" Grant	1328.50	I.H. Fourkiller	L B Bell	*on order of England & Kimbrough*
909	Fields, Andy J.				
910	" Ja^s P.				
911	" Andrew J.				
912	" John S.	1062.80	E.W. Buffington	G.W. Benge	
913	Four killer, Felix				
914	" Katie[sic]				
915	" Samson				
916	" Charles	8442			
917	" Larkin				
918	" W^m				
919	" Charlotte				
920	" Takey	2125.60	Katy Fourkiller	L B Bell	
921	Finley, Gean[sic]	265.70	Glean[sic] Finley	L B Bell	
922	Freeman, Jane	or 265.70 *Filed*	John Meigs	L B Bell	*check guardian*
923	Freeman, Cynthia L.	or 265.70 *Filed*	Magy[sic] E Meigs	L B Bell	*John Meigs wife*
924	Four killer, Cloud	265.70	Cloud Fourkiller	L B Bell	
925	Fields, Ben'j. F.	265.70	Ben F Fields	L B Bell	
926	Fields, Betsy	265.70	Betsy Fields	L B Bell	
927	Feelin, Watt				
928	" Nagie[sic]	531.40	Watt Feelin	L B Bell	
929	Fields, Charles				
930	" Carrie				
931	" George Dan'l				
932	" Betsy				
933	" W^m	1328.50	Charles O'Fields	L B Bell	*O'Fields was the correct name*

101

Starr Roll 1894

We, the undersigned citizens of the Cherokee Nation, by right of Cherokee blood, do hereby acknowledge to have received of E. E. Starr, National Treasurer of the Cherokee Nation, the sums set opposite our names respectively, in full of our shares in the per capita distribution authorized by an Act of the National Council, dated ___MAY 3 1894___ 1894.

Names of Head, and Members of Families	Amount $ cts	To Whom Paid	Witness to Payment	Remarks
934 Fields, Celia				
935 " Lucy	531.40	Celia Fields	L B Bell	
936 Fields, Jennie				
937 " Lydia	531.40	Jennie Fields	L B Bell	
938 Fields, Sam'l O	265.70	Sam¹ O'fields	L B Bell	
939 Fields, Jaˢ O	265.70	Jas O Fields	L B Bell	
940 Green, Mary J.				
941 " Sidney A				
942 " Margaret A				
943 " Jessie	1062.80	Mary Green	L B Bell	
944 Grigsby, Ellen				
945 " Dan'l.				
946 " Emmona				
947 " James				
948 " Henrietta	1328.50	William Grigsby	L B Bell	
949 Grant, Freddie	265.70	E.L. Grant	L B Bell	Eliza Grant
950 Guthrie, Wᵐ P.	265.70	Wᵐ P Guthrie	L B Bell	
951 Garrett, Lizzie A.				
952 " Bruce				
953 " Simeon				
954 " Mary				
955 " Allie				
956 " Lola				
957 " Willie				
958 " Thoˢ	2125.60	J Robt Garrett	L B Bell	
959 Garrett, Rachel C.				
960 " Mattie				
961 " Rob't				
962 " Claude				
963 " Frank				
964 " Fannie				

Starr Roll 1894

We, the undersigned citizens of the Cherokee Nation, by right of Cherokee blood, do hereby acknowledge to have received of E. E. Starr, National Treasurer of the Cherokee Nation, the sums set opposite our names respectively, in full of our shares in the per capita distribution authorized by an Act of the National Council, dated ___MAY 3 1894___ 1894.

	Names of Head, and Members of Families	Amount $ cts	To Whom Paid	Witness to Payment	Remarks
965	" Henry	1859.90	Joseph M Garrett	L B Bell	
966	Gritts, John				
967	" Nancy				
968	" Levi				
969	" Nicholas	1062.80	Nancy Gritts	L B Bell	
970	Guthrie, Lorin				
971	" Edna				
972	" Cora				
973	" Ethel				
974	" Charles	1328.50	Lorin Guthrie	L B Bell	
975	Going Wolfe[sic], Aaron				
976	" Julia	531.40	Aaron Going Wolf	L B Bell	
977	Gritts, Runabout				
978	" Sarah				
979	" Ezekial				
980	" Charles	1062.80	Runabout Gritts	L B Bell	
981	Groundhog, Tho[s]				
982	" Nancy				
983	" Lizzie	797.10	Nancy Groundhog	L B Bell	
984	Grease, Charles	265.70	Charley Grease	L B Bell	
985	Gritts, Annie	265.70	Annie Gritts	L B Bell	
986	Greace[sic], Alla				
987	Stealer, Lizzard	531.40	Alla Greece	L B Bell	*Insane*
988	Glenn, Jesse E				
989	" Mary E				
990	" Emma J.				
991	" Henry				
992	" Ethel M.				
993	" Franklin C.				
994	" Margaret A	1859.90	Jesse E Glenn	L B Bell	

Starr Roll 1894

We, the undersigned citizens of the Cherokee Nation, by right of Cherokee blood, do hereby acknowledge to have received of E. E. Starr, National Treasurer of the Cherokee Nation, the sums set opposite our names respectively, in full of our shares in the per capita distribution authorized by an Act of the National Council, dated ___MAY 3 1894___ 1894.

Names of Head, and Members of Families	Amount $ cts	To Whom Paid	Witness to Payment	Remarks
995 Goss, Ben'j. F.				
996 " W͞ᵐ R.	531.40	Benj F Goss	L B Bell	
997 Gordon, Caroline				
998 " Laura M.				
999 " Jaˢ F.	DEAD 797.10	W͞ᵐ Gordon	L B Bell	
1000 Gott, Jaˢ W.				
1001 " Ann				
1002 " Matilda				
1003 " Maggie				
1004 " Pickens				
1005 " Johnson	1594.20	J W Gott	L B Bell	
1006 Ghomley[sic], Sarah C	265.70	Sarah C Ghomly	L B Bell	
1007 Ghomley, Walter S				
1008 " Willeah	531.40	W S Ghomly	L B Bell	
				Sept 1894
1009 Gunpile, Annie	265.70	Annie Gunpile	Henry Eiffert	Sela Harlin
1010 Going Wolfe, Sylvester	265.70	Sylvester Goingwolf	L B Bell	
1011 Gibbs, Caroline				
1012 " Lillie O.				
1013 " W͞ᵐ P.				
1014 " Hattie E.				
1015 " Allan D.	1328.50	A.J. Gibbs	L B Bell	
1016 Grubb[sic], Minnie				
1017 " Earl				
1018 " Hiram	797.10	Minnie Grubbs	L B Bell	
1019 Goforth, Rachel				
1020 " Eu lem-ma				
1021 " Eu la ella	797.10	Rachel Goforth	L B Bell	
1022 Garner, May C.	order 265.70 Filed	J R Garrett	L B Bell	check on order

Starr Roll 1894

We, the undersigned citizens of the Cherokee Nation, by right of Cherokee blood, do hereby acknowledge to have received of E. E. Starr, National Treasurer of the Cherokee Nation, the sums set opposite our names respectively, in full of our shares in the per capita distribution authorized by an Act of the National Council, dated ____MAY 3 1894____ 1894.

Names of Head, and Members of Families	Amount $ cts	To Whom Paid	Witness to Payment	Remarks
1023 Holt, Mary M.				
1024 " Wᵐ L.				
1025 " Earls[sic] D.				
1026 " Mary E.	1062.80	Thoˢ J *(Illegible)*	L B Bell	*on order*
1027 Harlan[sic], George	265.70	Geo Harlin	L B Bell	
1028 Holland, Wᵐ G	265.70	Nancy ⁴³⁴⁸ Holland	L B Bell	*on order*
1029 Hamilton, Lugenia	265.70	Lugenia Hamilton	L B Bell	
1030 Herren, Rich'd F	265.70	Mattie Harlan	L B Bell	*mother of (blank)*
1031 Hays, Minnie L.				
1032 " Chaˢ J.	531.40	J.J. Hays	L B Bell	
1033 Hern, Peggy				
1034 " Helen P.				
1035 Foreman, Fannie				*Children of*
1036 " Willie				*Peggy Horn*
1037 " Lula E.	1328.50	Peggy Hern	L B Bell	
1038 Holland, Ples. H				
1039 " Nancy				
1040 " John Jr				
1041 " Alice				
1042 " Pleasant, Jr.				
1043 " Thoˢ L.				
1044 " Dennis W.				
1045 " Lugy				
1046 " Annie	2391.30	Nancy Holland	L B Bell	
1047 Hildebrand, James	265.70	*(Illegible)*	L B Bell	
1048 Holland, Nancy				
1049 " Spencer				
1050 " Dora B.	797.10	Nancy Holland	L B Bell	

105

Starr Roll 1894

We, the undersigned citizens of the Cherokee Nation, by right of Cherokee blood, do hereby acknowledge to have received of E. E. Starr, National Treasurer of the Cherokee Nation, the sums set opposite our names respectively, in full of our shares in the per capita distribution authorized by an Act of the National Council, dated ___MAY 3 1894___ 1894.

	Names of Head, and Members of Families	Amount $ cts	To Whom Paid	Witness to Payment	Remarks
1051	Holland, Jno W.				Jno. W. Holland
1052	" W<u>m</u>	␘			guardian for
1053	" Leonard	␘			Emma A Welch
1054	" James Jr	␘			
1055	" Rob't	␘			
1056	" Maggie	␘			on order
1057	Welch, Emma A.	1859.90	Jas L Holland	L B Bell	Jno W Holland
1058	Hummingbird, Isaac				
1059	" Mandy				
1060	" Willie				
1061	" Rider				
1062	" Josie				
1063	" Stan				
1064	" David				
1065	" Walter	2125.60	Isaac Hummingbird	L B Bell	
1066	Horseskin, Jennie	265.70	Jennie Horseskin	*(No name given)*	
1067	Horseskin, Ned	265.70	Ned Horseskin	L B Bell	on order of Tom *(Illegible)*
1068	Hart, John				
1069	" Willie				Chas Hart
1070	" Delilah	797.10	B.T. Chandler	G.W. Benge	on order
1071	Hammer, John				
1072	" Margaret				
1073	" Annie				
1074	" Julia				
1075	" Ella				
1076	" Tho<u>s</u>	1594.20	John Hammer	L B Bell	
1077	Harlin, Ellis				
1078	" George				
1079	" Caleb				
1080	" Jane	1062.80	Lydia Harlin	L B Bell	
1081	Hogner, Joseph				
1082	" Nancy				
1083	" Watt	797.10	H C Crittenden	L B Bell	check on order

Starr Roll 1894

We, the undersigned citizens of the Cherokee Nation, by right of Cherokee blood, do hereby acknowledge to have received of E. E. Starr, National Treasurer of the Cherokee Nation, the sums set opposite our names respectively, in full of our shares in the per capita distribution authorized by an Act of the National Council, dated ___MAY 3 1894___ 1894.

	Names of Head, and Members of Families	Amount $ cts	To Whom Paid	Witness to Payment	Remarks
1084	Harry, John Jr	265.70	John Harry	L B Bell	
1085	Hummingbird, Jacob				
1086	" Jennie				
1087	" Andrew				
1088	" Ella				
1089	" Emma	1328.50	Jacob Hummingbird	L B Bell	
1090	Bean, Raven	265.70	Lucy Blackwood	L B Bell	on order
1091	" Nannie	265.70	Lucy Blackwood	L B Bell	on order
1092	Harry, John				
1093	" An na lu ah				
1094	" Young pig				
1095	" Soldier				
1096	" Ske-kee				
1097	" Sarah	1594.20	John Harry or Hair	L B Bell	
1098	Hitcher, David				
1099	" Betsy				
1100	" Samson				
1101	" Willie				
1102	" John	1328.50	Betsy Hitcher	L B Bell	
1103	Harry, James	531.40	order H C Crittenden	L B Bell	check on order
1104	" Jennie				
1105	Harlan[sic], Jno. G.				
1106	" Eliza				
1107	" Nancy J.				
1108	" Edna				
1109	" Cherokee				
1110	" Sarah				
1111	" Eli	1859.90	Jno G. Harlin	L B Bell	
1112	Horseskin, Charlotte	458			
1113	" Louisa	458			
1114	" Mary Ann	797.10	Charlotte Horseskin	L B Bell	
1115	Hummingbird, Joshua				
1116	" Lizzie				

107

Starr Roll 1894

We, the undersigned citizens of the Cherokee Nation, by right of Cherokee blood, do hereby acknowledge to have received of E. E. Starr, National Treasurer of the Cherokee Nation, the sums set opposite our names respectively, in full of our shares in the per capita distribution authorized by an Act of the National Council, dated ____MAY 3 1894____ 1894.

	Names of Head, and Members of Families	Amount $ cts	To Whom Paid	Witness to Payment	Remarks
1117	" George				
1118	" Wilson	1062.80	Joshua Hummingbird	L B Bell	
1119	Hogner, Writer				
1120	" Charlotte				
1121	" George				
1122	" Lizzie				
1123	" Adam	1328.50	G.W. Benge	G.W. Benge	on order
1124	Hitcher, Sam'l	265.70 Order	H C Crittenden	L B Bell	
1125	Hyder, Peter	265.40[sic]	Peter Hyder	L B Bell	check on order
1126	Hogner, Wᵐ	265.70 Order	H C Crittenden	L B Bell	check on order
1127	Holland, Henry S.	265.70	Nancy Alberty	L B Bell	order
1128	Hawk, Jaˢ F.				
1129	" Ella F.				
1130	" Nannie F.				
1131	" Lydia F	590			
1132	" Cornelius F.				
1133	" Joseph F.	1594.20	G.W. Benge	Henry Eiffert	on order
1134	Harlan, Nelson	order Filed 265.70	Jno G. Harlin	L B Bell	Evans had order but gave it back
1135	Hawk, Joˢ F.				
1136	" Anna F.				
1137	" Katie F.				
1138	" Geegilly	1062.80	GW Benge	Henry Eiffert	on order
1139	Hendrix, Sam'l				
	" Susie	531.40	Susie Hendrix	L B Bell	
1140	Hicks, Ranzia	265.70	Ranzia Hicks	L B Bell	
1141	Harlan, Silas	501			
1142	" Mary	501			
1143	" Eli				
1144	" Lucinda	501			

108

Starr Roll 1894

We, the undersigned citizens of the Cherokee Nation, by right of Cherokee blood, do hereby acknowledge to have received of E. E. Starr, National Treasurer of the Cherokee Nation, the sums set opposite our names respectively, in full of our shares in the per capita distribution authorized by an Act of the National Council, dated ___MAY 3 1894___ 1894.

	Names of Head, and Members of Families	Amount $ cts	To Whom Paid	Witness to Payment	Remarks
1145	" Ellis	1328.50[1]	Silas Harlin	L B Bell	
1146	Hogner, Ellis				
1147	" Nellie	8678			
1148	" John				
1149	" Kinney				
1150	" Clem	1328.50	Nellie Hogner	L B Bell	
1151	Hogshooter, Ned				
1152	" Maria				
1153	" Caroline	797.10	Ned Hogshooter	L B Bell	
1154	Hogshooter, Osa[sic]				
1155	" Betsy				
1156	" Emma	797.10	Oce Hogshooter	L B Bell	
1157	Hammer, Rider				
1158	" Alsie				
1159	" Ellen	797.10	Alsie Hammer	L B Bell	
1160	Ham, Betsy				
1161	" David				
1162	" Perlie				
1163	" Dora	1062.80	Betsy Ham	L B Bell	
1164	Harless, Ophelia J.				
1165	" Guy				
1166	" Trenton	797.10	Scott Harless	L B Bell	
1167	Harless, Harrison	265.70	Arthur Harless	L B Bell	order of Wm Harless John
1168	Harless, Laura O.				
1169	" Anna				
1170	" Rufus				
1171	" Warren R.				
1172	" Louisa	1328.50	Arthur Harless	L B Bell	
1173	Hughes, George				
1174	" Linne				
1175	" Sarah				

Starr Roll 1894

We, the undersigned citizens of the Cherokee Nation, by right of Cherokee blood, do hereby acknowledge to have received of E. E. Starr, National Treasurer of the Cherokee Nation, the sums set opposite our names respectively, in full of our shares in the per capita distribution authorized by an Act of the National Council, dated _____MAY 3 1894_____ 1894.

	Names of Head, and Members of Families	Amount $ cts	To Whom Paid	Witness to Payment	Remarks
1176	" Joseph	1062.80	Geo Hughes	L B Bell	
1177	Hogshooter, James				
1178	" Sallie				
1179	" Dee	797.10	James Hogshooter	L B Bell	
1180	Hogshooter, Simon				
1181	" Annie				
1182	Bearpaw, W^m	797.10	Annie Hogshooter	L B Bell	
1183	Israel, David	265.70	David Isreal[sic]	L B Bell	
1184	Israel, W^m				
1185	" Sarah				
1186	" Roy				
1187	" Ira				
1188	" Chester				
1189	" Rufus R	1594.20	William Israel	L B Bell	
1190	Johnson, Rebecca				
1191	" Minnie Bell				
1192	" Clint	797.10	T B Johnson	L B Bell	
1193	Johnson, Jo^s M.				
1194	" Mary				
1195	" Jody				
1196	" Minnie				
1197	" Ella	1328.50	Mary Johnson	L B Bell	
1198	Johnson, Catherine	265.70	Catherine Johnson	L B Bell	
1199	Johnson, Dudley				
1200	" Laura				
1201	" Martha				
1202	" Nehemiah				
1203	" Isaac	1328.50	Adline Johnson	L B Bell	
1204	Johnson, Monroe	265.70	Catherine Johnson	L B Bell	

110

Starr Roll 1894

We, the undersigned citizens of the Cherokee Nation, by right of Cherokee blood, do hereby acknowledge to have received of E. E. Starr, National Treasurer of the Cherokee Nation, the sums set opposite our names respectively, in full of our shares in the per capita distribution authorized by an Act of the National Council, dated ____MAY 3 1894____ 1894.

Names of Head, and Members of Families	Amount $ cts	To Whom Paid	Witness to Payment	Remarks
1205 Johnson, Jesse				
1206 " Oscar	531.40	Jesse Johnson	L B Bell	
1207 Johnson, Peggy	265.70	Nancy Sixkiller	L B Bell	on order
1208 Jordan, Alice M.				
1209 " Birt				
1210 " Henry J.	797.10	Jeff Jourdan[sic]	L B Bell	
1211 Johnson, Rebecca C.				
1212 " Calvin				
1213 " Margaret	797.10	J R Johnson	L B Bell	
1214 Jackson, Still				
1215 " Minnie				
1216 " Jesse J.				
1217 " Johnson F.				
1218 " Annie	1328.50	Still Jackson	L B Bell	
1219 Jo hoo ster, Katie				
1220 Drywater, Polly	531.40	Katie Jo hooster	L B Bell	minor
1221 Kelly, Thos				wife white
1222 " Ja^s T				
1223 " Ida				
1224 " Rosanna				
1225 " Eva				
1226 " Willard				
1227 " Bessie	1859.90	Thos Kelly	L B Bell	
1228 Kelly, Nellie	265.70	Isaac Vanmater	L B Bell	
1229 Kirk, Susanna				
1230 " Charlotte				
1231 " Rob't.				
1232 " Sam'l.				
1233 " Wattie				
1234 " Asbury	1594.20	Thos Kirk	L B Bell	

111

Starr Roll 1894

We, the undersigned citizens of the Cherokee Nation, by right of Cherokee blood, do hereby acknowledge to have received of E. E. Starr, National Treasurer of the Cherokee Nation, the sums set opposite our names respectively, in full of our shares in the per capita distribution authorized by an Act of the National Council, dated ___MAY 3 1894___ 1894.

	Names of Head, and Members of Families	Amount $ cts	To Whom Paid	Witness to Payment	Remarks
1235	Kincade, Nancy M.				
1236	" Rob't. C.				
1237	" Ed'w. C.				
1238	" Francis N.				
1239	" W$\underline{m}$ R				
1240	" Cha$\underline{s}$ W.				
1241	" Andrew M.				
1242	" Ja$\underline{s}$ L.				
1243	" Martha L.	2391.30	Nancy Kincade	L B Bell	
1244	Kelly, Jno. M.				
1245	" Susan				
1246	" Charlie				
1247	" Susie				
1248	" Lacie				
1249	" Joel				
1250	" James				
1251	" Mary	2125.60	Jno M Kelly	L B Bell	
1252	Kirk, W$\underline{m}$				
1253	" Laura				
1254	" Sam'l.				
1255	" Della				
1256	" John				
1257	" Rebecca	1594.20	Laura Kirk	L B Bell	
1258	Leach, Peggy	265.70	John Harry *Hair* or	L B Bell	
1259	Leaf, Tho$\underline{s}$				
1260	" Nancy				
1261	" Willie				
1262	" Lydia				
1263	" Millie				
1264	" Caine				
1265	" Isaac				
1266	" Root	2125.60	Thomas Leaf	L B Bell	
1267	Lindsy, Margaret A.				
1268	" Jesse M.				
1269	" Annie W	797.10	Sallie E Duncan	L B Bell	*on order*

Starr Roll 1894

We, the undersigned citizens of the Cherokee Nation, by right of Cherokee blood, do hereby acknowledge to have received of E. E. Starr, National Treasurer of the Cherokee Nation, the sums set opposite our names respectively, in full of our shares in the per capita distribution authorized by an Act of the National Council, dated ___MAY 3 1894___ 1894.

	Names of Head, and Members of Families	Amount $ cts	To Whom Paid	Witness to Payment	Remarks
1270	Langley[sic], Zachary T	320			
1271	" Lock	318			
1272	" Marion J.	322			
1273	" Martha E.	320			
1274	" Chaˢ O.	320			
1275	" Susan J.	1594.20 320	Z T Langly	L B Bell	
1276	Langley[sic], Rob't R	265.70	Robt Langly	L B Bell	
1277	Langley[sic], Jno W.D.	316			
1278	" Sarah	316			
1279	" Joˢ O.	797.10 316	Jno W D Langly	L B Bell	
1280	Lacy, Adam L.				
1281	" Jennie A.				
1282	" Silas W.				
1283	" Rufus V.				
1284	" Charlotte C				
1285	" Myrtle M.	1594.20	Adam Lacy	L B Bell	
1286	Lee, Lydia				
1287	" Felix				
1288	" Sallie				
1289	" Katie				
1290	" Levi	1328.50	Lydia Lee	L B Bell	
1291	Lee, Nannie	265.70	Nannie Lee	L B Bell	
1292	Lee, Carrie				
1293	" James	531.40	Carrie Lee	L B Bell	
1294	Leaf, Lethe	265.70	Lethe Leaf	L B Bell	
1295	Leaf, Turn				
1296	" Peggy				
1297	" Henry				
1298	" Wᵐ	8647			
1299	" Jane	8195			
1300	" Scraper	1594.20	Turn Leaf	L B Bell	

113

Starr Roll 1894

We, the undersigned citizens of the Cherokee Nation, by right of Cherokee blood, do hereby acknowledge to have received of E. E. Starr, National Treasurer of the Cherokee Nation, the sums set opposite our names respectively, in full of our shares in the per capita distribution authorized by an Act of the National Council, dated ___MAY 3 1894___ 1894.

Names of Head, and Members of Families	Amount $ cts	To Whom Paid	Witness to Payment	Remarks
1301 Leaf, Jesse				
1302 " Tah-to-eh				
1303 " Louisa				
1304 " Coh-na-eh				
1305 " Jennie				
1306 " Co-he-nah	1594.20	Jesse Lee	L B Bell	*intend on roll wrong*
1307 Locust, Jackson				
1308 " Susan				
1309 " Abraham	797.10	Jackson Locust	L B Bell	
1310 Looney, John				
1311 " Jennie	531.40	John Looney	L B Bell	
1312 Leach, Phillips[sic]	265.70	Phillip Leach	L B Bell	
1313 Langley, Sidney				
1314 " Joseph				
1315 " Alice				
1316 " Loch				
1317 " Ollie	1328.50	Sidney Langly	L B Bell	
1318 Lane, Mary	265.70	Mary *(Illegible)*	Henry Eiffert *Oct 8th 1894*	*Lane or Lawe*
1319 Lee, Nellie				
1320 " Wayne	531.40	Leonard Lee	L B Bell	
1321 Lowry, Wa-lu-ky				
1322 " Ta-kie				
1323 " Nancy				
1324 " Thos				
1325 " Henry				
1326 " Susan				
1327 " Sallie				
1328 " Sut	2125.60	Takie Lowry	L B Bell	
1329 Langley, Andrew J.	R448 ENROLLMENT REFUSED.			
1330 " Mary J.	R448 ENROLLMENT REFUSED.			
1331 " Martha A	R448 ENROLLMENT REFUSED.			
1332 " John J	R448 ENROLLMENT REFUSED.			

114

Starr Roll 1894

We, the undersigned citizens of the Cherokee Nation, by right of Cherokee blood, do hereby acknowledge to have received of E. E. Starr, National Treasurer of the Cherokee Nation, the sums set opposite our names respectively, in full of our shares in the per capita distribution authorized by an Act of the National Council, dated ___ MAY 3 1894 ___ 1894.

	Names of Head, and Members of Families	Amount $ cts	To Whom Paid	Witness to Payment	Remarks
1333	" Rob't. E.	R448 ENROLLMENT REFUSED.			
1334	" Reno E	1594.20 R448	A J Langly	L B Bell	
1335	Morris, Silas	265.70	Jno D Buffington	L B Bell	
1336	Maupin, Carrie	265.70	Wᵐ Maupin	L B Bell	
1337	Moreland, Sarah J.				
1338	" Dora A.				
1339	" Martha J.				
1340	" Nancy M.				
1341	" Collins M.				
1342	" Jesse M.	1594.20	E W Buffington	L B Bell	*on order*
1343	Morris, Jno B				
1344	" Fannie				
1345	" Fred				
1346	" Bennie				
1347	" Burt				
1348	" Francis	1594.20	Jno B Morris	L B Bell	
1349	Marrs, Donas				
1350	" Iva N	531.40	Wᵐ H Morris	L B Bell	*on order*
1351	Mulcare, Tennessee				
1352	" Fred				
1353	" Ida				
1354	" Minnie				
1355	" Nora				
1356	" Sterling				
1357	" Rob't. Parris	1859.90	Mike Mulcare	L B Bell	*Mental imbecility*
1358	Mulcare, Emmet	265.70	Mike Mulcare	L B Bell	
1359	MᶜClain[sic], Sam'l.	265.70	Saml McLane	L B Bell	
1360	Martin, Mary G.				
1361	" Georgian	434			
1362	" Octavia				
1363	" Magaline[sic]				

Starr Roll 1894

We, the undersigned citizens of the Cherokee Nation, by right of Cherokee blood, do hereby acknowledge to have received of E. E. Starr, National Treasurer of the Cherokee Nation, the sums set opposite our names respectively, in full of our shares in the per capita distribution authorized by an Act of the National Council, dated ___MAY 3 1894___ 1894.

	Names of Head, and Members of Families	Amount $ cts	To Whom Paid	Witness to Payment	Remarks
1364	" Flora L.	1328.50	Mary G Martin		
1365	Morton, Noah	265.70	Joseph M. Grant *guardian*	L B Bell	
1366	Crittenden, Lydia	265.70	Lydia Harlin	L B Bell	*Lydia drew for herself having married* *Minors of the*
1367	" Charles	265.70	Johnson Mayes	L B Bell	*Mays family*
1368	" Jack	265.70	Johnson Mayes	L B Bell	*Book A* (54)
1369	Morris, Francis E.				
1370	" Thoˢ R.	531.40	Gabriel A Morris	L B Bell	
1371	Morris, Virgil C.				
1372	" Mary				
1373	" Laurie				
1374	" Minnie				
1375	" Willie				
1376	" Arthur	1859.90	V C Morris	L B Bell	
1377	McPherson, W^m R	265.70	W^m R McPherson	L B Bell	
1378	Morris, Wm H.				*W= H Morris*
1379	" Polly				*Guardian*
1380	" Fannie				*for*
1381	" George				*Reese*
1382	" Jeff				*Thornton*
1383	Thornton, Reese	1594.20	W^m H Morris	L B Bell	
1384	Moss, Mary M	265.70	Mary Moss *Investigate* B Bell		
1385	Morris, Glov				*Glov Morris*
1386	" Nannie				*Guardian*
1387	" Nicholas				*for*
1388	" Alice				*Lizzie*
1389	Bear, Lizzie	1328.50	Glov Morris	L B Bell	*Bear*
1390	Morton, Jack				
1391	" Hester A.				
1392	" Rob't. L.				
1393	" Grover C.				
1394	" W^m H	1328.50	Jack Morton	L B Bell	

116

Starr Roll 1894

We, the undersigned citizens of the Cherokee Nation, by right of Cherokee blood, do hereby acknowledge to have received of E. E. Starr, National Treasurer of the Cherokee Nation, the sums set opposite our names respectively, in full of our shares in the per capita distribution authorized by an Act of the National Council, dated ____MAY 3 1894____ 1894.

	Names of Head, and Members of Families	Amount $ cts	To Whom Paid	Witness to Payment	Remarks
1395	Morton, Newton				
1396	" John				
1397	" Vinny	order 411			
1398	" Lucy	Filed			
1399	" George				
1400	" Rebecca	1859.20[sic]	J R Garrett	L B Bell	check order
1401	Mixwater, Alex	265.70	Alex Mixwater	L B Bell	
1402	Morris, Charles				
1403	" Ja^{s} L.				
1404	" Bessie	797.10	Charles Morris	L B Bell	
1405	Martin, Mary A.				
1406	" Margaret H				
1407	" Dora J.				
1408	" Herman S.				
1409	" Ilo				
1410	" Susie	1594.20	Mary Ann Martin	L B Bell	
1411	Mays[sic], Johnson		6796		
1412	" Jessie				Continued on
1413	" George				Book A Page 55
1414	" Henry	1062.80	Johnson Mayes	L B Bell	
1415	Miller, W^{m}				
1416	" William	531.40	Wm Miller	L B Bell	
1417	Morris, Erasmus Parker				
1418	" Myrtie	order			
1419	" Phebe				
1420	" Jennie	Filed			
1421	" Eddie				
1422	" Mary	1594.20	EP Morris	L B Bell	
1423	Morris, Loyd	order Filed			
1424	" John				
1425	" W^{m}	797.10	Geo Furgeson	L B Bell	check on order
1426	Morris, Nolan	265.70	Nolan Morris	L B Bell	

Starr Roll 1894

We, the undersigned citizens of the Cherokee Nation, by right of Cherokee blood, do hereby acknowledge to have received of E. E. Starr, National Treasurer of the Cherokee Nation, the sums set opposite our names respectively, in full of our shares in the per capita distribution authorized by an Act of the National Council, dated ___MAY 3 1894___ 1894.

Names of Head, and Members of Families	Amount $ cts	To Whom Paid	Witness to Payment	Remarks
1427 Mames, John				
1428 " Jennie				
1429 " Co-tah-na				
1430 " Willie				
1431 " Wilson				
1432 Squirrel Nancy	1594.20	John Mames	L B Bell	Invalid
1433 McLaughlin, Gatsie				
1434 " Ella	531.40	Gatsie McLaughlin	L B Bell	
1435 Mounts, Rosanna				
1436 " Thos				
1437 Beavers, Wiley				Minor
1438 Smith, Jesse	1062.80	J W *(Illegible)*	L B Bell	
1439 Meper, Nancy				
1440 " Geo. Patten				
1441 " Ruth R.				
1442 " Mavina E				
1443 " Chas Anderson				
1444 " Lucinda	1594.20	J. M Messer	L B Bell	
1445 Morton, Lock				
1446 " Taka	531.40	Taka Morten[sic]	L B Bell	
1447 Morton, Geo.				
1448 " Cherokee				
1449 " Edna Anna				
1450 " Allen R.	1062.80	Cherokee Morton	L B Bell	
1451 Mc Donald, Collins	265.76 filed	C E Wetzel	L B Bell	check on order
1452 Martin, Susie J.				
1453 " Susan J.	531.40	Susie J Martin	L B Bell	
1454 Mc Pherson Mary	265.70	Mary McPherson	L B Bell	
1455 Mc Pherson, John V.				
1456 " Lucy C.				
1457 " Johnie				

Starr Roll 1894

We, the undersigned citizens of the Cherokee Nation, by right of Cherokee blood, do hereby acknowledge to have received of E. E. Starr, National Treasurer of the Cherokee Nation, the sums set opposite our names respectively, in full of our shares in the per capita distribution authorized by an Act of the National Council, dated ____MAY 3 1894____ 1894.

	Names of Head, and Members of Families	Amount $ cts	To Whom Paid	Witness to Payment	Remarks
1458	" Tho.ˢ J	1062.80	Ellis Starr Lee Payton	Henry Eiffert	
1459	Manus, W.ᵐ				
1460	" Sarah				
1461	" Richr'd	797.10 ᵃ²⁵⁷	W.ᵐ Manus	L B Bell	
1462	M.ᶜCrary, Louisa				
1463	Foreman, Rich'd.	531.40	Louisa M.ᶜCrary	L B Bell	Minor
1464	M.ᶜCrary, John				
1465	" W.ᵐ				
1466	" Viola	797.10	John M.ᶜCrary	L B Bell	
1467	Murphy, Sallie[sic]				
1468	" David				
1469	" Gertrude	797.10	Sally Murphy	L B Bell	
1470	Mann, Cary	265.70	Cary Mann	L B Bell	
1471	Mitchell, Martha J.				
1472	" Rob't. L.				
1473	" Levia L.				
1474	" Sevola L.				
1475	" Claude S				
1476	" Le Roy				
1477	" Joseph F.				
1478	" Clay A.	2125.60	Geo W Mitchell	L B Bell	
1479	Miller, David				
1480	" Lucy	531.40	Lucy Miller	L B Bell	
1481	Miller, Geo	265.70	Geo Miller	L B Bell	
1482	Mocker, Annie	265.70	Annie Mocker	L B Bell	
1483	Miller, Alfred				
1484	" Aggie				
1485	" Sarah J.				
1486	" Ola				
1487	" Susie				

119

Starr Roll 1894

We, the undersigned citizens of the Cherokee Nation, by right of Cherokee blood, do hereby acknowledge to have received of E. E. Starr, National Treasurer of the Cherokee Nation, the sums set opposite our names respectively, in full of our shares in the per capita distribution authorized by an Act of the National Council, dated ___MAY 3 1894___ 1894.

	Names of Head, and Members of Families	Amount $ cts	To Whom Paid	Witness to Payment	Remarks
1488	" Nannie	1594.20	Alfred Miller	L B Bell	
1489	Mann, David S.				
1490	" Elizabeth				
1491	" Minnie				
1492	" Bertha				
1493	" Henderson				
1494	" Pleasanton				
1495	" De Witt	1859.90	D S Mann	L B Bell	
1496	Mann, Maude[sic]	265.70	Maud Mann	L B Bell	
1497	Mann, Alzira	265.70	Alzira Mann	L B Bell	
1498	Mann, Pauline				
1499	" Lola	531.40	Marshall Mann	L B Bell	
1500	Mᶜ Coy, Rosanna W.			L B Bell	
1501	" Thoˢ				
1502	" Lucinda				
1503	" Sallie				
1504	" Ida	1328.50	*(No other information given.)*		
1505	Mᶜ Coy, Jaˢ W.				
1506	" Wᵐ				
1507	" Lelia				
1508	" Sina Alena	1062.80	Jas W MᶜCoy	L B Bell	
1509	Murphy, Emma C.				
1510	" Andrew T.				
1511	" Cora A.				
1512	" Henry E.				
1513	" Thoˢ	1328.50	J.T. Murphy	L B Bell	
1514	Mocker, Ben				
1515	" Polly				
1516	" Phelan				
1517	" Mary				
1518	" Fannie				
1519	" Maggie	1594.20	Ben Mocker	L B Bell	

Starr Roll 1894

We, the undersigned citizens of the Cherokee Nation, by right of Cherokee blood, do hereby acknowledge to have received of E. E. Starr, National Treasurer of the Cherokee Nation, the sums set opposite our names respectively, in full of our shares in the per capita distribution authorized by an Act of the National Council, dated ___MAY 3 1894___ 1894.

Names of Head, and Members of Families	Amount $ cts	To Whom Paid	Witness to Payment	Remarks
1520 Mᶜ Coy, Waddie				
1521 " Albert				
1522 " Myrthe	*order*			
1523 " Watt	1062.80	R J Alfrey	L B Bell	*check on order*
1524 Miller, Joseph	265.70 *order*	R J Alfrey	L B Bell	*check on order*
1525 Mannon[sic], John				
1526 " Jennie				
1527 " Nicholas				
1528 " Michael				
1529 " Sallie	1328.50	John Manus	L B Bell	
1530 Chu-wee, Sam'l	~~1328.50~~ 877.9	~~John Manus~~	L B Bell	*J.P. Carter has an order for this Oct 2/96 unpaid*
	$265.70	J.P. Carter	Wᵐ V Carey	*Pd on order of Oct 17ᵗʰ 1896*
1531 Mitchel, John	265.70	John Mitchel	L B Bell	
1532 Martin, Alman				
1533 " Elizabeth B.				
1534 " Henry				
1535 " Arazonia				
1536 " Alman, Jr.				
1537 " Olive				
1538 " Maude				
1539 " Ivea				
1540 " Jaˢ W.	2391.30	Alman Martin	L B Bell	
1541 Mitchell, Nannie				
1542 " Rachel	*order Filed*			
1543 " Lissie				
1544 " Donsia				
1545 " Caroline	1328.50	J L Newton	L B Bell	*check on order*
1546 Mitchel, Michael				
1547 " Arval	531.40	Michael Mitchel	L B Bell	
1548 Martin, Margaret A. *DEAD.*	265.70	V C Martin	L B Bell	
1549 Nugent, Jack				
1550 " Emiline[sic]				
1551 " Sarah				

121

Starr Roll 1894

We, the undersigned citizens of the Cherokee Nation, by right of Cherokee blood, do hereby acknowledge to have received of E. E. Starr, National Treasurer of the Cherokee Nation, the sums set opposite our names respectively, in full of our shares in the per capita distribution authorized by an Act of the National Council, dated ___MAY 3 1894___ 1894.

	Names of Head, and Members of Families	Amount $ cts	To Whom Paid	Witness to Payment	Remarks
1552	" Thursea				
1553	" Cornelius A.				
1554	" Millard				
1555	" Nelson				
1556	" Frank				
1557	" Jack	2391.30	Jack Nugent	L B Bell	
1558	Night, Le Roy	~~D867~~ R 770			Lizzie
1559	" Thos	~~D867~~ R 770			Night
1560	Wilkerson, Cora				Mother
1561	Shirley, Jas W.	1062.80	Lizzie Night	L B Bell	
1562	Noisewater, Nicholas	265.70	Katy Fourkiller	L B Bell	guardian
1563	Night, Ben				
1564	" Allie				
1565	" Annie				
1566	" John				
1567	" Starr				
1568	" Mary				
1569	" Charlie	1859.90	Ben Night	L B Bell	
1570	Night, Walker				
1571	" Jennie				
1572	" Lunnie				
1573	" Charlotte				
1574	" Robin	11328.50	Walker Night	L B Bell	
1575	Night, Polly				
1576	" Willie				
1577	" Lula				
1578	" Bird				
1579	" Susan A.				
1580	" Charlotte	1594.90	Polly Night	L B Bell	
1581	Neff, Florence				
1582	" James				
1583	" Mary Bell	797.10	T B Alberty	L B Bell	on order

122

Starr Roll 1894

We, the undersigned citizens of the Cherokee Nation, by right of Cherokee blood, do hereby acknowledge to have received of E. E. Starr, National Treasurer of the Cherokee Nation, the sums set opposite our names respectively, in full of our shares in the per capita distribution authorized by an Act of the National Council, dated ___MAY 3 1894___ 1894.

	Names of Head, and Members of Families	Amount $ cts	To Whom Paid	Witness to Payment	Remarks
1584	Newton, Sidney				
1585	" Della				
1586	" Rube				
1587	" Walter	1062.80	Jasper Newton	L B Bell	
1588	Noblet, Delilah				Delilah
1589	" Malinda				Noblet, mother
1590	" Newton				of
1591	Crittenden, John	1062.80 ²⁶⁰²	Delilah Noblet	L B Bell	John Crittenden
1592	Noisewater, Nancy	714			Wards of
1593	" Fannie				Katie
1594	" Betsy				Four-killer
1595	" Martha	1062.80	Katy Fourkiller	L B Bell	Guardian
1596	Oak-ball, Betsy	265.70	Betsy Oakball	L B Bell	
1597	Odle, Etta				
1598	" Louisa				
1599	" Margaret M.	797.10	Wᵐ Odle	L B Bell	
1600	Oak-ball, John	265.70	John Oakball	L B Bell	
1601	Oak-ball, White				
1602	" Susie				
1603	" Sallie	797.10	White Oakball	L B Bell	
1604	Paris, Ransom				
1605	" Celia				
1606	" George				
1607	" Eliza				
1608	" Ellen				
1609	" Malinda				
1610	" Sarah J.				
1611	" Ezekial				
1612	" Hick	2391.30	Ransom Paris	L B Bell	
1613	Paris[sic], Jesse J.	265.70	Jesse J Parris	L B Bell	Francis Beavers, Mother

123

Starr Roll 1894

We, the undersigned citizens of the Cherokee Nation, by right of Cherokee blood, do hereby acknowledge to have received of E. E. Starr, National Treasurer of the Cherokee Nation, the sums set opposite our names respectively, in full of our shares in the per capita distribution authorized by an Act of the National Council, dated ___MAY 3 1894___ 1894.

	Names of Head, and Members of Families	Amount $ cts	To Whom Paid	Witness to Payment	Remarks
1614	Padgett, Molly				
1615	" Ella				Children
1616	" Charlie				of
1617	Victory, Maggie				Lydia A.
1618	" Alfred J.	DEAD.			Victory
1619	" Fronia M.				
1620	" Caledonia	1859.90	Frank S Victory	L B Bell	
1621	Pierce[sic], Richr'd				
1622	" Nannie B.				
1623	" Walter H				
1624	" Roxie	797.10	Ricd Pearce	L B Bell	
1625	Pierce, John				
1626	" Willie	531.40	John Pierce	L B Bell	
1627	Pierce, Sallie	265.70	Richard Pierce	J.C. Starr	
1628	Phillips, Moses[sic]				
1629	" Robert				
1630	" Jennie				
1631	" Josie				
1632	" James				
1633	" Sallie				
1634	" Jeff	1859.90	Mose Phillips	L B Bell	
1635	Phillips, W$^{\underline{m}}$				
1636	" Martha				
1637	" Chris				
1638	" Lizzie	1062.80	Wm Phillips	L B Bell	
1639	Phillips, James				
1640	" Martha				
1641	" Rufus				
1642	" Sallie				
1643	" Jennie	1328.50	Martha Phillips	L B Bell	
1644	Paris, Jesse R.	265.70	Jesse R Paris	L B Bell	

124

Starr Roll 1894

We, the undersigned citizens of the Cherokee Nation, by right of Cherokee blood, do hereby acknowledge to have received of E. E. Starr, National Treasurer of the Cherokee Nation, the sums set opposite our names respectively, in full of our shares in the per capita distribution authorized by an Act of the National Council, dated ____MAY 3 1894____ 1894.

	Names of Head, and Members of Families	Amount $ cts	To Whom Paid	Witness to Payment	Remarks
1645	Paris, Jaˢ D.				
1646	" Nancy				
1647	" Wᵐ				
1648	" Nellie				
1649	" Margie				
1650	" Mary	1594.20	Jas D Parris	L B Bell	
1651	Path-killer, Johnson				
1652	" John	*order*			
1653	" Elizabeth				
1654	" Laura				
1655	" Jeannette	1328.50	J R Garrett	L B Bell	*check on order*
1656	Proctor, Ezekial, Jr.				
1657	" Sally				
1658	" Sam'l.				
1659	" Eli				
1660	" Charlie				
1661	" Wᵐ C.	1594.20	Ezekiel Proctor Jr	L B Bell	
1662	Payton, Emma				
1663	" Freddie L.	*order*			
1664	" Jno. M.	797.10	W B Rhea	L B Bell	*check on order*
1665	Polone, Adam				*Dead*
1666	" Mary				
1667	" Lacie				
1668	" Fred				
1669	" Tom				
1670	" Carrie A.			L B Bell	
1671	" John	1859.90	Mary Polone		
1672	Paris, Malachi	265.70	W B Rhea	L B Bell	*check on order*
1673	Pheasant, Mary				
1674	" George				
1675	" Wᵐ				
1676	" Alex				
1677	" Abraham	1328.50	Mary Pheasant	L B Bell	

125

Starr Roll 1894

We, the undersigned citizens of the Cherokee Nation, by right of Cherokee blood, do hereby acknowledge to have received of E. E. Starr, National Treasurer of the Cherokee Nation, the sums set opposite our names respectively, in full of our shares in the per capita distribution authorized by an Act of the National Council, dated ___MAY 3 1894___ 1894.

Names of Head, and Members of Families	Amount $ cts	To Whom Paid	Witness to Payment	Remarks
1678 Pheasant, Charles	265.70	Charles Pheasant	L B Bell	
1679 Proctor, Joseph	265.70	English[sic] & Kimbrough	L B Bell	
1680 Peach-eater				
1681 " Nellie	531.40	Peacheater	L B Bell	
1682 Peach-eater, Sukie[sic]	265.70	Sukey Peacheater	L B Bell	
1683 Peach, Stephen				Dead
1684 " Nancy		Adm		
1685 Cummins, Anna	797.10	John Pathkiller "	L B Bell	minor
1686 Padgett, Eliza				
1687 " Jacob				
1688 " Mariah				
1689 " Annie	1062.80	James Padgett	L B Bell	
1690 Proctor, Gene				
" Ned	531.40	Gene Proctor	L B Bell	
1691 Path-killer, John				
1692 " Fanny				
1693 " Willie	797.10	John Pathkiller	L B Bell	
1694 Paden, John Bell				Jno. Bell Paden
1695 " Maude				Guardian
1696 " Cha⁵ Lee				for
1697 " Ruth				George
1698 Hogner, George	1328.50	John Bell Paden	L B Bell	Hogner
1699 Paden, Lucinda	265.70	John Bell Paden	L B Bell	
1700 Polone, Frank				
1701 " Ruth	DEAD.			
1702 " Stephen				
1703 " Jesse				
1704 " Jane				
1705 " Cha⁵				
1706 " Eliza				

Starr Roll 1894

We, the undersigned citizens of the Cherokee Nation, by right of Cherokee blood, do hereby acknowledge to have received of E. E. Starr, National Treasurer of the Cherokee Nation, the sums set opposite our names respectively, in full of our shares in the per capita distribution authorized by an Act of the National Council, dated _____MAY 3 1894_____ 1894.

	Names of Head, and Members of Families	Amount $ cts	To Whom Paid	Witness to Payment	Remarks
1707	" Thoˢ	2125.60	Frank Polone	L B Bell	
1708	Payne, George	265.70	T. B Greer	L B Bell	check on order
1709	Petty, Elizabeth C.				
1710	" Michael G.	531.40	Elizabeth Petty	L B Bell	
1711	Phillips, Wᵐ	265.70	E W Buffington	Henry Eiffert	on order
1712	Petty, Mary				
1713	" Clarence	order Filed			
1714	" George				
1715	" Buna	1062.80	J T Evans	L B Bell	check on order
1716	Pheasant, James	265.70	James Pheasant	L B Bell	
1717	Pigeon, John	265.70	John Pigeon	L B Bell	
1718	Proctor, Linnie	265.70	Ezekiel Proctor	L B Bell	
1719	Proctor, Minnie	265.70	Minnie Proctor	L B Bell	
1720	Phillips, John	265.70	John Phillips	L B Bell	
1721	Proctor, Ezekial[sic]	265.70	Ezekiel Proctor	L B Bell	
1722	Proctor, Wᵐ	265.70	Wᵐ Proctor	L B Bell	
1723	Proctor, Francis J.	265.70	Jesse R Parris	L B Bell	husband
1724	Polone, Ollie				Ollie Polone
1725	" Charlotte				Guardian for
1726	" Andy				Willie
1727	Hog-shooter, Wᵐ	1062.80	Ollie Polone	L B Bell	Hog-shooter.
1728	Poor-boy, Ben'j.	265.70	Nakey Poor	L B Bell	
1729	Poor-boy, Bird				
1730	" Rachel				
1731	" Leach	797.10	Bird Poor boy	L B Bell	

127

Starr Roll 1894

We, the undersigned citizens of the Cherokee Nation, by right of Cherokee blood, do hereby acknowledge to have received of E. E. Starr, National Treasurer of the Cherokee Nation, the sums set opposite our names respectively, in full of our shares in the per capita distribution authorized by an Act of the National Council, dated ___MAY 3 1894___ 1894.

	Names of Head, and Members of Families	Amount $ cts	To Whom Paid	Witness to Payment	Remarks
1732	Quarles, Carrie E.	*order Filed*			
1733	" Susie Gritts				
1734	Bushyhead, Dennis				
1735	" Kate	1062.80	J R Garrett	L B Bell	*check on order*
1736	Quinton, Moses	DEAD. *order*			*Check & (Illegible)*
1737	" Sarah E	531.40	~~D402~~ 9826 C.H. Taylor	L B Bell	*on order $5.22*
1738	Russell, Jo⁵ L.	265.70	Jo L Russell	L B Bell	
1739	Ross, Daniel				
1740	" Ruth C.				
1741	" Florence E.				
1742	" Maggie M				
1743	" Cornelius				
1744	" Carrie	1594.20	Daniel Ross	L B Bell	
1745	Robinson, Anna				
1746	" Lizzie				
1747	" Willie	797.10	Wᵐ Robinson	L B Bell	
1748	Robins[sic], Woody				
1749	" Roxean[sic]				
1750	" Myrtie May				
1751	" Emma	1062.80	Woody Robbins	L B Bell	
1752	Reeves, Alice V.	*order* 265.70	John R Reeves	L B Bell	
1753	Reeves, Emma E.	265.70	U S Reeves	L B Bell	
1754	Redbird, Jackson				
1755	" Nancy				
1756	" Katie				
1757	" Swimmer	1062.80	Jackson Redbird	L B Bell	
1758	Reese, Joseph				
1759	" Ida				
1760	" Charles				
1761	" Andy	1062.80	Ida Reese	L B Bell	

128

Starr Roll 1894

We, the undersigned citizens of the Cherokee Nation, by right of Cherokee blood, do hereby acknowledge to have received of E. E. Starr, National Treasurer of the Cherokee Nation, the sums set opposite our names respectively, in full of our shares in the per capita distribution authorized by an Act of the National Council, dated ___MAY 3 1894___ 1894.

Names of Head, and Members of Families	Amount $ cts	To Whom Paid	Witness to Payment	Remarks
1762 Redden, Emeline				
1763 " Nannie				
1764 " Louisa M.	797.10	John Redden	L B Bell	
1765 Reese, Nancy J.				
1766 " Tho[s] J.				
1767 " Susan E.				
1768 " Mary A.				
1769 " John	1328.50	Nancy Jane Reese	L B Bell	
1770 Raper, Martin	265.70	Jas Brown	L B Bell	on order
1771 Raper, Martha	265.70	Jas Brown	L B Bell	on order
1772 Russell, Paul	265.70	Paul Russell	L B Bell	check
1773 Russell, Ja[s] B.				
1774 " Jo[s] M.	531.40	Jas B Russell	L B Bell	
1775 Russell, Francis E.	265.70	Jas B Russell	L B Bell	check
1776 Rider, Eve				
1777 Lewis, Rider				
1778 " Mary				
1779 Taylor, Chaddick	1062.80	Eve Rider	L B Bell	
1780 Richards, Susan M.				
1781 " Millie				
1782 " Jo[s] C.	797.10	Jas M Richards	L B Bell	
1783 Randolph, Mallie[sic]	265.70	Nellie Randolph	L B Bell	
1784 Rider, Joe				
1785 " Lena	321			
1786 Hall, Andrew	797.~~10~~01	Lena Rider	L B Bell	
1787 Redbird, Henry	265.70	Henry Redbird	L B Bell	
1788 Rattling Gourd[sic], Delilah				
1789 " Joseph				

Starr Roll 1894

We, the undersigned citizens of the Cherokee Nation, by right of Cherokee blood, do hereby acknowledge to have received of E. E. Starr, National Treasurer of the Cherokee Nation, the sums set opposite our names respectively, in full of our shares in the per capita distribution authorized by an Act of the National Council, dated ___MAY 3 1894___ 1894.

	Names of Head, and Members of Families	Amount $ cts	To Whom Paid	Witness to Payment	Remarks
1790	" Mollie	797.10	Delilah Ratlingourd	L B Bell	
1791	Redbird, White				
1792	" Betsy				
1793	" Catcher				
1794	" Betsy Jr				
1795	" Nellie	1328.50	White Redbird	L B Bell	
1796	Rider, John	265.70	John Rider 8212	L B Bell	
1797	Redbird, Jackson				
1798	" Mary				
1799	" Emma				
1800	" Ada				
1801	" Sarah				
1802	" Lizzie	1594.20	Mary Redbird	L B Bell	
1803	Redbird, Jesse				
1804	" Betsy				
1805	Stand, Ollie				
1806	Root, Mary	1062.80	Betsy Redbird	L B Bell	
1807	Redbird, George				
1808	" Peggy				
1809	Ground-hog, Susanna	797.10	Peggy Redbird	L B Bell	
1810	Rogers, Andrew J.				
1811	" Henry B.				
1812	" Levi H.				
1813	" Nannie				
1814	" John H.	1328.50	A J Rogers	L B Bell	
1815	Rattling-Gourd, Stay at home				
1816	" Aly				
1817	" John				
1818	" Geo.				
1819	" Mixwater				*Step-son of Stay at home*
1820	" John	1594.20	Stay at home Ratlingourd	L B Bell	
1821	Rider, Maggie M	265.70	A C Rider	L B Bell	

130

Starr Roll 1894

We, the undersigned citizens of the Cherokee Nation, by right of Cherokee blood, do hereby acknowledge to have received of E. E. Starr, National Treasurer of the Cherokee Nation, the sums set opposite our names respectively, in full of our shares in the per capita distribution authorized by an Act of the National Council, dated _____MAY 3 1894_____ 1894.

Names of Head, and Members of Families	Amount $ cts	To Whom Paid	Witness to Payment	Remarks
1822 Roberts, Margaret E.	265.70	Margaret E Roberts	L B Bell	
1823 Roberts, Alonzo	265.70	S.H. Roberts	L B Bell	
1824 Roberts, Sam'l W.	265.70	Saml Roberts	L B Bell	
1825 Reese, Murray[sic]				Murray
1826 " Sarah				Reese,
1827 " Richard				Guardian
1828 " Catherine				for
1829 " Ellis				Minor
1830 Stop, Jennie				children
1831 Whitmire, Mary J.	1859.90	Murry Reese	L B Bell	
1832 Reese, Charles				Chas Reese
1833 " Ollie				Guardian for
1834 Swimmer, Caroline	596			Minor
1835 Israel, W^m	1062.90	Charles Reese	L B Bell	children
1836 Ragsdale, Riley	265.70	J.R. Garrett	L B Bell	Check on order
1837 Rat, David				
1838 " Betsy	531.40	David Rat	L B Bell	
1839 Rider, Jennie				
1840 " Sallie				
1841 " Delilah	797.10	Jennie Rider	L B Bell	
1842 Rider, Augustus C.				
1843 " Ezekial				
1844 " Narcissa				
1845 " Vinnie				
1846 " Elizabeth				
1847 " Myrtle May				
1848 " Violet	1859.90	Augustus C Rider	L B Bell	
1849 Rogers, Sallie				
1850 " Chas H.	531.40	John Rogers	L B Bell	

131

Starr Roll 1894

We, the undersigned citizens of the Cherokee Nation, by right of Cherokee blood, do hereby acknowledge to have received of E. E. Starr, National Treasurer of the Cherokee Nation, the sums set opposite our names respectively, in full of our shares in the per capita distribution authorized by an Act of the National Council, dated ___MAY 3 1894___ 1894.

Names of Head, and Members of Families	Amount $ cts	To Whom Paid	Witness to Payment	Remarks
1851 Roberts, Esther S.				
1852 " Stephen C.				
1853 " Martha E.	797.10	S.H. Roberts	L B Bell	
1854 Rider, Thoˢ L.				
1855 " Ola				
1856 " Mary A.				
1857 " Ruth B.				
1858 " Phoebe				
1859 " Earl				
1860 " Roscoe C.				
1861 " Milton	2125.60	Thos L Rider	L B Bell	
1862 Reaves, Martha				
1863 " Stella				
1864 " Delilah				
1865 " John J.				
1866 " Myrtha[sic]	1328.50	C M Reaves	L B Bell	
1867 Rose, Anna				
1868 " Lola				
1869 " Belle				
1870 " Ada				
1871 " Bushyhead	1328.50	Anna Rose	L B Bell	
1872 Rogers, Nancy	265.70	Thomas Orz Adm	L B Bell	Administrator
1873 Russell, James				
1874 " Martha				
1875 " David				
1876 " Ira				
1877 " Darius				
1878 " Joseph				
1879 " Sevier				
1880 " Lydia	2125.60	Jas Russell	L B Bell	
1881 Rusk, Ella				Ella Rusk
1882 " Ned				Mother of
1883 " Roscoe				Florence Payne
1884 Payne, Florence	1062.80	John Rusk	L B Bell	

132

Starr Roll 1894

We, the undersigned citizens of the Cherokee Nation, by right of Cherokee blood, do hereby acknowledge to have received of E. E. Starr, National Treasurer of the Cherokee Nation, the sums set opposite our names respectively, in full of our shares in the per capita distribution authorized by an Act of the National Council, dated ___MAY 3 1894___ 1894.

	Names of Head, and Members of Families	Amount $ cts	To Whom Paid	Witness to Payment	Remarks
1885	Russell, Aaron				
1886	" Ollie				
1887	" Watt				
1888	" Richard				
1889	Dry, Anna	1328.50	Aaron Russell	L B Bell	
1890	Suwakie, Yellow-Hammer				
1891	" Betsy				
1892	" Tom				
1893	" James				
1894	" Nannie				
1895	" Elias				
1896	" Mary				
1897	" Annie				
1898	" Lennie				
1899	" Lawyer	2657.00	Betsy Suwakie	L B Bell	
1900	Six-killer Soldier				Soldier Six-killer
X	" Katie				guardian for
1901	Rat, Stand	797.10	Abraham Sixkiller	Henry Eiffert	on order from Father Stand Rat.
1902	Sanders, Delila				
1903	" James	531.40	Delila Sanders	L B Bell	on order
1904	Sixkiller, Sallie	265.70	Catherine Terrapin	L B Bell	
1905	Sam, Alex				
1906	" John				
1907	" Fred				
1908	Sanders, Jesse	1062.80	Alex Sam	L B Bell	
1909	Scraper, Charlotte				
1910	" Archilla	531.40	Charlotte Scraper	L B Bell	
1911	Stop, Bluford				
1912	" Tennie				
1913	" Polly	797.10	Blue Stop	L B Bell	
1914	Sanders, Sam'l.	265.70	Sam Sanders	L B Bell	

133

Starr Roll 1894

We, the undersigned citizens of the Cherokee Nation, by right of Cherokee blood, do hereby acknowledge to have received of E. E. Starr, National Treasurer of the Cherokee Nation, the sums set opposite our names respectively, in full of our shares in the per capita distribution authorized by an Act of the National Council, dated ____MAY 3 1894____ 1894.

Names of Head, and Members of Families	Amount $ cts	To Whom Paid	Witness to Payment	Remarks
1915 Shell, James				
1916 " Mary E	531.40	Jas Shell	L B Bell	
1917 Six-killer, Carrie				
1918 " Glover	531.40	Gabriel W. Morris	L B Bell	
1919 Simpson, Katie				
1920 " Ja^s A.				
1921 " Mary F.				
1922 " Hugh				
1923 " Grover	1328.50	Thos S Simpson	L B Bell	
1924 Soap, Rachel				*Rachel Soap*
1925 " Ben'j.				*guardian for*
1926 Leaf, Isaac				*Isaac Leaf and*
1927 " Caroline	1062.80	Rachel Soap	L B Bell	*guardian Caroline Leaf*
1928 Small-wood, Albert	265.70	Albert Smallwood	L B Bell	
1929 Shell, Charlotte	265.70	Jas Shell	L B Bell	*on order*
1930 Star, Johnnie	265.70	Jas Shell	L B Bell	*on order Invalid*
1931 Sanders, Mattie	265.70	Mattie Sanders	L B Bell	
1932 Sand, Stephen				
1933 " Lizzie				
1934 " Jennie	797.10	Stephen Sand	L B Bell	
1935 Six-killer, Johnson				
1936 " Louisa				
1937 " Lula				
1938 " Red-bird	1062.80	Johnson Sixkiller	L B Bell	
1939 Snip, Nick				
1940 " Annie				
1941 " Chas				
1942 " Nancy				
1943 " Lee				
1944 " Susanna	1594.20	Nick Snip	L B Bell	

Starr Roll 1894

We, the undersigned citizens of the Cherokee Nation, by right of Cherokee blood, do hereby acknowledge to have received of E. E. Starr, National Treasurer of the Cherokee Nation, the sums set opposite our names respectively, in full of our shares in the per capita distribution authorized by an Act of the National Council, dated ____MAY 3 1894____ 1894.

Names of Head, and Members of Families	Amount $ cts	To Whom Paid	Witness to Payment	Remarks
1945 Sloan, Mary	265.70	Charles Morris	L B Bell	on order
1946 Shell, Charles				
1947 " Rebecca				
1948 " Lula				
1949 " Jennie	1062.80	Charles Shell	L B Bell	
1950 Sanders, John				
1951 " W^{m}				
1952 " Callie				
1953 " Annie				
1954 " Polly	1328.50	John Sanders	L B Bell	
1955 Sanders, Betsy	265.70	Delilah Sanders	L B Bell	on order
1956 Sanders, Watt				
1957 " John				
1958 " Thos	797.10	Watt Sanders	L B Bell	
1959 Smallwood, Joe				
1960 " Jennie				
1961 " Lydia				
1962 " Mary				
1963 " Dick	1594.20	Jennie Smallwood	L B Bell	
1964 Spears, Lydia				
1965 " Josephine				
1966 " Mollie				
1967 " Willie				
1968 " Spencer	1328.50	Liberty Spears	L B Bell	
1969 Six-killer, Nancy	265.70	Nancy Sixkiller	L B Bell	
1970 Six-killer, Abraham				
1971 " Margaret				
1972 " Dennis				
1973 " Sarah				
1974 " Katie	1328.50	Abraham Sixkiller	L B Bell	

135

Starr Roll 1894

We, the undersigned citizens of the Cherokee Nation, by right of Cherokee blood, do hereby acknowledge to have received of E. E. Starr, National Treasurer of the Cherokee Nation, the sums set opposite our names respectively, in full of our shares in the per capita distribution authorized by an Act of the National Council, dated _____ MAY 3 1894 _____ 1894.

	Names of Head, and Members of Families	Amount $ cts	To Whom Paid	Witness to Payment	Remarks
1975	Still, Tom, Sr.				
1976	" Lucy				
1977	" Betsy				
1978	" Sam				
1979	" Tom, Jr.				
1980	" Wm S.				
1981	" Ada	2125.60	Thomas Still Sr.	L B Bell	
1982	Still, Lula	265.70	Thomas Still Sr	L B Bell	
1983	Sanders, Elizabeth				
1984	" Betsy				
1985	Wolfe, W^{m}				
1986	" Joseph	1062.80	Elizabeth Sanders	L B Bell	
1987	Stancil, John				
1988	" Sarah				
1989	" Hillman				
1990	" Louis				
1991	" Jo-Anna				
1992	" Wm Rob't.				
1993	" Joel B.				
1994	" Ja^{s}H.	2125.60	John Stancil	L B Bell	
1995	Spade, Watson	265.70	Watson Spade	L B Bell	
1996	Still, Nellie				
1997	" Willie				
1998	" Sam'l	797.10	Nellie Still	L B Bell	
1999	Speaker, Arch				
2000	" Jennie				
2001	" Calvin				
2002	Dick, W^{m}				
2003	" Geo.				
2004	" Betsy				
2005	" Fanny	1859.90	Jennie Speaker	L B Bell	
2006	Sanders, W^{m}	265.70	Wm Sanders	L B Bell	

Starr Roll 1894

We, the undersigned citizens of the Cherokee Nation, by right of Cherokee blood, do hereby acknowledge to have received of E. E. Starr, National Treasurer of the Cherokee Nation, the sums set opposite our names respectively, in full of our shares in the per capita distribution authorized by an Act of the National Council, dated ___MAY 3 1894___ 1894.

	Names of Head, and Members of Families	Amount $ cts	To Whom Paid	Witness to Payment	Remarks
2007	Squirrel, Ben				
2008	" Lucy				
2009	" Polly				
2010	" Sarah				
2011	" Jennie				
2012	" Alex	1594.20	Ben Squirrel	L B Bell	
2013	Spade, James				
2014	" Delilah				
2015	" Willie	797.10	James Spade	L B Bell	
2016	Scraper, Arch				
2017	" Jaˢ F.	531.40	Arch Scraper	L B Bell	
2018	Soap, Jack				
2019	" Betsy	*order*			
2020	" Ezekial				
2021	" Wᵐ				
2022	" Thoˢ				
2023	" Catherine	1594.20	Jack Soap	L B Bell	*on order of England & Kimbrough*
2024	Swimmer, Thoˢ				
2025	" Delilah				
2026	" Eve				
2027	" Nancy	1062.80	Thos Swimmer	L B Bell	
2028	Swimmer, Sallie				
2029	Blackwood, Lavina	531.40	Sallie Swimmer	L B Bell	
2030	Sanders Geo				
2031	" Caroline	531.40	Geo Sanders	L B Bell	
2032	Stinging, Tah-lah				
2033	" Alecy	531.40	Tah lah Stinging	L B Bell	
2034	Scott, Eli				
2035	" Delilah	531.40	Eli Scott	L B Bell	
2036	Six-killer, Mary	265.70	Mary Sixkiller	L B Bell	

Starr Roll 1894

We, the undersigned citizens of the Cherokee Nation, by right of Cherokee blood, do hereby acknowledge to have received of E. E. Starr, National Treasurer of the Cherokee Nation, the sums set opposite our names respectively, in full of our shares in the per capita distribution authorized by an Act of the National Council, dated ___MAY 3 1894___ 1894.

	Names of Head, and Members of Families	Amount $ cts	To Whom Paid	Witness to Payment	Remarks
2037	Scraper, Betsy				
2038	" Oliver				
2039	" John	797.10	Betsy Scraper	L B Bell	
2040	Star[sic], Jo⁵ M.				
2041	" Susie				
2042	" Joseph				
2043	" Maggie				
2044	" Sallie				
2045	" Nancy				
2046	" Delilah				
2047	" Jesse				
2048	" Alice	2391.30	J M Starr	L B Bell	
2049	Soap, George	265.70	Geo Soap	L B Bell	
2050	Spade, Johnson				
2051	" Rachel	531.40	Rachel Spade	L B Bell	
2052	Sixkiller, Jonas				
2053	" Winnie				
2054	" Ora				
2055	" Nannie	1062.80	Jonas Sixkiller	L B Bell	
2056	Shell, Laura	265.70	Laura Shell	L B Bell	
2057	Sheffield, Clementine				
2058	" Martha J.				
2059	" Walter J.				
2060	" Bula J.				
2061	" Iner[sic] M.				
2062	" Katie	1594.20	J T Evans	L B Bell	check on order
2063	Spade, Moses	265.70 Order	H C Crittenden	L B Bell	check on order
2064	Skitt, Lewis	265.70	Peggy *(Illegible)*	L B Bell	administrator
2065	Shell, Joshua				
2066	" Jane				
2067	" Wᵐ				

Starr Roll 1894

We, the undersigned citizens of the Cherokee Nation, by right of Cherokee blood, do hereby acknowledge to have received of E. E. Starr, National Treasurer of the Cherokee Nation, the sums set opposite our names respectively, in full of our shares in the per capita distribution authorized by an Act of the National Council, dated ___MAY 3 1894___ 1894.

	Names of Head, and Members of Families	Amount $ cts	To Whom Paid	Witness to Payment	Remarks
2068	" Lydia				
2069	" Sallie				
2070	" Swan				
2071	" Ada				
2072	" John Ann	2125.60	Joshua Shell	L B Bell	
2073	Scott, Jennie				
2074	" Elizabeth				
2075	" Sarah				
2076	" Henry				
2077	" Dennis				
2078	" Ella				
2079	" Susan				
2080	" Thos	2125.60	Jennie Scott	L B Bell	
2081	Stand, Rob't.				Rob't. Stand
2082	" Lucy				Guardian
2083	" Peggy				for
2084	" Sallie				Charles
2085	" Rich'd C.				Dick
2086	Dick, Chas	1594.20	Robt Stand	L B Bell	
2087	Spade, Anna	8625			
2088	Bean, Adam	8682 8682			
2089	Hitcher, W^m	8625 797.10	Anna Spade	L B Bell	
2090	Sturdevant, Martin B.				
2091	" Orrin				
2092	" John				
2093	" Joseph				
2094	" Richard	1328.50	M B Sturdevant	L B Bell	
2095	Sturdevant, Nancy				
2096	" Mollie	531.40	M B Sturdevant	L B Bell	
2097	Still, James	265.70	James Still	L B Bell	
2098	Snell, Cummin[sic]				
2099	" Nannie				
2100	" Lydia				

139

Starr Roll 1894

We, the undersigned citizens of the Cherokee Nation, by right of Cherokee blood, do hereby acknowledge to have received of E. E. Starr, National Treasurer of the Cherokee Nation, the sums set opposite our names respectively, in full of our shares in the per capita distribution authorized by an Act of the National Council, dated _____ MAY 3 1894 _____ 1894.

Names of Head, and Members of Families	Amount $ cts	To Whom Paid	Witness to Payment	Remarks
2101 " Bertha	1062.80	Cumming Snell	L B Bell	
2102 Snell, Sarah	265.70	Sarah Snell	L B Bell	
2103 Swimmer, Su-wake				
2104 " Nellie	531.40	Suwake Swimmer	L B Bell	
2105 Six-killer, Bluford				
2106 " Annie	531.40	Annie Sixkiller	L B Bell	
2107 Straight				
2108 " Wa-lu-kie	531.40	Straight	L B Bell	
2109 Straight, W$^{\underline{m}}$	265.70	W$^{\underline{m}}$ Straight	L B Bell	
2110 Smallwood, Ella	265.70	Ella Smallwood	L B Bell	
2111 Sand, Noyah				
2112 " Annie				
2113 " Willie				
2114 " John				
2115 Bearpaw, Daniel	1328.50	Noyah Sand	L B Bell	
2116 Still, W$^{\underline{m}}$	265.70	W$^{\underline{m}}$ Still	L B Bell	
2117 Still, Susan	265.70	Susan Still	L B Bell	
2118 San-ta-fee, Jennie	9069			
2119 " Joseph	9069			
2120 " Geo	797.10	9069 Jennie Santafee	L B Bell	
2121 Stover, Nellie 405	265.70	Nellie Stover	L B Bell	
2122 Stover, James DEAD.				
2123 " Lewis	531.40 815	James Stover	L B Bell	
2124 Sunday, Rachel	265.70	Rachel Sunday	L B Bell	
2125 Silcox, Sarah				
2126 " Jack				

Starr Roll 1894

We, the undersigned citizens of the Cherokee Nation, by right of Cherokee blood, do hereby acknowledge to have received of E. E. Starr, National Treasurer of the Cherokee Nation, the sums set opposite our names respectively, in full of our shares in the per capita distribution authorized by an Act of the National Council, dated _____ MAY 3 1894 _____ 1894.

	Names of Head, and Members of Families	Amount $ cts	To Whom Paid	Witness to Payment	Remarks
2127	" James				
2128	" Elizabeth	D 2784			
2129	" Susie				
2130	" Eliza M.	1594.20	Sarah Silcox	L B Bell	
2131	Shelly, Lucy				
2132	" Vertie				
2133	" Oscar				
2134	" Maggie	1062.80	Alper Shelly	L B Bell	
2135	Turtle, Arch				
2136	" Fannie				
2137	" Nancy				
2138	" Ned				
2139	" Bessie				
2140	" Charlotte				
2141	" Charlie				
2142	" Adam				
2143	" W$^{\underline{m}}$				
2144	" Emma	2657.00	Arch Turtle	L B Bell	
2145	Three-killer, Tho$^{\underline{s}}$	265.70	Tho$^{\underline{s}}$ Three Killer	L B Bell	
2146	Thornton, Emily				*Emily Thornton*
2147	Scraper, Mary				*guardian for*
2148	" John				*minor*
2149	Fodder, Stephen	1062.80	Emly[sic] Thornton	L B Bell	*children*
2150	Thompson, Rachel M.				
2151	" Lizzie Lee				
2152	" Ella A.				
2153	" Jo$^{\underline{s}}$ C.				
2154	" W$^{\underline{m}}$ C.				
2155	" Lusie[sic]				
2156	" Calvin	1859.90	J.C. Thompson	L B Bell	
2157	Thompson, Narcissa				
2158	" Andrew M				
2159	" Rob't. H.				
2160	" Ja$^{\underline{s}}$ C.				

Starr Roll 1894

We, the undersigned citizens of the Cherokee Nation, by right of Cherokee blood, do hereby acknowledge to have received of E. E. Starr, National Treasurer of the Cherokee Nation, the sums set opposite our names respectively, in full of our shares in the per capita distribution authorized by an Act of the National Council, dated ___MAY 3 1894___ 1894.

	Names of Head, and Members of Families	Amount $ cts	To Whom Paid	Witness to Payment	Remarks
2161	" Clem				
2162	" Lody				
2163	" OOma[sic]				
2164	" Ethel	2125.60	R H L Thompson	L B Bell	check
2165	Thornton, Nannie	265.70	J L W Williams	Henry Eiffert	
2166	Thomason, Tammie M				
2167	" Maggie B				
2168	" Dan'l W.				
2169	" Clarence	1062.80	W H Thomason	L B Bell	
2170	Thornton, Joe				
2171	" Peggy				Peggy Thornton
2172	" Delilah				Mother
2173	" Jesse				of
2174	" Willie				George Archie
2175	" Wiley				and
2176	Archie, Geo				Eli
2177	" Eli	2125.60	Peggy Thornton	L B Bell	Archie
2178	Troth, Susan E.				Susan E. Troth
2179	" Mary M.				mother of
2180	Hart, Maggie I.	797.10	Danie V Troth	L B Bell	Maggie I Hart
2181	Terrapin, Joe				
2182	" Wildie				
2183	" Jesse				
2184	" Ellen	1062.80	Joe Tarrapin[sic]	L B Bell	
2185	Twilly, Lucy J.				
2186	" W$^{\underline{m}}$ D.				
2187	" Dora	797.10	J W Twilly	L B Bell	
2188	Thurman, Mary				Mary Thurman
2189	" Lillie				mother of
2190	" Salina				John Kirk
2191	Kirk, John				and
2192	" Widdie	1328.50	Mary Thurman	L B Bell	Widdie Kirk

Starr Roll 1894

We, the undersigned citizens of the Cherokee Nation, by right of Cherokee blood, do hereby acknowledge to have received of E. E. Starr, National Treasurer of the Cherokee Nation, the sums set opposite our names respectively, in full of our shares in the per capita distribution authorized by an Act of the National Council, dated _____ MAY 3 1894 _____ 1894.

	Names of Head, and Members of Families	Amount $ cts	To Whom Paid	Witness to Payment	Remarks
2193	Thornton, Nancy J.	265.70	Delila Sanders	L B Bell	on order
2194	" Susan E.	265.70	Nancy J Thornton	L B Bell	
2195	Terrapin, Car-se-la-wee				
2196	" Lizzie				
2197	" Chaˢ				
2198	" Abraham				
2199	" Eve				
2200	" Gabriel				
2201	" Betsy				
2202	" Aggie				
2203	" Jennie				
2204	" Jinsey	2657.00	Carselawey Terrapin	L B Bell	on order of J.T. Evans
2205	Tieasky[sic], Alsie				
2206	" Lizzie				
2207	" George	797.10	Arline Tiesky	L B Bell	
2208	Terrapin, Thomas	D2902			
2209	" Jennie	D2902			
2210	" Lydia	D2902			
2211	" Daniel	1062.80	Thoˢ Terrapin	L B Bell	
2212	Tyner, Nancy				
2213	" Mary				
2214	" George				
2215	" James				
2216	" Jenanna				
2217	" Frank				
2218	" Alice				
2219	" Carrie	2125.60	Jefferson Tyner	L B Bell	
2220	Tieasky[sic], George				
2221	" Annie				
2222	" Elias	797.10	Elizabeth Tiesky	L B Bell	
2223	Terrill, Wͫ				
2224	" Lizzie	order			
2225	" Sarah				
2226	" Chaˢ				

Starr Roll 1894

We, the undersigned citizens of the Cherokee Nation, by right of Cherokee blood, do hereby acknowledge to have received of E. E. Starr, National Treasurer of the Cherokee Nation, the sums set opposite our names respectively, in full of our shares in the per capita distribution authorized by an Act of the National Council, dated ___MAY 3 1894___ 1894.

	Names of Head, and Members of Families	Amount $ cts	To Whom Paid	Witness to Payment	Remarks
2227	" W^{m}				
2228	" Dennis	1594.20	Wm Terrell	L B Bell	on order of England & Kimbrough
2229	Terrapin, Nelson				Catherine Terrapin
2230	" Catherine	531.40	Catherine Terrapin		mother of David
2231	Downing, David	265.70	Catherine Terrapin		Downing
2232	Tidwell, Sophronia				
2233	" Chamerell[sic]				married again
2234	" Jno. W.	797.10	Sophronia Leaford	L B Bell	& changed names
2235	Tidwell, Versnoy				
2236	" Celia E	531.40	Versnoy Tidwell	L B Bell	
2237	Tidwell, Ada				
2238	" Charity	531.40	Ada Tidwell	L B Bell	
2239	Tah-lah, Johnson	265.70	Johnson Tahlah	L B Bell	
2240	Taylor, Lydia	265.70	Lydia Taylor	L B Bell	
2241	Twist, Touneat[sic]				
2242	" Sarah				
2243	" Albert	797.10	Tozuneat Twist	L B Bell	
2244	Twist, John				
2245	" Abraham				
2246	" Isaac				
2247	" Jane				
2248	" Bertha	1328.50	John Twist	L B Bell	
2249	Twist, Wm J.	265.70	W J Twist	L B Bell	
2250	Ta-nu-wee, Naked				
2251	" Minnie				
2252	" Jennie				
2253	" Ah-ne-la	1062.80	Naked Tanuwee	L B Bell	
2254	Twist, Martha Ann	265.70	To zu neat Twist	L B Bell	

144

Starr Roll 1894

We, the undersigned citizens of the Cherokee Nation, by right of Cherokee blood, do hereby acknowledge to have received of E. E. Starr, National Treasurer of the Cherokee Nation, the sums set opposite our names respectively, in full of our shares in the per capita distribution authorized by an Act of the National Council, dated ____MAY 3 1894____ 1894.

	Names of Head, and Members of Families	Amount $ cts	To Whom Paid	Witness to Payment	Remarks
2255	Twist, Henry	265.70	Tozouneat[sic] Twist	L B Bell	
2256	Tidwell, John	265.40[sic]	Ada Tidwell	L B Bell	on order
2257	Three-killer, Jos				
2258	" Mary				
2259	" Daniel				
2260	" Emma				
2261	" Jennie				
2262	" James				
2263	" Che-na-sa				
2264	" Addie	2125.60	Jos Three Killer	L B Bell	
2265	Thomas, Martha J				
2266	" Ella				
2267	" Watt				
2268	" Bulah				
2269	" Jno. B.				
2270	" Burt				
2271	" James	1859.90	Geo W Ward	L B Bell	
2272	Turtle, Charles				
2273	" Peggy	531.40	Peggy Turtle	L B Bell	
2274	Turtle, Wm	265.70	Peggy Turtle	L B Bell	order
2275	Turtle, Mary	265.70	Mary Turtle	L B Bell	
2276	Thompson, Emma	DEAD.			
2277	" Thomas				
2278	" Joseph				
2279	Fields, Jno. O.	1062.80	Emma Thompson	L B Bell	Infant
2280	Thompson, Olla	265.70	Emma Thompson	L B Bell	
2281	Thompson, Wm	265.70	Wm 9069 Thompson	L B Bell	
2282	Thompson, Peggy				
2283	" Felix				
2284	" Wm				

145

Starr Roll 1894

We, the undersigned citizens of the Cherokee Nation, by right of Cherokee blood, do hereby acknowledge to have received of E. E. Starr, National Treasurer of the Cherokee Nation, the sums set opposite our names respectively, in full of our shares in the per capita distribution authorized by an Act of the National Council, dated ____MAY 3 1894____ 1894.

	Names of Head, and Members of Families	Amount $ cts	To Whom Paid	Witness to Payment	Remarks
2285	" Dorinda				
2286	" Flora				
2287	" Joel				
2288	" Paulina	1859.90	E (?) Thompson	L B Bell	
2289	Thompson, Anna C.	DEAD.			
2290	" Jno. L.				
2291	" Martha J.				
2292	" Oliver N.				
2293	" Nathaniel A.				
2294	" Clarence E	1594.20	T.J.C. Thompson	L B Bell	
2295	Thompson, Julia				
2296	" Geo. R.				
2297	" Delilah				
2298	" John				
2299	" Benj.				
2300	" Mary A.				
2301	" Jo^s, Jr.				
2302	" Ja^s T.	2125.60	Joseph Thompson	L B Bell	
2303	Thurman, Della				
2304	" Virginia	531.40	L L Duckworth	L B Bell	
2305	Twist				
2306	" Jennie				
2307	" Levi	797.10	Jennie Twist	L B Bell	
2308	Vickory, John H.				
2309	" Clara A.				
2310	" Wm P.				
2311	" Sarah C.				
2312	" Florence				
2313	" Cora				
2314	" Richard				
2315	" Ruth E.	2125.60	John H Vickory	L B Bell	
2316	Vickory, Frank S.				
2317	" Lydia A.	DEAD. 531.40	Frank S Vickry[sic]	L B Bell	

146

Starr Roll 1894

We, the undersigned citizens of the Cherokee Nation, by right of Cherokee blood, do hereby acknowledge to have received of E. E. Starr, National Treasurer of the Cherokee Nation, the sums set opposite our names respectively, in full of our shares in the per capita distribution authorized by an Act of the National Council, dated ___MAY 3 1894___ 1894.

	Names of Head, and Members of Families	Amount $ cts	To Whom Paid	Witness to Payment	Remarks
2318	Vickory, James				
2319	" Martha E.				
2320	" Mary A.				
2321	" Martha	1062.80	Jas Vickory	L B Bell	
2322	Van-ma-tra[sic], Martha				*Martha Van-ma-tra*
2323	" Jno. Thos				*Mother of*
2324	Martin, Gertrude	797.10	Isaac Van matia	L B Bell	*Gertrude Martin*
2325	Vann, Isaac				
2326	" Sarah				
2327	" Charles				
2328	" Nelson				
2329	" Edna	1328.50	Isaac Vann	L B Bell	
2330	Whelcher[sic], Mary				
2331	" Lou-Ella	531.40	J H Welcher	L B Bell	
2332	Wilkie, John				
2333	" Jno. W.				
2334	" Geo. H.				
2335	" Cherokee	8636			
2336	" Margaret	445			
2337	" Laura J.	445			
2338	" Nancy E.	1859.90 445	John Wilkie	L B Bell	
2339	Wilkie, George	248			
2340	" Iffie				
2341	" Sidney				
2342	" Belle				
2343	" Jno. W.				
2344	" Nancy M.	1594.20	Geo Wilkie	L B Bell	
2345	Walker, James				
2346	Bear-paw, Rob't.	531.40	Jas Walker	L B Bell	*guardian*
2347	Ward, Margaret A.	265.70	W G Ward	L B Bell	
2348	Walking-stick, S.R.	265.70	S R Walkingstick	L B Bell	

147

Starr Roll 1894

We, the undersigned citizens of the Cherokee Nation, by right of Cherokee blood, do hereby acknowledge to have received of E. E. Starr, National Treasurer of the Cherokee Nation, the sums set opposite our names respectively, in full of our shares in the per capita distribution authorized by an Act of the National Council, dated ___MAY 3 1894___ 1894.

	Names of Head, and Members of Families	Amount $ cts	To Whom Paid	Witness to Payment	Remarks
2349	Weaver, John				
2350	" Ellen	531.40	John Weaver	L B Bell	
2351	Wright, Jesse	265.70	Charlotte Wright	L B Bell	*drawn by mother on order*
2352	Wolfe[sic], Rich'd. M	6852			
2353	" Susan E.				
2354	" Jesse B				
2355	" Mitchell W.				
2356	" Mary J.				
2357	" Alice				
2358	" Rich'd. T.	1859.90	R M Wolf	Henry Eiffert	
2359	Wilkie, David	319			
2360	" Jno. W.	319			
2361	" Olla N.	797.10 319	David Wilkie	L B Bell	
2362	Whisenhunt, Brunette				
2363	" W$^{\underline{m}}$				
2364	" Ben'j.				
2365	" Mary				
2366	" Josie				
2367	" Joseph	1594.20	Brunette Whisenhunt	L B Bell	
2368	Weaver, Joe	265.70	Jo Weaver	L B Bell	
2369	Weaver, Jo-Anna	265.70	Joanna Weaver	L B Bell	
2370	Williams, Walter W.				
2371	" Eliza L.				
2372	" Blanche	797.10	J B Alberty	L B Bell	*on order*
2373	Williams, Rob't. B.	265.70	Martha Williams	L B Bell	*on order*
2374	Wolfe, Arch	265.70	Arch Christy	L B Bell	
2375	Wright, Martha J.	265.70	Jesse V Wright	L B Bell	*order*
2376	Wright, Nannie E.	265.70	Jesse V Wright	L B Bell	*order*

148

Starr Roll 1894

We, the undersigned citizens of the Cherokee Nation, by right of Cherokee blood, do hereby acknowledge to have received of E. E. Starr, National Treasurer of the Cherokee Nation, the sums set opposite our names respectively, in full of our shares in the per capita distribution authorized by an Act of the National Council, dated _____MAY 3 1894_____ 1894.

	Names of Head, and Members of Families	Amount $ cts	To Whom Paid	Witness to Payment	Remarks
2377	Witt, Georgie				
2378	" Eula L.	531.40	Jesse C Alberty	L B Bell	on order
2379	Williams, Martha				
2380	" Lee				
2381	" Ellis				
2382	" Ellen				
2383	" Fred	1328.50	Martha Williams	L B Bell	
2384	Wilkie, Jesse W.	265.70	Jesse W Wilkie	L B Bell	
2385	Wilkie, Sidney	265.70	Sidney Wilkie	L B Bell	
2386	Wagner, Thos F.				
2387	" Lucinda				
2388	" Marshal				
2389	" Edith				
2390	" Nannie				
2391	" Emma J.				
2392	" Ja^s F				
2393	" Maude				
2394	" Thos				
2395	" Ada	2657.00	Chas F Wagner	L B Bell	
2396	Williams, Chas M.	265.701	Martha Williams	L B Bell	on order
2397	Whitmire, Walter S.				
2398	" Ellen				
2399	" W^m				
2400	" Dan'l				
2401	" James				
2402	" Dennis				
2403	" Thos				
2404	" Johnathan				
2405	" Nellie	2391.30	J W Alberty	L B Bell	
2406	Weaver, Hettie				See Hettie Weaver's protest against her Husband
2407	" Jo Anna				
2408	" Mary				
2409	" Annie				

149

Starr Roll 1894

We, the undersigned citizens of the Cherokee Nation, by right of Cherokee blood, do hereby acknowledge to have received of E. E. Starr, National Treasurer of the Cherokee Nation, the sums set opposite our names respectively, in full of our shares in the per capita distribution authorized by an Act of the National Council, dated ___MAY 3 1894___ 1894.

	Names of Head, and Members of Families	Amount $ cts	To Whom Paid	Witness to Payment	Remarks
2410	" Katie				
2411	" Rachel				
2412	" Thoˢ				
2413	" Sallie				
2414	Martin, Nellie	2391.30	Hettie Weaver	L B Bell	
2415	Williams, Lula L.	265.70	J L W Williams	Henry Eiffert	
2416	Williams, Elizabeth	265.70	J L W Williams	Henry Eiffert	
2417	Williams, Jaˢ L.	265.70	J L W Williams	Henry Eiffert	
2418	Watt, Johnson				
2419	" Susan				
2420	" Ned				
2421	" Walter	1062.80	Johnson Watt	L B Bell	
2422	Woodall, Chaˢ				
2423	" Roxie				
2424	" Katie				
2425	" Emma				
2426	" Thoˢ				
2427	" Watie	1894.20	Charles Woodall	L B Bell	
2428	Whitmire, Johnson	265.70	J R Whitmire	L B Bell	*on order*
2429	Wright, Willie	265.70	Polly Crowder	L B Bell	*on order*
2430	Wilkerson, Joe	265.70	Jo Wilkerson	L B Bell	
2431	" Amanda	665.70[sic]	Amanda Wilkerson	L B Bell	
2432	Whitmire, Chaˢ				
2433	" Palmyra				
2434	" Ellis				
2435	" Andrew				
2436	" Jaˢ W.				
2437	" Noah				
2438	" Jack				
2439	" Wᵐ	2125.60	Charles Whitmire	L B Bell	

Starr Roll 1894

We, the undersigned citizens of the Cherokee Nation, by right of Cherokee blood, do hereby acknowledge to have received of E. E. Starr, National Treasurer of the Cherokee Nation, the sums set opposite our names respectively, in full of our shares in the per capita distribution authorized by an Act of the National Council, dated ___MAY 3 1894___ 1894.

	Names of Head, and Members of Families	Amount $ cts	To Whom Paid	Witness to Payment	Remarks
2440	Winton, Alice				*Wm Winton*
2441	" Ella				*father*
2442	" Elizabeth				
2443	" Stand W.	1062.80	W^m P 2684 Winton	L B Bell	
2444	Williams, Wm D.	265.70	J L W Williams	Henry Eiffert	
2445	Wright, Jesse V.				
2446	" Harriet A.				
2447	" Alex D.				
2448	" Eli				
2449	" Jesse J.				
2450	" Mary A.	1594.20	Jesse V Wright	L B Bell	
2451	Watt, Dan'l.				
2452	" Nancy				
2453	" Stephen				
2454	" Eliza				
2455	" W^m				
2456	" John				
2457	Thornton, Sallie	1859.90	Danl Watt	L B Bell	*guardian of Sallie Thornton*
2458	Watt, Jonas	265.70	Jonas Watt	L B Bell	
2459	Watt, Mush				
2460	" Rachel				
2461	" Chas				
2462	" Polly				
2463	" Isaac				
2464	" Lizzie				
2465	" Jennie				
2466	" Wilson				
2467	" Henry	2391.30	Mush Watt	L B Bell	
2468	Watt, Jackson				
2469	" Willie	531.40	Jackson Watt	L B Bell	
2470	Whittington, Cynthia	265.70	Cinthia[sic] Whittington	L B Bell	

151

Starr Roll 1894

We, the undersigned citizens of the Cherokee Nation, by right of Cherokee blood, do hereby acknowledge to have received of E. E. Starr, National Treasurer of the Cherokee Nation, the sums set opposite our names respectively, in full of our shares in the per capita distribution authorized by an Act of the National Council, dated ___MAY 3 1894___ 1894.

	Names of Head, and Members of Families	Amount $ cts	To Whom Paid	Witness to Payment	Remarks
2471	Willis, John				
2472	" Hugh	531.40	Wm Maupin	L B Bell	on order
2473	Wolfe[sic], Mattie				Mattie Wolfe
2474	Wofford, Geneva				Mother
2475	Sanders, Peggy	797.10	Mattie Wolf	L B Bell	
2476	Walker, Sallie	265.70	Thomas Still Sr	L B Bell	on order
2477	Wilkerson, Lucy	265.70	Jo Wilkerson	L B Bell	order
2478	Wright, Charlotte				
2479	" Cornelius				
2480	Wright, Johnathan				
2481	" Jack				
2482	" Sallie	1328.50	Charlotte Wright	L B Bell	
2483	Wright, George	265.70	Charlotte Wright	L B Bell	drawn by his mother
2484	Whitmire, Eli H.				
2485	" Geo C				
2486	" Mary	797.10	EH Whitmire	L B Bell	
2487	Whitmire, Geo G.	265.70	S R Walkingstick	G W Benge	on order
2488	Wright, Tillman	265.70	Tillman Wright	L B Bell	
2489	Wolfe[sic], Jackson				
2490	" Betsy				
2491	" Eliza				
2492	" Maggie				
2493	" Alsie	1328.50	Jackson Wolf	L B Bell	
2494	Wolfe[sic], Jennie	265.70	Jennie Wolf	L B Bell	20 yrs
2495	Wolfe[sic], Jennie	265.70	Jennie Wolf	L B Bell	60 yrs
2496	Wolfe[sic], Lacy				Guardian for 3
2497	" Polly	531.40	Lacy Wolf	L B Bell	Adair children

152

Starr Roll 1894

We, the undersigned citizens of the Cherokee Nation, by right of Cherokee blood, do hereby acknowledge to have received of E. E. Starr, National Treasurer of the Cherokee Nation, the sums set opposite our names respectively, in full of our shares in the per capita distribution authorized by an Act of the National Council, dated ___MAY 3 1894___ 1894.

	Names of Head, and Members of Families	Amount $ cts	To Whom Paid	Witness to Payment	Remarks
2498	Wolfe[sic], James	265.70	James Wolf	L B Bell	
2499	Wolfe[sic], John				
2500	" Nannie				
2501	" Mary				
2502	" Jack				
2503	" Lucy				
2504	" Alsie				
2505	" John, Jr.				
2506	" Charlotte				
2507	" Polly	2391.30	John Wolf	L B Bell	
2508	Willis, Hester	229			
2509	" Jesse R.				
2510	" Geo. G.	229			
2511	" Claude C.	229			
2512	" Lula	229			
2513	" Thula A.	1594920	Hugh P Willis	L B Bell	
2514	Walking-stick, Leon	order 265.70	S R Walkingstick	L B Bell	
2515	Whitmire, Charlotte	265.70	J R Whitmire	L B Bell	on order
2516	Whitmire, Sarah J.	265.70	J R Whitmire	L B Bell	on order
2517	Wolfe[sic], Alex				
2518	" Elizabeth				
2519	" Lincoln				
2520	" Charles	1062.80	Alex Wolf	L B Bell	
2521	Wolfe[sic], Jack				
2522	" Catherine				
2523	" Sarah				
2524	" Dick				
2525	" Cynthia				
2526	" Hummingbird	1594.20	Jack Wolf	L B Bell	
2527	Wolfe[sic], David				
2528	" Louisa				
2529	" Stephen				

153

Starr Roll 1894

We, the undersigned citizens of the Cherokee Nation, by right of Cherokee blood, do hereby acknowledge to have received of E. E. Starr, National Treasurer of the Cherokee Nation, the sums set opposite our names respectively, in full of our shares in the per capita distribution authorized by an Act of the National Council, dated ___MAY 3 1894___ 1894.

	Names of Head, and Members of Families	Amount $ cts	To Whom Paid	Witness to Payment	Remarks
2530	" Soloman				
2531	" Red-Cloud				
2532	" Josie				
2533	Scraper, W$^{\underline{m}}$				
2534	Sanders, Cha$^{\underline{s}}$	2125.60	David Wolf	L B Bell	
2535	Woodall, Clara	265.70	Clara Woodall	L B Bell	
2536	Webster, Alice	265.70	Charles Ance	L B Bell	order
2537	Walking-stick, Susie				Susie Walking S
2538	Tucker, Maggie	} order			guardian for
2539	" Lennie	797.10	J M Starr	L B Bell	Tucker children
2540	Ward, Yell				
2541	" Nancy				
2542	" John	797.10	Yell Ward	L B Bell	
2543	Whitmire, Johnathan J	265.70	Johnathan Whitmire	L B Bell	
2544	Watt, Henry				
2545	" Mary				
2546	" Louisa				
2547	" Anna				
2548	" Ollie				
2549	" Carrie	1594.20	Henry Watt	L B Bell	
2550	Wolfe[sic], David				
2551	" Catherine				
2552	" Mary				
2553	" Sallie				
2554	" Nancy	1328.50	David Wolf	L B Bell	
2555	Walking-stick, Susie	265.70	Susie Walkingstick	L B Bell	
2556	Wofford, Jennie	265.70	Jackson Locust	L B Bell	on order
2557	Walking-stick, Edw.				
2558	" Sarah				
2559	" James				

154

Starr Roll 1894

We, the undersigned citizens of the Cherokee Nation, by right of Cherokee blood, do hereby acknowledge to have received of E. E. Starr, National Treasurer of the Cherokee Nation, the sums set opposite our names respectively, in full of our shares in the per capita distribution authorized by an Act of the National Council, dated ___MAY 3 1894___ 1894.

	Names of Head, and Members of Families	Amount $ cts	To Whom Paid	Witness to Payment	Remarks
2560	" Lydia	9			
2561	" Hugh M.	1			
2562	" Ben'j.	2			
2563	" Geneva	0			
2564	" John				
2565	" Catherine	2391.30	J.T. Evans	L B Bell	*check on order*
2566	Walking-stick, Henry				
2567	" Betsey				
2568	" Charlotte	797.10	Henry Walkingstick	L B Bell	
2569	Walking-stick, Mary				
2570	" Ezekial	531.40	J M Starr		*order*
2571	Whitmire, White				
2572	" Annie				
2573	" W^{m}				
2574	" Walter	1062.80	E.W. Buffington	L B Bell	*check on order*
2575	Wolfe[sic], Jennie				
2576	" W^{m}				
2577	" Lucy				
2578	" Young Beaver				
2579	" Martha				
2580	" Nancy				
2581	" Polly	8206			
2582	" Henry	2125.60	Wm Wolf	L B Bell	
2583	Welch, Sarah E	265.70	S J Starr	L B Bell	*check on order*
2584	Watt, Aggie	265.70	Aggie Watt	L B Bell	
2585	Whitmire, Johnathan A				*Johnathan Whitmire*
2586	" Temperance				*guardian for*
2587	" Henry				*Henry Whitmire and guardian*
2588	Conrad, Minnie	1062.80	J A Whitmire	L B Bell	*Minnie Conrad*
2589	Walking-stick, Ben'j.	265.70	Ben Walkingstick	L B Bell	

155

Starr Roll 1894

We, the undersigned citizens of the Cherokee Nation, by right of Cherokee blood, do hereby acknowledge to have received of E. E. Starr, National Treasurer of the Cherokee Nation, the sums set opposite our names respectively, in full of our shares in the per capita distribution authorized by an Act of the National Council, dated ___MAY 3 1894___ 1894.

	Names of Head, and Members of Families	Amount $ cts	To Whom Paid	Witness to Payment	Remarks
2590	Wilkerson, Ollie				
2591	" Henry				
2592	" Jennie				
2593	" Alfred				
2594	" Nannie	1328.50	Ollie Wilkerson	L B Bell	
2595	Walking-stick, Isaac				Isaac Walking-S
2596	" Catherine				guardian for
2597	" Felix				
2598	" Jesse				Annie
2599	" Jennie				Cloud
2600	Cloud, Annie	1594.20	Isaac Walkingstick	L B Bell	
2601	Walking-stick, Flint				
2601	" Peggy				
2603	" Dan'l.				
2604	" Eddie	1062.80	Flint Walkingstick	L B Bell	
2605	Welch, George				
2606	" Lizzie				
2607	" Moses	313			
2608	" Geo. Jr.	313			
2609	" Bruce	313			
2610	" Mary	1594.20	Geo Welch	L B Bell	
2611	Winget, Nannie				
2612	" Chas				
2613	" Marsh	797.10	William Wright	L B Bell	
2614	Wolfe[sic], Eli				
2615	" Caroline				
2616	" Sallie				
2617	" Henry				
2618	" Rich'rd.	1328.50	Eli Wolf	L B Bell	
2619	Williams, Newton				
2620	" Watie				
2621	" Mattie				
2622	" Maggie				
2623	" Addie				

156

We, the undersigned citizens of the Cherokee Nation, by right of Cherokee blood, do hereby acknowledge to have received of E. E. Starr, National Treasurer of the Cherokee Nation, the sums set opposite our names respectively, in full of our shares in the per capita distribution authorized by an Act of the National Council, dated ____MAY 3 1894____ 1894.

	Names of Head, and Members of Families	Amount $ cts	To Whom Paid	Witness to Payment	Remarks
2624	" Lottie				
2625	" David	1859.90	Jennie Williams	L B Bell	
2626	Williams, Joˢ	265.70 ᵒʳᵈᵉʳ ᶠⁱˡᵉᵈ	J T Evans	L B Bell	*check on order*
2627	Whitmire, George	265.70	George Whitmire	L B Bell	
2628	Ward, Carrie A	265.70	Carrie Ward	L B Bell	
2629	Winton, Fagin				
2630	" Chaˢ H.	531.40	Fagin Winton	L B Bell	
2631	Welch, Thoˢ				
2632	" Fannie				
2633	" Maude				
2634	" Brice				
2635	" Reese	1328.50	C H Allen	L B Bell	
2636	Welch, Mack Jr	265.70	Mack Welch	L B Bell	
2637	Welch, Scott				
2638	" Lizzie				
2639	" Mary	797.10	Scott Welch	L B Bell	
2640	Wofford, Chaˢ	265.70	John Beck	L B Bell	*check to Julia Beck*
2641	Welch, John				
2642	" Carrie				
2643	" Frank	797.10	John Welch	L B Bell	
2644	Ward, James	265.70	J.C. Starr	L B Bell	
2645	" Dan'l. M.	265.70	Danl M. Ward	L B Bell	
2646	Welch, Marshal[sic] N.				
2647	" John				
2648	" Minnie	797.10	Marshall N Welch	L B Bell	
2649	Ward, Frank				
2650	" Marion				
2651	" George				

Starr Roll 1894

We, the undersigned citizens of the Cherokee Nation, by right of Cherokee blood, do hereby acknowledge to have received of E. E. Starr, National Treasurer of the Cherokee Nation, the sums set opposite our names respectively, in full of our shares in the per capita distribution authorized by an Act of the National Council, dated ___MAY 3 1894___ 1894.

	Names of Head, and Members of Families	Amount $ cts	To Whom Paid	Witness to Payment	Remarks
2652	" Nettie				
2653	" Mary				
2654	" John	1594.20	Frank Ward ~~J. R. Johnson~~	L B Bell	
2655	Webster, Fannie				
2656	" Arthur				
2657	" Charles				
2658	" Silas	1062.80	Bird Webster	L B Bell	
2659	Welch, Mack				
2660	" Cleo	531.40	J W Alberty	L B Bell	
2661	Ward, Geo. W.	265.70	Geo W Ward	L B Bell	
2662	Washington, Elizabeth				
2663	" Sallie M.				
2664	" Chas L.				
2665	" Edw'd. T.				
2666	" Mary Elizabeth	1328.50	Levi Folsom	L B Bell	*on order*
2667	Ward, John	265.70	John Ward	L B Bell	
2668	Wolfe[sic], Thomas				
2669	" Nannie				
2670	" Lou- Ella				
2671	" John				
2672	" Jesse				
2673	" Sam'l.	1594.20	Thos Wolf	L B Bell	
2674	Young-bird, W^m				
2675	" Lola				
2676	" Susie				
2677	" Peggy				
2678	" Sallie				
2679	" Laura	1594.20	Wm Youngbird	L B Bell	
2680	Young-bird, Isaac				
2681	" Nancy				
2682	" Nancy, Jr.				
2683	" Lizzie				

Starr Roll 1894

We, the undersigned citizens of the Cherokee Nation, by right of Cherokee blood, do hereby acknowledge to have received of E. E. Starr, National Treasurer of the Cherokee Nation, the sums set opposite our names respectively, in full of our shares in the per capita distribution authorized by an Act of the National Council, dated ___MAY 3 1894___ 1894.

	Names of Head, and Members of Families	Amount $ cts	To Whom Paid	Witness to Payment	Remarks
2684	" Lucy	1328.50	Nancy Youngbird *Isaac*	L B Bell	
2685	Young-bird, Susie				
2686	" Lennie				
2687	" Nellie				
2688	" Nannie				
2689	" Sam'l				
2690	" James	1594.20	Susie Youngbird	L B Bell	
2691	Young-bird, White	265.70	White Youngbird	L B Bell	

****

Executive Department, Cherokee Nation.
Tahlequah.

I, C. J. Harris, Principal Chief of the Cherokee Nation, and I, E. E. Starr, Treasurer, do hereby certify that the foregoing enrollment of persons resident in Going Snake district is a correct transcript from the original census of said district, as ordered by the Act of the National Council, approved May 15th, 1893, and that the number, so ascertained, to participate in the per-capita distribution of the $6,640,000 as ordered by the Act of the National Council, approved May 3, 1894, is 2695.

C. J. Harris Prin Chief.
E. E. Starr Treasurer.

****

Illinois *(District)*

Starr Roll 1894

We, the undersigned citizens of the Cherokee Nation, by right of Cherokee blood, do hereby acknowledge to have received of E. E. Starr, National Treasurer of the Cherokee Nation, the sums set opposite our names respectively, in full of our shares in the per capita distribution authorized by an Act of the National Council, dated ___MAY 3 1894___ 1894.

	Names of Head, and Members of Families	Amount	To Whom Paid	Witness to Payment	Remarks
1	Andre Eliza				
2	Cunningham Thos F				
3	Andre Paul M	797.10	Eliza Andre	G W Benge	
4	Anderson Louisa				
5	" Nancy J				
6	" John D				
7	" William M				
8	" Joe E				
9	" Mark				
10	" Fannie	1859.90	Louisa Anderson	G W Benge	
11	Adair James F	265.70 order	Christian Gulager	Henry Eiffert	Ck on order
12	Aird Lizzie	265.70	Lizzie Aird	G W Benge	
13	Anderson Jennie[sic]	order	Jenny Anderson	L B Bell Willy	Willy
14	Minnie B.	531.50	~~J W Willy~~	~~Henry Eiffert~~	Willy withdrew order on order
15	Alcom Mary E	order			Patrick
16	Wilson James	531.40	J J Patrick	Henry Eiffert	Ck Pd
17	Alcom Joseph	265.70	J J Patrick	Henry Eiffert	Ck Pd
18	Ackley Mary				
19	Oliver				
20	Maggie				
21	Letta	1062.80	Mary Ackley	Henry Eiffert	
22	Allen Johnston			Fannie Allen	
23	Allen Fannie				
24	Annie				
25	Nannie	1062.80	Fannie Allen	G W Benge	
26	Adair Henry G				
27	Caroline				
28	Minta				
29	George				
30	Sallie				
31	Lucinda	1594.20	Henry G. Adair	L B Bell	

160

Starr Roll 1894

We, the undersigned citizens of the Cherokee Nation, by right of Cherokee blood, do hereby acknowledge to have received of E. E. Starr, National Treasurer of the Cherokee Nation, the sums set opposite our names respectively, in full of our shares in the per capita distribution authorized by an Act of the National Council, dated ___MAY 3 1894___ 1894.

Names of Head, and Members of Families	Amount	To Whom Paid	Witness to Payment	Remarks
32 Arch Lucinda				
33 Ey-ah-na				
34 Sit-oo-wa-qu				
35 Lizzie				
36 Iue le-ya-kah				
37 Wah li				
38 James	1859.90	Ey ah na Arch	G W Benge	
39 Arch Phills				
40 Nancy				
41 Johnston				
42 John				
43 James	1328.50	Branan & Hayes	G W Benge	*by order*
44 Arch Stephen	*order* 265.70	Branan & Hayes	Henry Eiffert	*B & Hayes on order*
45 Ah mi ga[sic] Coh-sah-hela	265.70	Ah mi ja Coh sah hela	G W Benge	
46 Anderson Dick	265.70	Dick Anderson	J P Carter	
47 Anderson Dick Jr.	265.70	J F Wells	Henry Eiffert	*Wells*
48 *(Name and amount erased)* *order*		J F Wells	Henry Eiffert	*Miller*
49 Lovely				
50 Chas.	531.40	Dick Anderson	J P Carter	
51 Adair Jno M	265.70	J.M. Adair	G W Benge	
52 Armstrong Victor	*order* 265.70	W S Nash	Henry Eiffert	*on order W S Nash*
53 Archilla Lucy				
54 Sam Watt	531.40	L.R. Madden	G W Benge	*by order*
55 Adair Mary				
56 Jennie	531.40	Mary Adair	G.W. Benge	
57 Adair Emma	265.70	Mary Adair	Henry Eiffert	*5 mo old minor*
58 Brimmer Mary	*order* 265.70	T R Madden	Henry Eiffert	*Check Madden*

161

Starr Roll 1894

We, the undersigned citizens of the Cherokee Nation, by right of Cherokee blood, do hereby acknowledge to have received of E. E. Starr, National Treasurer of the Cherokee Nation, the sums set opposite our names respectively, in full of our shares in the per capita distribution authorized by an Act of the National Council, dated _____ MAY 3 1894 _____ 1894.

Names of Head, and Members of Families	Amount	To Whom Paid	Witness to Payment	Remarks
59 Brown Isabella				
60 " Ada				
61 " Mary	797.10	Wm Brown	G W Benge	
62 Burns Nancy	265.70	Nancy Burns	Henry Eiffert	
63 Barker Jennie	265.70	Walsh and Shutts[sic]	Henry Eiffert	order W & S
64 Blake Katie				
65 " Mary				
66 " Houston	797.10	Katie Blake	L B Bell	
67 Brown Ann	265.70	Ann Brown	G W Benge	
68 Brown Wm D.				
69 Pearly				
70 W^m D Jr				
71 Albert				
72 Nellie	1328.50	W.D. Brown	G W Benge	
73 Burger Riddle				
74 Takey[sic]				
75 Lewis R.				
76 Jack				
77 Picken	1328.50	Taly Burger	G W Benge	
78 Benge Ross L.	265.70	Ross L Benge	G W Benge	
79 Bean Fannie	265.70	Robin Bean	G W Benge	Dead
80 Benge Robert				
81 Annie	531.40	Robert Benge	G W Benge	
82 Brown Robert				
83 Nellie				
84 Irene				
85 Elma	1062.80	Robt Brown	L B Bell	
86 Boon Volney				
87 Frank				

162

Starr Roll 1894

We, the undersigned citizens of the Cherokee Nation, by right of Cherokee blood, do hereby acknowledge to have received of E. E. Starr, National Treasurer of the Cherokee Nation, the sums set opposite our names respectively, in full of our shares in the per capita distribution authorized by an Act of the National Council, dated ____MAY 3 1894____ 1894.

	Names of Head, and Members of Families	Amount	To Whom Paid	Witness to Payment	Remarks
88	Earl				
89	Emma	1062.80	Emily Harngu[sic]	Henry Eiffert	
90	Bowden Jane				
91	McDonald Bradley				
92	" " Chas	797.10	Jane Bowden	G W Benge	
93	Brady Lucinda				
94	Quilliams[sic] Samuel				
95	Southerland Jesse	797.10	Lucinda Brady	G W Benge	
~~96~~	~~" Abraham~~				*enrolled on*
~~97~~	~~" Betsy~~				*orphan rolls*
98	Benge S. H. Sr				
99	" Theodore				
100	" Jennie				
101	" Nancy				
102	" S H Jr	1328.50	S.H. Benge Sr.	G W Benge	
103	Brewer W. S.				
104	Jack				
105	Brown				
106	Dick				
107	Nannie	1328.50	W.S. Brewer	G W Benge	
108	Brewer Thos F.				
109	Chowie				
110	W^m S	797.10	T F Brewer	G W Benge	
111	Benge M. V.				
112	Maybelle				
113	Amy				
114	Martin V. Jr				
115	John				
116	Emma	1594.20	M V Benge	L B Bell	
117	Benge George				
118	Betsy				
119	John				
120	Dick				

Starr Roll 1894

We, the undersigned citizens of the Cherokee Nation, by right of Cherokee blood, do hereby acknowledge to have received of E. E. Starr, National Treasurer of the Cherokee Nation, the sums set opposite our names respectively, in full of our shares in the per capita distribution authorized by an Act of the National Council, dated ___MAY 3 1894___ 1894.

	Names of Head, and Members of Families	Amount	To Whom Paid	Witness to Payment	Remarks
121	Mary				
122	Jennie				
123	Riddle				
124	James	2125.60	Betsy Benge	G W Benge	
125	Baldridge Susan				
126	Gritts William	531.40	Susan Baldridge	Henry Eiffert	
127	Boudinot Dick F	order			Madden
128	" Catharine				
129	" Carrie				
130	" Elinor N.	1062.80	T R Madden	Henry Eiffert	check order
131	Ballard Jennie	265.70	Jennie Ballard	G W Benge	
132	Beartail Polly	265.70	Beartail	L B Bell	Father of Polly Beartail
133	Ballard Tuxie				
134	" Mary				
135	" Black Fox				
136	" Crab Grass				
137	" Dewit	1328.50	Tuxie Ballard	G W Benge	
138	Blaylock John	order			Madden
139	" Nancy DEAD.				
140	Cristie Mattie				
	(Bowleyn Illegible)				Enrolled at Orphan Asylum
141	Bushyhead Betsy	1062.80	John Blaylock P 2924	L B Bell	
142	Bowleyn Arch	265.70	T E Donham	Henry Eiffert	T E Donham Ck
143	Birdtail Jim				
144	" Annie				
145	" Anderson				
146	" David	1062.80	Jim Birdtail	G W Benge	
147	Brown John L.				
148	Sallie	DEAD.			
149	Brown Robert	DEAD.			
150	" Jack				

Starr Roll 1894

We, the undersigned citizens of the Cherokee Nation, by right of Cherokee blood, do hereby acknowledge to have received of E. E. Starr, National Treasurer of the Cherokee Nation, the sums set opposite our names respectively, in full of our shares in the per capita distribution authorized by an Act of the National Council, dated ____MAY 3 1894____ 1894.

	Names of Head, and Members of Families	Amount	To Whom Paid	Witness to Payment	Remarks
151	" Narcissas				
152	" John Jr				
153	" Kalah	1859.90	John Brown	G W Benge	
154	Barnes James				
155	" Mattie				
156	" Myrtle				
157	" Jennie E.				
158	" Charlotte A	1328.50	James Barnes	G W Benge	
159	Bean Hulbert				
160	Elizabeth				
161	Mary D.	797.10	E.S. Ellis	Henry Eiffert	*check order E.S. Ellis*
162	Boyles George	*order*			*W & S*
163	Margaret				
164	Passon Cisero	797.10	Walsh & Shutt	Henry Eiffert	*check order*
165					
166	Bowlen Charles				
167	" Lizzie				
168	" William				
169	" Ah y hoi ka				
170	" Red Bird	1328.50	Chas Bowlen	Henry Eiffert	
171	Ballard Arch	265.70	Arch Ballard	G W Benge	

****

(The information below was inserted in the logbook before the page containing George Bushyhead #181 and Susan Bushyhead #182 and was originally handwritten and is typed as given.)

Personally appeared this 11th day of July AD 1894 before the undersigned authority, Susie Bushyhead, and made oath in due form of law that ~~that~~ she was registered as a Cherokee citizen for the Cherokee Strip Payment as the wife of George Bushyhead of Illinois District, that

Starr Roll 1894

We, the undersigned citizens of the Cherokee Nation, by right of Cherokee blood, do hereby acknowledge to have received of E. E. Starr, National Treasurer of the Cherokee Nation, the sums set opposite our names respectively, in full of our shares in the per capita distribution authorized by an Act of the National Council, dated ___MAY 3 1894___ 1894.

Names of Head, and Members of Families	Amount	To Whom Paid	Witness to Payment	Remarks

thereafter she and her husband separated and have since lived apart because of his inteseparate habits and failure to support the family, and that said separation took place in January AD 1894. And that at the time of said separation she took with her three children the issue of said marriage with the said Bushhead, named respectively Charles, Mary, and Everett Bushhead, all minors, and has since ~~has~~ had their care custody and support, and also one child of hers by a former marriage with George Crawford said child also being a minor and named George Crawford, and that she is entitled to draw the per capita payment due her four children aforesaid as well as her own. And further that said George Bushyhead is wholly incapable to take charge of of or care for said children or the money coming to them, by reason of his inteseparate and indolent habits, and she protests against the payment of any part of said money to him or his assigns.

before me this 11th day of July AD 1894.

Test:

R.S. Baugh

Susie ✝ Bushyhead

Geo. E. Nelson

Sworn and subscribed to before me a Notary Public in and for the First Judicial Division of the Indian Territory this 11th day of July AD 1894.

J F Chandler

Notary Public

****

166

Starr Roll 1894

We, the undersigned citizens of the Cherokee Nation, by right of Cherokee blood, do hereby acknowledge to have received of E. E. Starr, National Treasurer of the Cherokee Nation, the sums set opposite our names respectively, in full of our shares in the per capita distribution authorized by an Act of the National Council, dated ____MAY 3 1894____ 1894.

Names of Head, and Members of Families	Amount	To Whom Paid	Witness to Payment	Remarks

Fort Gibson IND. TER., *July 11th* 1894

To the HON. E. E. STARR, Treasurer of the Cherokee Nation:

SIR: I, *Susie Bushyhead*, a citizen of the Cherokee Nation by blood and resident of *Illinois* District, for myself and family, consisting of ~~my wife~~ *myself* ~~and a Cherokee by blood~~, and *four children by blood namely, George Crawford by her former husband and Charles, Mary and Everett Bushyhead and* ~~children~~, do hereby authorize, appoint and empower and by these presents do constitute and appoint THOMAS R. MADDEN my true and lawful attorney, without revocation, and revoking all former power of attorney whatever to collect, receive and receipt for the per capita distribution due myself and family, as provided in an Act of the National Council, approved May 3rd, 1894, for the reason that my attendance at home is very necessary in order that I may protect and harvest my crop heretofore planted which is in great danger of waste in case I am not present, besides the expense of remaining at the place of payment until I can procure my money. This I deem of good and sufficient cause as contemplated in Section 6, of an Act approved May 3rd, 1894:

ATTEST: SIGNED:

Geo E Nelson   *Susie* ✝ *Bushyhead*

R.S. Baugh

Subscribed to and sworn to before me, this *11th* day of *July* 1894.

....Notary Public

....1894

Received of THOMAS R. MADDEN, ...DOLLARS, in full payment of the per capita distribution for myself, wife and .... children, as per the foregoing Power of Attorney.

IN THE PRESENCE OF

....

....

****

167

Starr Roll 1894

We, the undersigned citizens of the Cherokee Nation, by right of Cherokee blood, do hereby acknowledge to have received of E. E. Starr, National Treasurer of the Cherokee Nation, the sums set opposite our names respectively, in full of our shares in the per capita distribution authorized by an Act of the National Council, dated ___MAY 3 1894___ 1894.

	Names of Head, and Members of Families	Amount	To Whom Paid	Witness to Payment	Remarks
172	Balou Josie	265.70	Josie Balou	Henry Eiffert	
173	Balou Joseph H				
174	" Thomas J	531.40	Marian Balou	Henry Eiffert	
175	Ballard Mary				
176	Cyntha				
177	Andrew				
178	Ruth				
179	Henry	1328.50	Mary Ballard	Henry Eiffert	
180	Beck William F.	265.70	Annie Shult	*Annie Shults is Annie Beck*	
181	Bushyhead George	265.70	Walsh and Shutt	Henry Eiffert	*check*
182	" Susan	265.70	Susan Bushyhead	L B Bell	
183	Crawford George	265.70 *order*	Susan Bushyhead	L B Bell	
184	Bushyhead Chas	265.70	Susan Bushyhead	L B Bell	
185	" Mary	265.70	Susan Bushyhead	L B Bell	
186	" John	265.70	Walsh and Shutt	Henry Eiffert	*check*
187	Buckhanan[sic] Martha				
188	" James				
189	" Carrie	797.10	Carrie Buchanan	L B Bell	*admn order*
190	Buster Rachel	*order*			*B & H*
191	Cornelius				
192	David				
193	Eyna				
194	Di ga no tsas li	1328.50	Branan & Hayes	Henry Eiffert	*order on check*
195	Buster Nellie	*order*			*B & H*
196	Quatie	*paid*			
197	Buster Thomas				
198	Too stoo				
199	Clubbs				
200	Etsa-ka	1328.50	Branan & Hayes	G W Benge	*on order*
201	Bearpaw Sarah	265.70 *order*	Branan & Hayes	J.C. Starr	*pd check on B & H July 24, 1894*

168

Starr Roll 1894

We, the undersigned citizens of the Cherokee Nation, by right of Cherokee blood, do hereby acknowledge to have received of E. E. Starr, National Treasurer of the Cherokee Nation, the sums set opposite our names respectively, in full of our shares in the per capita distribution authorized by an Act of the National Council, dated ___MAY 3 1894___ 1894.

	Names of Head, and Members of Families	Amount	To Whom Paid	Witness to Payment	Remarks
202	Bullet James		D 2565		
203	Lucy		D 2565		
204	Walker		D 2565		
205	Nellie		D 2565		
206	John		D 2565		
207	Dagee	1594.20	James Bullet	L B Bell	
208	Barricks Minnie				
209	David A	~~531.40~~ ~~265.70~~	Minnie Barricks	G W Benge	
210	Bark John				
211	Lizzie				
212	Perry				
213	Levi	1062.80	John Bark	L B Bell	
214	Cloud William	265.70	Wᵐ Cloud	G W Benge	
215	Bark Chas				
216	Lydia				
217	Nancy				
218	Robert				
219	Scruggs				
220	Samuel	1594.20	Chas Bark	G W Benge	
221	Barry Lizzie	order			Bonham
222	Billie	531.40	T.E. Bonham	G W Benge	on order
223	Brown Mollie				
224	Maud				
225	Adda				
226	Bertha				
227	Mary				
228	Roach	1594.20	Caleb Starr	G W Benge	
229	Bullet[sic] Arch				R.B. Choate
230	" Annie				
231	" Ned				
232	" Eliza	1062.80	Arch Bullette	L B Bell	

169

Starr Roll 1894

We, the undersigned citizens of the Cherokee Nation, by right of Cherokee blood, do hereby acknowledge to have received of E. E. Starr, National Treasurer of the Cherokee Nation, the sums set opposite our names respectively, in full of our shares in the per capita distribution authorized by an Act of the National Council, dated _____ MAY 3 1894 _____ 1894.

	Names of Head, and Members of Families	Amount	To Whom Paid	Witness to Payment	Remarks
233	Bird Ave				
234	" Cyntha				
235	Sa-ne los gah				
236	James	1062.80	Ave Bird	G W Benge	
237	Bolen Lizzie				
238	Waters[sic] Willie	531.40	James Water	Henry Eiffert	one day old
239	Byers David				
240	Annie				
241	Lucy				
242	Mary				
243	Sallie	order			J F Wills
244	Eliza	1594.20	J F Wells	Henry Eiffert	on order
245	Byers William H				
246	" Elizabeth				
247	" Henry				
248	" Eliza				
249	" Rosa DEAD.				
250	" Charles				
251	" Sarah				
252	" Leona				
253	" Mary	2391.30	W.H. Byers	G W Benge	
254	Byers Wilson	265.70	Wilson Byers	Henry Eiffert	
255	Blute John				
256	" Esther	8289			
257	" John Jr.	8289			
258	" Thompson	1062.80	T.E. Bonham	J.C. Starr	Paid check on order
259	Bonham Adda				
260	Vaughan E.				
261	Nannie A.	797.10	T.E. Bonham	G W Benge	
262	Blair William	order 265.70	Walsh and Shutt	Henry Eiffert	ck order
263	Kellah	265.70	Kellah Blair	G W Benge	
264	Buster Betsy	order 265.70	T E Bonham	Henry Eiffert	TE Bonham

170

Starr Roll 1894

We, the undersigned citizens of the Cherokee Nation, by right of Cherokee blood, do hereby acknowledge to have received of E. E. Starr, National Treasurer of the Cherokee Nation, the sums set opposite our names respectively, in full of our shares in the per capita distribution authorized by an Act of the National Council, dated ___MAY 3 1894___ 1894.

Names of Head, and Members of Families	Amount	To Whom Paid	Witness to Payment	Remarks
265 Buster Lydia	263.70	Branan & Hayes	J.C. Starr	check on order Branan & Hayes
266 Bearpaw Cyntha	order			Carlile
267 Lillie B.	531.40	Thoms Carlisle	Henry Eiffert	check on order

****

(The information below was inserted in the logbook before the page containing Katie Bowden #271 and was originally handwritten and is typed as given.)

Cherokee Nation ⎫
Illinois District ⎭

    Before me personally appeared Kattie Bowden, who says under oath that through misrepresentations made by one Tho⁺ Carlile of Campbell Station I was induced to give him an order upon the Hon E E Starr Treasurer to draw my per capita distribution that said order was so given without consideration and consequently void. I therefore desire the same cancelled. Further that I am the daughter of Lucy McNerney, and a member of her family, and being supported in her family, and she is entitled to draw my said money.

Katie her X mark Bowden

Sworn to and subscribed before me this 12 day of July 1894

Henry C. Meigs
Clerk Illinois District

****

E E Starr
   Treasurer
      Sir

    Please take notice that I, Lucy McNerney, a Cherokee by Blood, am the natural mother of Kattie Bowden, that she is under age, and unable to transact business. The said Kattie is a member of my

Starr Roll 1894

We, the undersigned citizens of the Cherokee Nation, by right of Cherokee blood, do hereby acknowledge to have received of E. E. Starr, National Treasurer of the Cherokee Nation, the sums set opposite our names respectively, in full of our shares in the per capita distribution authorized by an Act of the National Council, dated ___MAY 3 1894___ 1894.

Names of Head, and Members of Families	Amount	To Whom Paid	Witness to Payment	Remarks

family and is supported by myself and husband. That I am informed said Kattie has given an order to one Carlisle to draw her per capita. Said order was given under misrepresentations and without consideration, and is therefore void.

I therefore notify you not to pay said order, so I will collect or draw the same myself.

Dated at Fort Gibson on July 12 1894

In presence of

Geo H Walsh

W.H. Mayes

Lucy *her* M<sup>c</sup>Nerney
mark

****

Names of Head, and Members of Families	Amount	To Whom Paid	Witness to Payment	Remarks
268 Blackburn Malzana	order			W & S
269 " Lon	531.40	Walsh and Shutt	Henry Eiffert	check on order
270 Bragg Elizabeth	265.70	Solomon Bragg	G W Benge	
271 Bowden Katie	order 265.70	Thoms[sic] Carlisle	Henry Eiffert	Carlisle check on order
272 Bushyhead Jennie				
273 Collier Mary	531.40	Jennie Bushyhead	Henry Eiffert	
274 Bell Minnie				
275 " Ella L.				
276 Alfred E				
277 Vann John C.				
278 Napoleon B.				
279 Fannie	1594.20	S.E. Bell	G W Benge	
280 Beedle Rena	DEAD. 265.70	Rena Beedle	Henry Eiffert	
281 Cordrey William L	order			Martin
282 Jennetta				
283 Ella	797.10	W.N Martin	E.W. Buffington	check on order
284 Cordrey Frank	order 265.70	Walsh and Shutt	Henry Eiffert	Pd check order W & S

172

Starr Roll 1894

We, the undersigned citizens of the Cherokee Nation, by right of Cherokee blood, do hereby acknowledge to have received of E. E. Starr, National Treasurer of the Cherokee Nation, the sums set opposite our names respectively, in full of our shares in the per capita distribution authorized by an Act of the National Council, dated ___MAY 3 1894___ 1894.

Names of Head, and Members of Families	Amount	To Whom Paid	Witness to Payment	Remarks
285 Crossland Richard	order			W S Nash
286 Lada				
287 Samuel	797.10	W S Nash	Henry Eiffert	check order
288 Crossland William	order 265.70	Walsh and Shutt	Henry Eiffert	Pd W H - check on order
289 Jennie	265.70	Jennie Crossland	G W Benge	
290 Crane Nancy	265.70	Nancy Crane	G W Benge	
291 Casey John	265.70	R L Baugh	Henry Eiffert	check on order R.L. Baugh
292 Casey Arch	265.70	Sam Severs by	Henry Eiffert	order
293 Campbell Lucy A				
294 George L.				
295 Mary E.	797.10	Lucy A Campbell	G W Benge	
~~Lowery Minnie~~				Enrolled at Orphan Asylum
296 Cochran Ellen				
297 Dolly				
298 Maud				
299 Hooley				
300 Ada	1328.50	Ellen Cochran	G W Benge	
301 Coleman James A.				
302 Nannie				
303 Emma				
304 Willie				
305 Minnie				
306 Eva				
307 Fanny				
308 Ella				
309 Timothy W.	2391.30	J.A. Coleman	G W Benge	
310 Cookson Thos J.				
311 Delila				
312 Levi				
313 Andrew	1062.80	T.J. Cookson	G W Benge	

173

Starr Roll 1894

We, the undersigned citizens of the Cherokee Nation, by right of Cherokee blood, do hereby acknowledge to have received of E. E. Starr, National Treasurer of the Cherokee Nation, the sums set opposite our names respectively, in full of our shares in the per capita distribution authorized by an Act of the National Council, dated ____MAY 3 1894____ 1894.

	Names of Head, and Members of Families	Amount	To Whom Paid	Witness to Payment	Remarks
314	Coody Joseph S.				
315	Ella				
316	William S.				
317	Jess				
318	Sarah E.				
319	Annie F.	1594.20	Ja^s O. Coody	Henry Eiffert	
320	Cookson John H.	265.70	J.H. Cookson	L B Bell	
321	Candy Nellie	order			Madden
322	Jesse				
323	Dave				
324	Rachel	1062.80	T R Madden	Henry Eiffert	check on order
325	Candy Sallie				
326	George				
327	Nancy	797.10	Sallie Candy	G W Benge	
328	Cochran Arch				
329	Mary				
330	Lizzie				
331	Mattie				
332	Carrie	1328.50	Arch Cochran	G W Benge	
333	Chooie Ned	order			Madden
334	" Rachel				
335	" Eyahtsaka				
336	" Tah-skee kee tee hee	1062.80	T R Madden	Henry Eiffert	check on order
337	Cookson E. L.				
338	Aggie				
339	Thomas				
340	Ogden				
341	Elinor				
342	Lovett John				orphan
343	George	1859.90	E.L. Cookson	G W Benge	orphan
344	Chooie Big				
345	Nancy				
346	Robert	797.10	Big Chooie	G W Benge	

Starr Roll 1894

We, the undersigned citizens of the Cherokee Nation, by right of Cherokee blood, do hereby acknowledge to have received of E. E. Starr, National Treasurer of the Cherokee Nation, the sums set opposite our names respectively, in full of our shares in the per capita distribution authorized by an Act of the National Council, dated ____MAY 3 1894____ 1894.

	Names of Head, and Members of Families	Amount	To Whom Paid	Witness to Payment	Remarks
347	Choate George				
348	Lizzie				
349	Susan F.				
350	Lewis				
351	Lillan[sic]				
352	George W.				
353	Phelix				
354	Callie				
355	Rufus				
356	Jennie	2657.00	George Choate	G W Benge	
357	Cookson Joseph				
358	Eliza				
359	Jack				
360	Levi				
361	Clem				
362	Ella	1594.20	Joseph Cookson	Henry Eiffert	
363	Crawford James	265.70	Nellie Johnson	Henry Eiffert	
364	Catcher Charles	265.70	~~Cha Catcher~~ T B Green	Henry Eiffert	ord ck.
365	Carlisle Stephen F[sic].				
366	William A.	531.40	Stephen T Carlisle	Henry Eiffert	
367	Costen[sic] Elmire	265.70	C.W. Costin	G W Benge	
368	Crawford George				
369	Susan				
370	Jennie	paid			
371	Crawford Katie				
372	Robert	1328.50	Susan Crawford	Henry Eiffert	
373	Conrad George				
374	Mary	531.40	Mary Conrad	G W Benge	
375	Cookson Nellie				
376	Johnston Everett				
377	Madden Eunice M.				
378	" Thomas R.				

Starr Roll 1894

We, the undersigned citizens of the Cherokee Nation, by right of Cherokee blood, do hereby acknowledge to have received of E. E. Starr, National Treasurer of the Cherokee Nation, the sums set opposite our names respectively, in full of our shares in the per capita distribution authorized by an Act of the National Council, dated _____ MAY 3 1894 _____ 1894.

	Names of Head, and Members of Families	Amount	To Whom Paid	Witness to Payment	Remarks
379	Constantee	1328.50	Nellie Cookson	Henry Eiffert	
380	Cookson Andrew G				
381	Mary J.				
382	Lizzie M.				
383	Maggie L.				
384	Levi M.				
385	Mary A				
386	Annie	1859.90	Andrew G. Cookson	L B Bell	
387	Craig Nannie				
388	Adna	531.40	A H Craig	G W Benge	
389	Collins John H.				
390	Jennie				
391	Mollie	797.10	John H Collins	Henry Eiffert	
392	Chonstotic Nancy	~~order~~ 265.70	T R Madden	Henry Eiffert	~~Madden~~ order check
393	Candy Deertrack	order			Nash
394	Wah ki koo	531.40	W S Nash	E.W. Buffington	on order
395	Campbell William W.				
396	Hugh W.				
397	Nannie	797.10	W.W. Campbell	G W Benge	
398	Campbell William L.	265.70	Wᵐ L Campbell	Henry Eiffert	
399	Crapo Nelson L	265.70	N L Crapo	L B Bell	
400	Carlile Thomas				
401	Myrthe[sic]				
402	Auther[sic]	797.10	Thomas Carlile	G W Benge	
403	Crapo Lewis				
404	Lindie				
405	Eliza				
406	Albert				
407	Akey				
408	Katie				

Starr Roll 1894

We, the undersigned citizens of the Cherokee Nation, by right of Cherokee blood, do hereby acknowledge to have received of E. E. Starr, National Treasurer of the Cherokee Nation, the sums set opposite our names respectively, in full of our shares in the per capita distribution authorized by an Act of the National Council, dated ___MAY 3 1894___ 1894.

	Names of Head, and Members of Families	Amount	To Whom Paid	Witness to Payment	Remarks
409	George				
410	Polly	2125.60	Branan & Hayes	G W Benge	*by order*
411	Choate Silas	265.70 *1052*	W︔ P. Thompson	G W Benge	*329.10 by order*
412	Choate Chas.	265.70 *order*	Dave Smallwood	E.W. Buffington	*check on order Dave Smallwood*
413	Calvert Nannie				
414	Samuel A.			Nannie Calvert	
415	Calvert Roberty				
416	Willie N.	1062.80	Nannie Calvert	G W Benge	
417	Carslile[sic] William				
418	William A. Jr				
419	Leo A				
420	Maud	1062.80	W︔ Carslile	G W Benge	
421	Childers William	D 744	10331		
422	Sophie	D 744	10331		
423	Willie S	D 744	10331		
424	Tandy S.	1062.80	D 744 William Childers	Henry Eiffert	
425	Cloud Chow ah you ka	*order*			T.E. Bonham
426	Spoon Nancy				
427	" Goround	797.10	T E Bonham	E W Buffington	*check on order*
428	Chaney Arty				
429	William I.				
430	Margaret				
431	Florence				
432	Eliza				
433	Ragsdel John				
434	Williams Jeanie	1859.90	Jasper Chaney	G W Benge	
435	Campsey Jim				
436	Lucy				
437	Betsy				
438	Nannie				
439	John R.	*Paid*			

Starr Roll 1894

We, the undersigned citizens of the Cherokee Nation, by right of Cherokee blood, do hereby acknowledge to have received of E. E. Starr, National Treasurer of the Cherokee Nation, the sums set opposite our names respectively, in full of our shares in the per capita distribution authorized by an Act of the National Council, dated ___MAY 3 1894___ 1894.

	Names of Head, and Members of Families	Amount	To Whom Paid	Witness to Payment	Remarks
440	Campsey Sallie				
441	Cochran				
442	Robin	2125.60	Jim Campsey	Henry Eiffert	
443	Campsey Joseph				
444	Lowler Takey	531.40	Joe Campsey	L B Bell	
445	Cumings[sic] Wilson				
446	Nancy				
447	Sadie	797.10	Wilson Cumming	L B Bell	
448	Coleman Arch	order	witness required		Blue Housebug
449	Nannie				
450	Richard				
451	Emma				
452	Kiah	1328.50	Blue Housebug	Henry Eiffert	
453	Cumings[sic] Robert				
454	Maggie				
455	Evans				
456	Francis				
457	Jesse				
458	Rebeca[sic]	1594.20	Robt Cummings	Henry Eiffert	
459	Cristie[sic] William				
460	Nellie				
461	Polly				
462	Jack				
463	Nellie				
464	John	Paid			
465	Cristie Lydia				
466	Jennie				
467	Thomas M.				
468	Chickentoter	2657.00	William Christy	Henry Eiffert	
469	Cowell Lucy				
470	Bullet				
471	Minnie				
472	Charlott				
473	Sadie	1328.50	J.N. Cowell	G W Benge	

Starr Roll 1894

We, the undersigned citizens of the Cherokee Nation, by right of Cherokee blood, do hereby acknowledge to have received of E. E. Starr, National Treasurer of the Cherokee Nation, the sums set opposite our names respectively, in full of our shares in the per capita distribution authorized by an Act of the National Council, dated ____MAY 3 1894____ 1894.

Names of Head, and Members of Families	Amount	To Whom Paid	Witness to Payment	Remarks
474 Colby James				Colby James *Standing*
475 Barnes Stella DEAD.	531.40	James Colby	G W Benge	orphan
476 Chambers Lorenzo D.				
477 Elsie	1138			
478 Cristie Isreal				
479 " Arch	1062.80	Elsie Chambers	G W Benge	
480 Coston Mariah	265.70	Geo Elders	L B Bell	
481 Crawford Sally	order			W.S. Nash
482 " Jack				
483 " Katie				
484 Palone Nancy	1062.80	W S Nash	Henry Eiffert	ck order
485 Campbell Nancy				
486 Gibbs Berenice[sic]	531.40	Nancy Campbell	G W Benge	
487 Cochran Alex	265.70	J J Patrick	Henry Eiffert	see #1147 Ck Pd
488 Clapp James	order			D L Scott
489 Frank	531.40	A B Clapp	L B Bell	withdrawn order
490 Crawling Sunday				
491 Jesse	531.40	Sunday Crawling	L B Bell	
492 Childers John Jr	265.70	H.C. Lowrey	E.W. Buffington	check on order H.C. Lowrey
493 Casey William	265.70	William Casey	Henry Eiffert	T.B. Sivers guardian
494 Cordry John	265.70	Henry Eiffert Guard Robt B Ross.		Pd unpaid Dec 11/96
495 Day light Ellis	265.70	Walsh & Shutt	G W Benge	on order W & S -
496 Day light Laura	265.70	Walsh and Shutt	G W Benge	on order W & S -
497 Duvall Mary R	265.70	Hubbard Ross	L B Bell	
498 Davis Dosh	265.70	Christian Gulager	G W Benge	on order

179

Starr Roll 1894

We, the undersigned citizens of the Cherokee Nation, by right of Cherokee blood, do hereby acknowledge to have received of E. E. Starr, National Treasurer of the Cherokee Nation, the sums set opposite our names respectively, in full of our shares in the per capita distribution authorized by an Act of the National Council, dated ___MAY 3 1894___ 1894.

Names of Head, and Members of Families	Amount	To Whom Paid	Witness to Payment	Remarks
499 Daniel Catharine B	265.70	Catherine B Daniel	Henry Eiffert	
500 Dowell Sarah				
501 " Charles M.				
502 " Mammie				
503 " Henry H				
504 " Bessie				
505 " Claud E				
506 Hynes Frank				
507 " Henry	2125.60	Sarah Dowell	G W Benge	
508 Dims more[sic] Belle	265.70	Belle Demsmore	G W Benge	
509 De armond Rachal[sic]	265.70	Alex Ballard	G W Benge	
510 Downing Wash	order			Blackstone & Co
511 " Eliza				
512 " Laura	797.10	Blackstone & Co	G W Benge	on order
513 Dave Sampson	order			Madden
514 " Nancy				
515 Stoo is tie	4 yrs old paid	8929		
516 Dave Lucy				
517 " Gane	1328.50	Sampson Dave	L B Bell	
518 Bushyhead Constalogie	265.70	Mary Waters	L B Bell	Child is not a child of Sampson Dave
519 Davis Polly	order			Madden
520 " Minerva	531.40	T.R. Madden	G W Benge	on order
521 Daugherty Willie	order 265.70	Walsh and Shutt	G W Benge	W&S – on order
522 Deer in water Keener	order			Madden
523 " Susan				
524 " Louis				
525 " Stan	1062.80	T.R. Madden	G W Benge	on order
526 Deer in water George	order			Madden
527 " Annie				
528 " " Richard				
529 " " Charles				

Starr Roll 1894

We, the undersigned citizens of the Cherokee Nation, by right of Cherokee blood, do hereby acknowledge to have received of E. E. Starr, National Treasurer of the Cherokee Nation, the sums set opposite our names respectively, in full of our shares in the per capita distribution authorized by an Act of the National Council, dated ___MAY 3 1894___ 1894.

	Names of Head, and Members of Families	Amount	To Whom Paid	Witness to Payment	Remarks
530	" " Nellie				
531	" " Mary	1594.20	T.R. Madden	G W Benge	on order
532	Dassler Akey				
533	" Rachal[sic]				
534	" John W.				
535	" James L.				
536	" Osie				
537	" Lizzie				
538	" Charles	1859.90	Lewis Dassler	G W Benge	
539	Deer in water James	265.70 order	T R Madden	G.W. Benge	on order
540	Dun back Nancy				
541	" " Henryetta				
542	" " John				
543	" " Effie	1062.80	Nancy Dunback	G W Benge	
544	Drum Lizzie	265.70	Branan[sic] & Hayes	G W Benge	on order
545	Du val[sic] Huston	265.70	Branan & Hayes	G W Benge	on order
546	Dassler Mary	265.70 order			B.& H.
547	" Robert	531.40	Branan and Hayes	G W Benge	on order
548	Daugherty Jack	order		order withdrawn	J.R. Skaggs
549	" Susan				
550	" James				
551	" Nancy				
552	" Kate	1328.50	Jack Daugherty	G W Benge	
553	Du val Joseph	265.70 order	T.E. Bonham	G W Benge	on order
554	Downing Elizabeth	265.70 order	N.S. Drake	G W Benge	N.S. Drake on order
555	Double tooh Lucy				
556	Bud Mary	531.40	Roach & Young	G W Benge	
557	Du val John	265.70 order	Thomas Carlisle	G W Benge	on order
558	" Lilla	order			B & H

181

Starr Roll 1894

We, the undersigned citizens of the Cherokee Nation, by right of Cherokee blood, do hereby acknowledge to have received of E. E. Starr, National Treasurer of the Cherokee Nation, the sums set opposite our names respectively, in full of our shares in the per capita distribution authorized by an Act of the National Council, dated _____ MAY 3 1894 _____ 1894.

	Names of Head, and Members of Families	Amount	To Whom Paid	Witness to Payment	Remarks
559	" Charley				
560	" Maggie				
561	" Floria	1062.80	Banon[sic] and Hayes	G W Benge	on order
562	Duval William				enrolled at
563	Ben				Orphan Asylum
564	Duval Sam	order 265.70	Thomas Carlisle	G W Benge	on order
565	Drake Emma				
566	" Emma E	531.40	J.W. Drake	G W Benge	
567	Duval Isaac	order 265.70	Thomas Carlile	G W Benge	Carlile
568	Downing Ben	265.70	J J Patrick	Henry Eiffert	order Oct 15/94
569	Downing Return	265.70	N.S Drake	L B Bell	Aug 17,1894 Sequoyah C.H. on order adm
570	Dassler Henry	order 265.70	Thomas Carlisle	G W Benge	Gordialer
571	Elleage[sic] Andrew M	order	Given by Mary Eldrige	See letters	minors
572	" Ruth M.				children of
573	" Hattie P.				Marrion Elledge
574	" James A				
575	" Mary A	1328.50	Walsh and Shutt	G W Benge	on order W&S
576	Elledge Rebeca	265.70	Rebeca Elledge	G W Benge	
577	Ethrige[sic] Miza				
578	John				
579	Rachal	797.10	Jeff Ethridge	L B Bell	
580	Elk McCoy				
581	" Celia				
582	" Mary				
583	" Lillia				
584	Foreman Nellie		9192		
585	Elk Bettsie	1594.20	McCoy Elk	Henry Eiffert	
586	Elk Bettsie	$265.70	Bettsie Elk	Robt B Ross.	by check
587	Elders George W	265.70	Geo Elders	L B Bell	

Starr Roll 1894

We, the undersigned citizens of the Cherokee Nation, by right of Cherokee blood, do hereby acknowledge to have received of E. E. Starr, National Treasurer of the Cherokee Nation, the sums set opposite our names respectively, in full of our shares in the per capita distribution authorized by an Act of the National Council, dated ___MAY 3 1894___ 1894.

Names of Head, and Members of Families	Amount	To Whom Paid	Witness to Payment	Remarks
588 Elowee Jennie	265.70	Branan & Hayes	G W Benge	by order
589 Elk William				
590 Peggie	531.40	Blackstone & Co	Henry Eiffert	ck on order
591 ~~Collins Abraham~~				enrolled at
592 ~~Fannie~~				Orphan Sylum[sic]
593 Elgin Loucinda				
594 " Fenton F.				
595 " Ester C				
596 Tiffany Wallace				
597 " Andrew G.				
598 " Alexander	1594.20	Lucinda Elgin	Henry Eiffert	
599 Faulkner Nora				
600 " Jack				
601 Owen Eugene				
602 " Elizabeth G				
603 " Lillie	1328.50	Nora Faulkner	G W Benge	
604 Fox Eliza	265.70 Creek CREEK. Walsh & Shutt		G W Benge	on W&S order
605 Fox Sarah A.	CREEK.	Enrolled on Creek Cencus[sic] Card Field #862 D 1942		
606 Mose	CREEK.			
607 Pessey	CREEK.			
608 Dave	order CREEK.			W & S
609 Susan	CREEK.			
610 Loucinda	1594.20	Walsh and Shutt	G W Benge	on order
611 Fuller Rosa L				
612 Nellie				
613 James T.	797.10	W.S. Fuller	G W Benge	
614 Fields Nellie	265.70	Alex McCoy	Henry Eiffert	
615 Fields John M.	265.70	Eliza Andre	G W Benge	on order
616 Fodder Charles				
617 Jennie				
618 Towie Hattie				

Starr Roll 1894

We, the undersigned citizens of the Cherokee Nation, by right of Cherokee blood, do hereby acknowledge to have received of E. E. Starr, National Treasurer of the Cherokee Nation, the sums set opposite our names respectively, in full of our shares in the per capita distribution authorized by an Act of the National Council, dated _____ MAY 3 1894 _____ 1894.

Names of Head, and Members of Families	Amount	To Whom Paid	Witness to Payment	Remarks
619 Alexander Sohnie	1062.80	Charles Fodder	L B Bell	
620 Fallen Alexander				
621 Samuel A.	531.40	Alex Fallen	Henry Eiffert	
622 Foreman Jesse				
623 " Quatie				
624 " Luke	797.10	Jesse Foreman	G W Benge	
625 Fields Samuel	*order*		*order with drawn by Carlisle*	
626 " Takey				
627 " Oo-tah-nee-too-ti				
628 " Ridge	1,062.80	Sam¹ Fields	G W Benge	
629 Fagans James A	*order*			*W S Nash*
630 " Luther	531.40	W.S. Nash	G W Benge	*on order*
631 Fallen Sarah				
632 Kelly Mary A.				
633 Chabbuck Ross				
634 Williams Andrew	1062.80	Sarah Fallen	G W Benge	
635 Foreman Cephas W	265.70	Cephas W Foreman	Henry Eiffert	
636 Fields Timothy	265.70	Timothy Fields	Henry Eiffert	
637 Fields Kellah M				
638 Robert B.				
639 Samuel F.				
640 Lugie P.				
641 George B.				
642 Kiah R.	1,594.20	Kellah M Fields	G W Benge	
643 Foreman Nannie E.				
644 George B DEAD.				
645 Percy J.				
646 Susan F.				
647 Alexander				
648 Ada				
649 George D.	1,859.90	N.E. Foreman	G W Benge	

184

Starr Roll 1894

We, the undersigned citizens of the Cherokee Nation, by right of Cherokee blood, do hereby acknowledge to have received of E. E. Starr, National Treasurer of the Cherokee Nation, the sums set opposite our names respectively, in full of our shares in the per capita distribution authorized by an Act of the National Council, dated ___MAY 3 1894___ 1894.

Names of Head, and Members of Families	Amount	To Whom Paid	Witness to Payment	Remarks
650 Foster James	265.70	James Foster	G W Benge	
651 Fields George W.				
652 Mattie J.				
653 George W. Jr				
654 James F.				
655 Charles H				
656 Mattie M.	1,59.90	G.W. Fields	G W Benge	
657 Feather Watts				
658 Nancy				
659 Nellie				
660 Coo-tlaw-sti	1062.80	T.E. Bonham	J.C. Starr	Pd check on order JUL 24 18
661 Foreman Thomas	order			Ellis
662 Lizzie				
663 Susan	797.10	E.S. Ellis	G W Benge	on order
664 Ford Rosa	order			Martin W.N.
665 Grayham Nancy	531.40	W N Martin	Henry Eiffert	order Ck
666 Foreman William H.				
667 William H. Jr.	order			
668 Susan A.				O.W. Willy
669 Johnston	1,062.80	O.W. Willy	G W Benge	on order
670 Fallen George	order			A. Foyil
671 Ellis	531.40	A Foyil	Henry Eiffert	ord check
672 French Dora F.	265.70 order	W.S. Nash	G W Benge	on order W.S.Nash
673 Foreman Shorey	265.70	Shorey Foreman	G W Benge	
674 Foreman Ned	265.70 order	Branan & Hayes	G W Benge	B&H mother whi on order
674 Gunter George	265.70 1327 order	A.R. Matherson	G W Benge	A.R. Matherson
675 Gott Jack B.				
676 Susan				
677 Margaret				

Starr Roll 1894

We, the undersigned citizens of the Cherokee Nation, by right of Cherokee blood, do hereby acknowledge to have received of E. E. Starr, National Treasurer of the Cherokee Nation, the sums set opposite our names respectively, in full of our shares in the per capita distribution authorized by an Act of the National Council, dated ____MAY 3 1894____ 1894.

	Names of Head, and Members of Families	Amount	To Whom Paid	Witness to Payment	Remarks
678	John				
679	Alphonso				
680	Laura				
681	James				
682	Sophie A.	2,215.60	J.B. Gott	G W Benge	
683	Griffin Jack	order			Willy
684	Charles	531.40	C W Willy	Henry Eiffert	Ck order
685	Gunter Kee Kee	265.70	W.S. Nash	Henry Eiffert	Nash
686	Griffin Andrew J.	265.70	Andrew J Griffin	Henry Eiffert	Oct 4 94
687	Greer Hannah				
688	Mary P.				
689	Thomas O.				
690	Joseph	1,062.80	(Illegible) Greer	G W Benge	
691	Gritts Samuel				Madden
692	Kate				
693	Robert	797.10	T R Madden	Henry Eiffert	Ck order
694	Grass Nannie	order			Madden
695	Peggie	531.40	T R Madden	Henry Eiffert	Ck order
696	Grease William				
697	Nancy	531.40	William Grease	Henry Eiffert	
698	Gonzaley[sic] Frank				
699	Kate	531.40	Frank Gonzalus[sic]	Henry Eiffert	
700	Grapes Mary				Patrick
701	Ballard Brice				
702	Clay Lovely	2106			
703	" Henry	order			
704	Patrick Jessie	1328.50	J J Patrick	Henry Eiffert	Ck Pd
705	George Lizzie	order			B&H
706	Susie	531.40	Brannan & Hayes	Henry Eiffert	Ck - order.

186

Starr Roll 1894

We, the undersigned citizens of the Cherokee Nation, by right of Cherokee blood, do hereby acknowledge to have received of E. E. Starr, National Treasurer of the Cherokee Nation, the sums set opposite our names respectively, in full of our shares in the per capita distribution authorized by an Act of the National Council, dated ____MAY 3 1894____ 1894.

Names of Head, and Members of Families	Amount	To Whom Paid	Witness to Payment	Remarks
707 Girty Polly				B&H
708 " Susie				
709 " Eliza				
710 " Simon				
711 " Tobacco				
712 Albert John	1594.20	Branan & Hayes	Henry Eiffert	B&H Ck order
713 Garard Margaret				
714 " Ida	1140			
715 " Ebie				
716 " Daniel				
717 " Major	1328.50	Wm Garard	G W Benge	
718 Garrison Nancy	265.70	Nancy Garrison	Henry Eiffert	
719 Gritts Anderson W.				
720 " Lizzie				
721 " Wessley[sic] A.				
722 " George W.	1062.80	Anderson W Gritts	L B Bell	
723 Girty John	265.70	Tom Carlisle	Henry Eiffert	Carlisle ck order
724 Green Joseph	(No other information given.)			
725 Griffin Andrew	265.70	A.J. Griffin	G W Benge	
726 Glass Thomas				
727 Nancy				
728 Alsie				
729 Staley[sic]	1,062.80	Thomas Glass	G W Benge	
730 Girty James	265.70	E.S. Ellis	Henry Eiffert	ck order Ellis
731 Gibbs William	265.70	Nancy Campbell	G W Benge	
732 Girty Taylor	order			B & H
733 Betsy				
734 Cherokee	797.10	Branan & Hayes	Henry Eiffert	ck order

187

Starr Roll 1894

We, the undersigned citizens of the Cherokee Nation, by right of Cherokee blood, do hereby acknowledge to have received of E. E. Starr, National Treasurer of the Cherokee Nation, the sums set opposite our names respectively, in full of our shares in the per capita distribution authorized by an Act of the National Council, dated ___MAY 3 1894___ 1894.

Names of Head, and Members of Families	Amount	To Whom Paid	Witness to Payment	Remarks
735 Gilstrap Louisa	order			Madden
736 Louis				
737 Jennie	797.10	T R Madden	Henry Eiffert	Ck order
738 Gillispie Louisa				
739 William M	paid			
740 Harris Katie	797.10	Lousa[sic] Gillispie	G W Benge	
741 Hawk Adam	order			Madden
742 Sallie				
743 John				
744 Alice				
745 Jennie	1328.50	T R Madden	Henry Eiffert	Ck order
746 Harnage Emily W.	265.70	Emily W Harnage	Henry Eiffert	
747 Hanan Maggie L.				W&S
748 Joseph E				
749 Newton E				
750 James T	1062.80	Walsh & Shutt	Henry Eiffert	Ck order
751 Hart Sallie	265.70	G.W. Benge	G W Benge	
752 Hughes Maggie				
753 Belle	531.40	Maggie Hughes	G W Benge	
754 Higgins Lydia E	265.70	Frank T H Higgins	G W Benge	
755 Hopson Clara H				
756 Thornton Percy M	531.40	Clem H. Hopson	L B Bell	
757 Hicks Emma I	265.70	P W Hicks	L B Bell	
758 Haley Nellie				
759 Arnee				
760 Albert J	797.10	Nellie Haley	G W Benge	
761 Hicks Herbert W				
762 Ethel				
763 Homer W	797.10	Herbert W Hicks	L B Bell	

188

Starr Roll 1894

We, the undersigned citizens of the Cherokee Nation, by right of Cherokee blood, do hereby acknowledge to have received of E. E. Starr, National Treasurer of the Cherokee Nation, the sums set opposite our names respectively, in full of our shares in the per capita distribution authorized by an Act of the National Council, dated ___MAY 3 1894___ 1894.

Names of Head, and Members of Families	Amount	To Whom Paid	Witness to Payment	Remarks
764 Hicks Percy W.	265.70	Percy W Hicks	L B Bell	
765 Horn Samuel	order			W.S. Nash
766 Malzarine	DEAD.			Dead.
767 David				
768 George				
769 Collins Henry	1328.50	8603 W S Nash P186 Henry Eiffert		Ck Pd
770 Harrison Mattie E				
771 Mary	531.40	Mattie E Harrison	Henry Eiffert	
772 Hensley Margaret				
773 " Carrie				
774 " John W.				
775 " Tennessee C				
776 " Samuel				
777 " Houston				
778 " George				
777 " James				
780 " Joseph	2391.30	Margaret Hensley	G W Benge	
781 Hilderbrand Lem	order	9077		Branan & Hayes
782 Lizzie	531.40	Branan & Hayes	Henry Eiffert	Ck order
783 Hilderbrand John	order			
784 John Jr	531.40	T R Madden	Henry Eiffert	Madden
785 Hilderbrand Brice	order			Madden
786 " Stephen				
787 " Hooley				
788 " Julie (?)	1062.80 1385	T R Madden	Henry Eiffert	Ck order
789 Hannan Andrew				Patrick
790 Jennie				
791 Maggie				
792 Edward	order			
793 Mary				
794 Girtie				
795 Andrew Jr.	1859.90	J.J. Patrick	Henry Eiffert	ck Pd

189

Starr Roll 1894

We, the undersigned citizens of the Cherokee Nation, by right of Cherokee blood, do hereby acknowledge to have received of E. E. Starr, National Treasurer of the Cherokee Nation, the sums set opposite our names respectively, in full of our shares in the per capita distribution authorized by an Act of the National Council, dated ___MAY 3 1894___ 1894.

	Names of Head, and Members of Families	Amount	To Whom Paid	Witness to Payment	Remarks
796	Hicks Lewis				
797	Peggie				
798	Samantha	797.10	Lewis Hicks	G W Benge	
799	Hicks Ahlie				
800	Lovett Lydia				
801	Miller William	797.10	Ahlie Hicks	G W Benge	
802	Headrick Lucy				
803	Michael				
804	Wutty	797.10	Lucy Headrick	G W Benge	
805	Housebug Blueford	order			E.C. Thompson
806	Kizzie				
807	Lydia				
808	Warren 73				
809	Dora N 26	1328.50	E C Thompson	Henry Eiffert	Ck order
810	Hogtoter Sunday				
811	Nancy				
812	Young Joe				
813	Ross Ida	1062.80	Sunday Hogtoter	G W Benge	
814	Hair John				
815	" George				
816	" Medley	797.10	John Hair	G W Benge	
817	Huggins Kate				
818	Robinson Dora				
819	Lillie		D 2959		
820	Irving				
821	Lucy	1328.50	Kate Huggins	G W Benge	no check
822	Hildabrand[sic] Daniel	265.70	J.E. Hayes	G W Benge	
823	Hair Jesse DEAD.				
824	Mary				
825	Martha				
826	Emaline				
827	Walter				

Starr Roll 1894

We, the undersigned citizens of the Cherokee Nation, by right of Cherokee blood, do hereby acknowledge to have received of E. E. Starr, National Treasurer of the Cherokee Nation, the sums set opposite our names respectively, in full of our shares in the per capita distribution authorized by an Act of the National Council, dated ___MAY 3 1894___ 1894.

	Names of Head, and Members of Families	Amount	To Whom Paid	Witness to Payment	Remarks
828	Betsy				
829	Oscar				
830	Josie	2125.60	Jesse Hair	G W Benge	
831	Horn Charlott[sic]				
832	Lafayette				
833	Ella				
834	Chas W.	*paid*			
835	Horn Nancy				
836	Thomas				
837	Mattie				
838	Susan	2125.60	Charlotte Horn	G W Benge	
839	Horn Louisa				
840	John				
841	Robert				
842	Fannie				
843	Cristie Isaac	1328.50	Louisa Horn	G W Benge	
844	Horn Jery[sic] DEAD.	*order*			*Ellis*
845	Minnie				
846	Callie				
847	Maud	1062.80	E S Ellis	Henry Eiffert	*Ck order*
848	~~Foreman Ned~~		*Transferred to letter F.*		*Orphan*
849	Halcomb[sic] Dick				
850	Nannie				
851	Jennie				
852	George				
853	Ester				
854	Charles				
855	Dick Johnston	1859.90	Dick Holcomb	Henry Eiffert	
856	Holt Polly				
857	Lizzie				
858	Jennie				
859	Nancy				
860	Sarah	1328.50	Polly Holt	Henry Eiffert	
861	Hall William F.	265.70 *order*	ES Ellis	Henry Eiffert	*ck Ellis*

191

Starr Roll 1894

We, the undersigned citizens of the Cherokee Nation, by right of Cherokee blood, do hereby acknowledge to have received of E. E. Starr, National Treasurer of the Cherokee Nation, the sums set opposite our names respectively, in full of our shares in the per capita distribution authorized by an Act of the National Council, dated ___MAY 3 1894___ 1894.

	Names of Head, and Members of Families	Amount	To Whom Paid	Witness to Payment	Remarks
862	Henson Thomas	order			J.R. Skaggs
863	Annie				
864	Myrtle				
865	Levina	1062.80	J R Skaggs	Henry Eiffert	ck Pd
866	Henson Scott	order 265.70	J R Skaggs	Henry Eiffert	ck order J.R. Skaggs
867	Hayes Tilden H	order 265.70	Walsh & Shutt	Henry Eiffert	ck W&S order
868	Henson William	order 265.70	E S Ellis	L B Bell	J.R. Skaggs Check
869	Horn John C.	order 265.70	T.E. Bonham ~~John C Horn~~	Henry Eiffert	ck order Bonham
870	Hilderbrand Reese				
871	Mary				
872	Martha				
873	Lelia				
874	William				
875	Tommie				
876	Johnie	1859.90	Branan & Hayes	G W Benge	by order
877	Henson Zeke	$265.70	Zeke Henson	Robt B Ross.	
878	Henson Buck	265.70 order	J R Skaggs	Henry Eiffert	order Ck
879	Henson Powhattan	265.70	CW Starr	Henry Eiffert	CW Starr
880	Henson Downing	265.70	Blackstone & Co	Henry Eiffert	Check Pd
881	Margaret	265.70 order	JR Skaggs	Henry Eiffert	J R Skaggs order
882	Henson George	265.70 order	JR Skaggs D1218	Henry Eiffert	J.R. Skaggs ck order
883	Henson Caleb DEAD.	265.70 order	J R Skaggs	Henry Eiffert	J.R. Skaggs ck order
884	Hall Eliza	order 265.70	N S Drake	Henry Eiffert	N S Drake ck -
885	" Rosabella	265.70	Blackstone & Co	Henry Eiffert	Blackstone & Co
886	Hall Ester L.				
887	Ussrey Luvenia				
888	Ezekiel				

Starr Roll 1894

We, the undersigned citizens of the Cherokee Nation, by right of Cherokee blood, do hereby acknowledge to have received of E. E. Starr, National Treasurer of the Cherokee Nation, the sums set opposite our names respectively, in full of our shares in the per capita distribution authorized by an Act of the National Council, dated ___MAY 3 1894___ 1894.

Names of Head, and Members of Families	Amount	To Whom Paid	Witness to Payment	Remarks
889 Price Willie				
890 Hall Mattie			.	
891 Watie				
892 Floyd	1859.90	W.D. Hall	G W Benge	
893 Harland William	order 265.70	Walsh and Shutt	Henry Eiffert	ord W&S Ck
894 Hampton John W.	order 265.70	W. N. Martin	G W Benge	on order
895 Hicks Racheal[sic]				
896 Bowden Sallie	531.40	Rachael Hicks	G W Benge	
897 Doctor Nancy	265.70	Rachael Hicks	G W Benge	
898 Hair James	265.70	Thomas Carlile	G W Benge	on order
899 Hosmer John	265.70	Geo King	G W Benge	see Letters of Administration
900 Howard Allie	order			Nash
901 Bessie B.	531.40	NS Nash	Henry Eiffert	order Ck
902 Hicks Abbie	265.70	L.C. Ross	S.W. Mayfield	
903 Isreal Ella	order			Nash
904 Candy Mary G.	531.40	W.S. Nash	G W Benge	on order
905 Isreal John	order	D1231		
906 Sarah				Nash
907 Phillip				
908 Millie	1062.80	W.S. Nash	G W Benge	on order
909 Ice Nancy	order 265.70	T.R. Madden	G W Benge	Madden on order
910 Irving William				
911 George				
912 Fannie				
913 Ewing				
914 Stella	1328.50	William Irving	G W Benge	
915 Irving Joseph				Patrick
916 " Watie	order 531.40	J.J. Patrick	Henry Eiffert	Ck Pd

Starr Roll 1894

We, the undersigned citizens of the Cherokee Nation, by right of Cherokee blood, do hereby acknowledge to have received of E. E. Starr, National Treasurer of the Cherokee Nation, the sums set opposite our names respectively, in full of our shares in the per capita distribution authorized by an Act of the National Council, dated _____ MAY 3 1894 _____ 1894.

Names of Head, and Members of Families	Amount	To Whom Paid	Witness to Payment	Remarks

****

(The information below was inserted in the logbook before the page containing William Johnson #919. This transcriber assumes this is the concerned party mentioned since there is no reference given to this number.)

Letters of Guardianship.

CHEROKEE NATION, I.T.⎫
Illinois **District.** ⎬

OFFICE DISTRICT JUDGE. ⎫
Illinois District. ⎬

To Whom it May Concern:

KNOW YE, That I *E L Cookson* Judge of the District Court of the District and Nation aforesaid, do, by virtue of authority in me vested by law, this day make, constitute and appoint in the name and by the authority of the CHEROKEE NATION *Alex Petitte* as guardian of *Willie Johnson*

minor child............ of *Johnson Jack* deceased, late of *Illinois* District, Cherokee Nation, the said *Alex Petitte* having complied with and performed all the duties required by law of *him* precedent to the appointment.

In testimony whereof I hereunto set my hand on this the **12** day of *July* 189 **4**

```
.........
: SEAL. :
:.......:
```

E L Cookson
Judge District Court.

Attest: *Henry C. Meigs*
Clerk *Illinois* District.

****

194

Starr Roll 1894

We, the undersigned citizens of the Cherokee Nation, by right of Cherokee blood, do hereby acknowledge to have received of E. E. Starr, National Treasurer of the Cherokee Nation, the sums set opposite our names respectively, in full of our shares in the per capita distribution authorized by an Act of the National Council, dated ____MAY 3 1894____ 1894.

Names of Head, and Members of Families	Amount	To Whom Paid	Witness to Payment	Remarks
917 Jackson Walter H	265.70	W H Jackson	G W Benge	
918 John Thomas	265.70	Jesse Foreman	G W Benge	
919 Johnson William	order 265.70	Walsh and Shutt	G W Benge	on W&S
920 Jumper Sam				
921 " Annie	531.40	Branan & Hayes	G W Benge	by order
922 Jack Wattie				
923 " Wahli sa				
924 " Dave				
925 " Quahleyouka				
926 " Polly				
927 " Jesse				
928 " Tah da-yi	1859.90	Branan & Hayes	G W Benge	by order
929 Johnson David	order			Carlisle
930 " Akey				
931 " Levi		D 2949		
932 McCoy Ezekiel	1062.80	Thomas Carlile	G W Benge	on order
933 Johnson Betsie	order			T E Bonham
934 " Weekee	531.40	T.E. Bonham	G W Benge	on order
935 Jairrel[sic] Maggie	265.70	J.F. Wells	G W Benge	Wells on order
936 Jack James	265.70	Thomas Carlile	G W Benge	Carlile on order
937 " Lucy				
938 Still Polly	531.40	Thomas Carlile	G W Benge	on Carlile
939 Johnston Peter	265.70	Sunday Hogtoter	G W Benge	
940 Jim Wilson				
941 " Nannie				
942 " Susan				
943 " Akey				
944 " Josiah				
945 " Tee nee sus	1594.20	Jim Wilson	Henry Eiffert	

195

Starr Roll 1894

We, the undersigned citizens of the Cherokee Nation, by right of Cherokee blood, do hereby acknowledge to have received of E. E. Starr, National Treasurer of the Cherokee Nation, the sums set opposite our names respectively, in full of our shares in the per capita distribution authorized by an Act of the National Council, dated ____MAY 3 1894____ 1894.

Names of Head, and Members of Families	Amount	To Whom Paid	Witness to Payment	Remarks
946 Johnston Cloud	order			Madden
947 Nellie				
948 Phillips Quatie	797.10	T.R. Madden	G W Benge	on order
949 Crawford Ned	265.70	Nelly Johnson	Henry Eiffert	
950 Keyes Levi				
951 Viola W				
952 Carrie M.	797.10	Levi Keys	Henry Eiffert	
953 Knee land Fannie				
954 " Ross Harry				
955 " Louis G	797.10	Herbert Kneeland	G W Benge	
956 Kennard Martha				
957 Raper Mose	531.40	Martha Kennard	L B Bell	
958 Keener Jennie	order			Madden
959 Sanders Pearl	531.40	T. R. Madden	G W Benge	on order
960 Keys James T.				
961 Margaret E				
962 James M.				
963 Mary J.				
964 John D.				
965 Walter S.				
966 Levi H				
967 Spears Lizziebelle	2125.60	James T Keys	Henry Eiffert	
968 Keys Levi R.				
969 Elizabeth				
970 Carslile[sic] Henry	797.10	Levi Keys	L B Bell	
971 Ki yah nah Jennie	265.70	TE Bonham	Henry Eiffert	
972 Losson Comingdeer	265.70	Henry Eiffert	Robt B Ross	
973 Willis Wah-sin-noe	265.70	TE Bonham	Henry Eiffert	
974 Kidney Fannie	265.70	Fannie Kidney	G W Benge	Census Roll says Kiddy -
975 Lacy Polly	order 265.70	W.S. Nash	G W Benge	WhSoNbeh

196

Starr Roll 1894

We, the undersigned citizens of the Cherokee Nation, by right of Cherokee blood, do hereby acknowledge to have received of E. E. Starr, National Treasurer of the Cherokee Nation, the sums set opposite our names respectively, in full of our shares in the per capita distribution authorized by an Act of the National Council, dated ___MAY 3 1894___ 1894.

Names of Head, and Members of Families	Amount	To Whom Paid	Witness to Payment	Remarks
976 Lowrey Daniel W.				
977 " Ellen				
978 " Florence				
979 " George				
980 " Richard				
981 " James	1594.20	D.W. Lowrey	G W Benge	
982 Long Nakey	265.70	Nakey Long	G W Benge	
983 Lannon[sic] Zora				
984 Camille				
985 Harrell James H				orphan
986 " Mary				
987 Parchmeal Akey	1,328.50	H D Lonnon	G W Benge	
988 Levi Eli	265.70	T.R. Madden	G W Benge	on order Madden
989 Locust Obadiah				
990 William	531.40	Obadiah Locust	G W Benge	
991 Lyman[sic] Lewis				
992 Charlott				
993 Elimire[sic]				
994 Livi[sic]	1,962.80	Lewis Lymon	G W Benge	
995 Lyman Polly				
996 William				
997 Patrick	797.10	Polly Lyman	G W Benge	
998 Lyman Henry	265.70	Polly Lyman	G W Benge	
999 Lewis Amanda M.				
1000 Effie	531.40	A.M. Lewis	G W Benge	
1001 Lewis Elimire J.	265.70	A.M. Lewis	G W Benge	
1002 Lovett James Jr	265.70	J.J. Patrick	Henry Eiffert	order Oct 15 94 orphan
1003 Lovett James Sr	265.70	See Protest	Henry Eiffert	Patrick Ck
1004 Susan	265.70	Annie Martin	L B Bell	
1005 William	265.70	J J Patrick	Henry Eiffert	Ck

197

Starr Roll 1894

We, the undersigned citizens of the Cherokee Nation, by right of Cherokee blood, do hereby acknowledge to have received of E. E. Starr, National Treasurer of the Cherokee Nation, the sums set opposite our names respectively, in full of our shares in the per capita distribution authorized by an Act of the National Council, dated _____ MAY 3 1894 _____ 1894.

	Names of Head, and Members of Families	Amount	To Whom Paid	Witness to Payment	Remarks
1006	Elimire	265.70	J J Patrick	Henry Eiffert	Ck
1007	Rose	265.70	J J Patrick	Henry Eiffert	Ck
1008	Lyman Peggy				
1009	Nora	531.40	Peggy Lyman	Henry Eiffert	
1010	Lillard Zack				
1011	Ella				
1012	Susan				
1013	William				
1014	Charles	1328.50	Zack Lillard	Henry Eiffert	
1015	Lovett[sic] Richard	~~order~~	withdrawn		~~Madden~~
1016	Racheal				
1017	Eliza	797.10	Racheal Lovette	Henry Eiffert	
1018	Lunosford[sic] Racheal				
1019	Andrew				
1020	Eliza				
1021	Ellen				
1022	Lucy				
1023	Jesse				
1024	Mary				
1025	Calvin	2,125.60	Ed Lunsford	G W Benge	
1026	Linder Martha A	~~265.70~~	T.R. Madden	G W Benge	~~Madden~~
1027	" Mallie A	~~265.70~~	Thos Carlile	G W Benge	Madden
1028	Linder Hiram V.				
1029	" Charles C	531.40	T.R. Madden	G W Benge	by order
1030	Linder Finis	order			Carlisle
1031	" Viola DEAD.	531.40	Thomas Carlile	G W Benge	on order
1032	Lindsey Nettie				
1033	" Josephine				
1034	" Jesse				
1035	" John				
1036	" Thomas	1328.50	Joseph Lindsey	G W Benge	

Starr Roll 1894

We, the undersigned citizens of the Cherokee Nation, by right of Cherokee blood, do hereby acknowledge to have received of E. E. Starr, National Treasurer of the Cherokee Nation, the sums set opposite our names respectively, in full of our shares in the per capita distribution authorized by an Act of the National Council, dated ____MAY 3 1894____ 1894.

	Names of Head, and Members of Families	Amount	To Whom Paid	Witness to Payment	Remarks
1037	Lifter DEAD.				no given name
1038	" Betsy DEAD.	531.40	Lifter	Henry Eiffert	
1039	Lizzard Thomas				
1040	Susan				
1041	Johnston Sallie	797.10	Thomas Lizzard	L B Bell	orphan Thomas Lizzard guardian
1042	Low cut Fish				
1043	" Peggy				
1044	" Alice				
1045	" George				
1046	" Ned				
1047	" Sallie	1594.20	T.E. Bonham	G W Benge	T E Bonham By order
1048	Low cut James	265.70	TE Bonham	Henry Eiffert	T E Bonham Ck
1049	Lizzard Cat	265.70	Thos Lizzard adm	L B Bell	In jail in Detroit
1050	Jennie	265.70	Jennie Lizzard	Henry Eiffert	
1051	Lawly Noose				
1052	Martha				
1053	Gunseen				
1054	Penoskie Cat				Orphan
1055	" Serdie				"
1056	Sem-i-ha-la				"
1057	Leach	1859.90	Mose Lawly	Henry Eiffert	"
1058	Lawly Marheach	265.70	Mose Lawly	Henry Eiffert	
1059	Leigh Racheal				
1060	Mamie	531.40	Racheal Leigh	Henry Eiffert	
1061	Lee Calvin	order			W S Drake
1062	Martha				
1063	Hannah	797.10	N.S. Drake	G W Benge	by order
1064	Lacey Calvin	order			
1065	Cornelius	531.40	Wm Thompson	G W Benge	by order
1066	Lee Crossland	265.70	Crossland Lee	L B Bell	

Starr Roll 1894

We, the undersigned citizens of the Cherokee Nation, by right of Cherokee blood, do hereby acknowledge to have received of E. E. Starr, National Treasurer of the Cherokee Nation, the sums set opposite our names respectively, in full of our shares in the per capita distribution authorized by an Act of the National Council, dated ____MAY 3 1894____ 1894.

Names of Head, and Members of Families	Amount	To Whom Paid	Witness to Payment	Remarks
1067 Lowcat Maggie	order			T E Bonham
1068 Wilson George				
1069 Lizzard Lizzie	797.10	T.E. Bonham	G W Benge	by order
1070 Lawley Taky	265.70	W.M. Gulager	Robt B Ross. Aug 29/96	
1071 Leaf John				
1072 Sushoy	8304			
1073 James				
1074 Wah-lee-yer	1062.80	John Leaf	Henry Eiffert	
1075 Locust Ice	265.70	J R Mayfield	L B Bell	
1076 Lyons Annie E				Henry C Meigs
1077 Willie	531.40	H.C. Meigs	G W Benge	guardian
1078 King Sophie	265.70	Sophie King	Henry Eiffert	
1079 Leaf John	order			Carlile
1080 Nellie				
1081 Mary				
1082 Adam				orphan
1083 Downing Richard	1328.50	John Leaf	G W Benge	
1084 Morgan Olney	order			Wm Martin
1085 Samuel				
1086 Barnes C.				
1087 Vicary Lillie				
1088 " Nettie M.	1328.50	Wm N Martin	G W Benge	by order
1089 Meigs Henry C.				
1090 Josephine				
1091 Robert H				
1092 James McD				
1093 Maud				
1094 Josephine	1594.20	HC Meigs	L B Bell	
1095 Meigs Annie	265.70	Annie Meigs	L B Bell	

Starr Roll 1894

We, the undersigned citizens of the Cherokee Nation, by right of Cherokee blood, do hereby acknowledge to have received of E. E. Starr, National Treasurer of the Cherokee Nation, the sums set opposite our names respectively, in full of our shares in the per capita distribution authorized by an Act of the National Council, dated ___MAY 3 1894___ 1894.

	Names of Head, and Members of Families	Amount	To Whom Paid	Witness to Payment	Remarks
1096	Martin Dollie E				
1097	Hercules				
1098	Mary				
1099	Matilda				
1100	Edgar				
1101	Calvin	1594.20	D.E. Martin	G W Benge	
1102	Mackey Florence	265.70 *order*	Florence Mackey	L B Bell	*Nash*
1103	Martin Eliza J.				
1104	Annie	531.40	E.J. Martin	G W Benge	
1105	Matheson Maud				
1106	Ruby R				
1107	Floyd	797.10	Henry Eiffert	G W Benge	
1108	Martin Warren M				
1109	Mary J				
1110	Roy D.	797.10	M J Martin	G W Benge	
1111	Martin Lewis A.				
1112	Gertrude	On Choctaw Card No 4764 *2997*			
1113	Edward	" " " " " D2953 *2997*			
1114	Oscar				
1115	Tandy	1328.50 On Choctaw Card No 4764	L A Martin	G W Benge D2953 *2997*	
1116	Martin Parmelia	265.70	Parmelia Martin	G W Benge	
1117	McCracken Cooper				
1118	" Nancy				
1119	" Walter S				
1120	French Bernice				
1121	" Maggie				
1122	" Cricket	1594.20	Cooper McCracken	G W Benge	
1123	Maxwell Armstead				
1124	Nancy				
1125	Lenard				
1126	Joseph	265.70	A. Foyil	G W Benge	*by order A. Foyil*
1127	Sarah E.				

Starr Roll 1894

We, the undersigned citizens of the Cherokee Nation, by right of Cherokee blood, do hereby acknowledge to have received of E. E. Starr, National Treasurer of the Cherokee Nation, the sums set opposite our names respectively, in full of our shares in the per capita distribution authorized by an Act of the National Council, dated _____ MAY 3 1894 _____ 1894.

	Names of Head, and Members of Families	Amount	To Whom Paid	Witness to Payment	Remarks
1128	Charles				
1129	Cristopher[sic] C.	1594.20	Nancy Maxwell	G W Benge	
1130	McDaniel Geo W.	order			Madden
1131	Mary				
1132	Georgia	paid			
1133	McDaniel Mattie				
1134	James				
1135	Rosa				
1136	Choate Ellen	1859.90	T R Madden	G W Benge	by order
1137	McLemon Joe	265.70	Walsh & Shutt	G W Benge	by order
1138	Martin Andrew J.	265.70	Andrew J Martin	Henry Eiffert	
1139	Morris Maggie	265.70	T H Morris	G W Benge	
1140	McLain Joseph				
1141	William DEAD.				
1142	Floyd	797.10	Joseph McLain	G W Benge	
1143	McLain[sic] Henry	265.70	Henry McClain	G W Benge	
1144	McLain Jesse				
1145	Maggie				
1146	Susan				
1147	Frank				
1148	Nannie				
1149	Samuel				
1150	Calvin				
1151	Eliza	2125.60	Jesse McLain	G W Benge	
1152	McLain John				
1153	Edwin				
1154	Nannie				
1155	Mary			John McLain	GWB
1156	McLain Jesse				
1157	James	1594.20	John McLain	G W Benge	

Starr Roll 1894

We, the undersigned citizens of the Cherokee Nation, by right of Cherokee blood, do hereby acknowledge to have received of E. E. Starr, National Treasurer of the Cherokee Nation, the sums set opposite our names respectively, in full of our shares in the per capita distribution authorized by an Act of the National Council, dated ___MAY 3 1894___ 1894.

	Names of Head, and Members of Families	Amount	To Whom Paid	Witness to Payment	Remarks
1158	Madden Emily				
1159	Jennetta				
1160	Lilly bale				
1161	Victor E.				
1162	Leo B.	1328.50	Emily Madden	Henry Eiffert	
1163	Madden Annie L				
1164	Georgie				
1165	Annie				
1166	Clarence W.				
1167	Jack C.	1328.50	Annie L Madden	Henry Eiffert	
1168	Manning Johnston[sic]				
1169	Nancy	531.40	Johnson Manning	G W Benge	by order
1170	McLain John				
1171	Elnora				
1172	Cyntha				
1173	Henry	1062.80	Thomas Carlisle	G W Benge	
1174	Macky[sic] John D.	265.70	J.D. Mackey	G W Benge	
1175	McCoy Ellen	265.70	Ellen McCoy	G W Benge	
1176	Ned E	265.70	B.O. Reed	G W Benge	on order
1177	James L	265.70	Wash Mayes	L B Bell	paid Wash Mayes is warden of Nat^l prison
1178	Fannie J DEAD.	265.70	Walsh & Shutt	G W Benge	by order
1179	Fannie L	265.70	Ellen McCoy	G W Benge	
1180	McCoy Jefferson	265.70	N.S. Drake	G W Benge	N.S. Drake by order
1181	McCoy Mayse	order			Drake
1182	Grover C.	531.40	NS Drake	Henry Eiffert	ck – on order
1183	Mitchell Luella				
1184	Johanna				
1185	Lelia				
1186	Maggie				
1187	James H	1328.50	Luella Mitchell	Henry Eiffert	
1188	Morris John	265.70	John Morris	L B Bell	

203

Starr Roll 1894

We, the undersigned citizens of the Cherokee Nation, by right of Cherokee blood, do hereby acknowledge to have received of E. E. Starr, National Treasurer of the Cherokee Nation, the sums set opposite our names respectively, in full of our shares in the per capita distribution authorized by an Act of the National Council, dated ___ MAY 3 1894 ___ 1894.

	Names of Head, and Members of Families	Amount	To Whom Paid	Witness to Payment	Remarks
	~~Morris Joseph~~				*Enrolled at Orphan Asylum*
1189	McCoy Lizzie	*order*			*B Housebug*
1190	Alex				
1191	Mark				
1192	Betsy				
1193	Oo-te-sut-tah				
1194	Ross Nannie				
1195	Shell Jennie	1859.90	Blue Housebug	G W Benge	*by order*
1196	McNunny Lucy				
1197	" Robert				
1198	McClannahan Thomas	797.10	Lucy McNunny	G W Benge	
1199	McLain Austin[sic]				
1200	Lou				
1201	Ellen			Ostin McLain	*G W Benge*
1202	McLain Jesse				
1203	Flossie				
1204	John A.	1594.22	Ostin McLain	G W Benge	
1205	Mayfield John R				
1206	" Ross				
1207	" Gratchen[sic]				
1208	" Blanch	1062.80	J R Mayfield	L B Bell	
1209	Maxwell Charles L	265.70	C L Maxwell	G W Benge	
1210	Maxwell Marcus	265.70	Marcus Maxwell	G W Benge	
1211	Maxwell Benjaman				
1212	" Alfred L.				
1213	" Blanche	797.10	Benj. Maxwell	L B Bell	
1214	McCoy Alex				
1215	Alex Jr.				
1216	Ned				
1217	Girty Jess				
1218	McCoy Sallie				
1219	" Ester				

204

Starr Roll 1894

We, the undersigned citizens of the Cherokee Nation, by right of Cherokee blood, do hereby acknowledge to have received of E. E. Starr, National Treasurer of the Cherokee Nation, the sums set opposite our names respectively, in full of our shares in the per capita distribution authorized by an Act of the National Council, dated ____MAY 3 1894____ 1894.

	Names of Head, and Members of Families	Amount	To Whom Paid	Witness to Payment	Remarks
1220	" Thomas	1859.90	Alex McCoy	Henry Eiffert	
1221	Moore Mary E				
1222	" Charles W. Jr				
1223	Scruggs Henry		D2679		
1224	James				
1225	John G.	1328.50	H.D. Lonnon	G W Benge	
1226	McLemore Eliza				
1227	Jackson Annie				
1228	" Lizzie	797.10	Richard Vann	G. W. Benge	on order
1229	Mink Runabout				
1230	" Jinsey				
1231	" William				
1232	" Eliza	1062.80	Mink Runabout	Henry Eiffert	
1233	More[sic] Henry W	265.70	Saml S Moore	Henry Eiffert	Guardian Dr Sam'l S. Moore –
1234	Mathis Lydia	265.70	Lydia Mathis	G W Benge	
1235	Myers Emma				
1236	" Isaac				
1237	" Mary A				
1238	" George E				
1239	Lee Elizabeth	1328.50	James Myers	Henry Eiffert	
1240	McPherson Robert	order			W.S. Nash
1241	" Mollie				
1242	" Jennie				
1243	" Joanna				
1244	" Willis				
1245	" Della	1594.20	W.S. Nash	G W Benge	by order
1246	Martin William H				
1247	" Sarah J.				
1248	" Frank				
1249	" Eugene			W H Martin	G W Benge
1250	Martin William H Jr.				
1251	Susan L.				

Starr Roll 1894

We, the undersigned citizens of the Cherokee Nation, by right of Cherokee blood, do hereby acknowledge to have received of E. E. Starr, National Treasurer of the Cherokee Nation, the sums set opposite our names respectively, in full of our shares in the per capita distribution authorized by an Act of the National Council, dated ___MAY 3 1894___ 1894.

	Names of Head, and Members of Families	Amount	To Whom Paid	Witness to Payment	Remarks
1252	Thereasa[sic] J.				
1253	Cordilia[sic]				
1254	Hubbard Joanna				
1255	" Mary	2657.00	Wm Martin	G W Benge	
1256	Mitchell Frank R	order D 49 265.70	Christian Gulegar	G W Benge	C Guleger by order
1257	McBride Mary J	265.70	Mary J McBride	L B Bell	
1258	Miller Leslie	265.70	W.S. Nash	G W Benge	on Sondash
1259	Miller Susan				
1260	James				
1261	Moses				
1262	John				
	Raincrow Thos.				On Orphan Roll
1263	Raincrow Johnston	1328.50	Susan Miller	Henry Eiffert	
1264	Miller Cabin	265.70	Cabin Miller	L B Bell	
1265	McCoy Ida	order 265.70	Branan & Hayes	G W Benge	B By Hayes
1266	Murphy Lafayette	order 265.70	J.R. Skaggs	G W Benge	J R Skaggs
1267	Mills Annie	order 265.70	J.F. Wells	G W Benge	Wells by order
1268	Maples Racheal DEAD.	order			Nash
1269	Bettie H.	531.40	W.S. Nash	G W Benge	by order
1270	Muskrat Peggie				
1271	" Lucy				
1272	" Katie	797.10	Peggie Muskrat D:2951	Henry Eiffert	
1273	McDonald Emma	265.70	C.C. Lipe	G W Benge	
1274	Moore Loucinda[sic]	265.70	Lucinda Moore	G W Benge	
1275	Mitchell Joe	265.70	Joe Mitchell	Henry Eiffert	

Starr Roll 1894

We, the undersigned citizens of the Cherokee Nation, by right of Cherokee blood, do hereby acknowledge to have received of E. E. Starr, National Treasurer of the Cherokee Nation, the sums set opposite our names respectively, in full of our shares in the per capita distribution authorized by an Act of the National Council, dated ____MAY 3 1894____ 1894.

	Names of Head, and Members of Families	Amount	To Whom Paid	Witness to Payment	Remarks
1276	Nash Tookah				
1277	Nellie				
1278	Bertha				
1279	Carroll	1062.80	Tookah Nash	G W Benge	
1280	Nash Ida V.	265.70	W T Thompson	G W Benge	
1281	Nash Fanny E.				
1282	Frank A				
1283	Florian H				
1284	Lucy N				
1285	Corrine				
1286	Hilda				
1287	Edwin O.	1859.90	W. T. Thompson	G W Benge	
1288	Nash Harry F.	265.70	H. F. Nash	G W Benge	
1289	Nunally[sic] Mary A.				
1290	Margaret T.				
1291	Minnie D				
1292	John H				
1293	Walter S.				
1294	Maud A				
1295	Kate	1859.90	Mary A Nunnally	Henry Eiffert	
1296	Nunnally Jennie B	265.70	Jennie Nunnally	Henry Eiffert	
1297	Newton Elizabeth				
1298	Hoyd[sic] E.	531.40	Elizabeth Newton	G W Benge	
1299	Noisey Thomas	265.70	Thomas Carlile	G W Benge	by order Carlisle
1300	Noisey Mack	265.70 order	Branan & Hayes	G W Benge	B by blatos
1301	Noisey Nellie	265.70 ck	Thomas Carlisle[sic]	Henry Eiffert	ck order
1302	Buzzard Joe	265.70	Thomas Carlile	G W Benge	by order Carlisle
1303	Noisy Car-der-you-ill	order			B & Hayes
1304	John	531.40	Branan & Hayes	G W Benge	by order

207

Starr Roll 1894

We, the undersigned citizens of the Cherokee Nation, by right of Cherokee blood, do hereby acknowledge to have received of E. E. Starr, National Treasurer of the Cherokee Nation, the sums set opposite our names respectively, in full of our shares in the per capita distribution authorized by an Act of the National Council, dated _____ MAY 3 1894 _____ 1894.

	Names of Head, and Members of Families	Amount	To Whom Paid	Witness to Payment	Remarks
1305	Osage Katie	order			*Madden*
1306	West Cornelius	531.40	T.R. Madden	G W Benge	*by order*
1307	Oer Samuel				
1308	Eliza				
1309	Polly				
1310	John				
1311	Belle				
1312	Nannie				
1313	Sophie	1859.90	Samuel Oer	G W Benge	
1314	Oer Wesley	265.70	Wesley Oer	G W Benge	
1315	Oer Annie				
1316	Elizabeth	531.40	Branan & Hayes	G W Benge	*on order*
1317	Oer Lucy	265.70	Branan & Hayes	G W Benge	*on order*
1318	Price Fannie				
1319	William M.	531.40	Fannie Price	L B Bell	
1320	Poindexter Maggie				
1321	William				
1322	Benjamin				
1323	Paralee	1062.80	J.R. Poindexter	G W Benge	
1324	Phipps Amanda	*order*			*Nash*
1325	Bettie				
1326	John				
1327	Carrie				
1328	Joe				
1329	Martha	1594.20	W.S. Nash	G W Benge	*by order*
1330	Perry Ellen				
1331	John F				
1332	Lizzie J.				
1333	Della				
1334	Effie				
1335	Mary	1594.20	Ellen Perry	G W Benge	

Starr Roll 1894

We, the undersigned citizens of the Cherokee Nation, by right of Cherokee blood, do hereby acknowledge to have received of E. E. Starr, National Treasurer of the Cherokee Nation, the sums set opposite our names respectively, in full of our shares in the per capita distribution authorized by an Act of the National Council, dated ___MAY 3 1894___ 1894.

	Names of Head, and Members of Families	Amount	To Whom Paid	Witness to Payment	Remarks
1336	Petit William Jr.	265.70	W.S. Nash	G W Benge	by order Nash
1337	Poorbear Fanny	order			J J Kelly
1338	Clark Willie	531.40	J.J. Kelly	G W Benge	by order
1339	Pettit Frank				
1340	Polly				
1341	Andrew	797.10	Frank Pettit	Henry Eiffert	
1342	Petit Watie	265.70	E.S. Ellis	J.C. Starr	check by Ellix order
1343	Petit[sic] Robert				
1344	Tennie				
1345	Cyntha				
1346	Belle	1062.80	Robert Petitt	G W Benge	
1347	Petit John R.	order			J Thompson
1348	Rufus				
1349	Richard	797.10	J Thompson	G W Benge	by order
1350	Parnell Celia				
1351	Lula				
1352	Samuel				
1353	Benjamin				
1354	Henrietta	1324.50	J R Garrett	G W Benge	by order Garrett
1355	Patrick Eliza	265.70	Eliza Patrick	Henry Eiffert	
1356	Parnell Mary	order			Madden
1357	Grover				
"	Annie	797.10	T.R. Madden	G W Benge	by order
1358	Petit[sic] Amelia	265.70	Amelia Pettitt	Henry Eiffert	
1359	Petit George	order			Madden
1360	Dolly				
1361	George Jr				
1362	Richard				
1363	Emma	1328.50	T.R. Madden	G W Benge	by order

Starr Roll 1894

We, the undersigned citizens of the Cherokee Nation, by right of Cherokee blood, do hereby acknowledge to have received of E. E. Starr, National Treasurer of the Cherokee Nation, the sums set opposite our names respectively, in full of our shares in the per capita distribution authorized by an Act of the National Council, dated ___MAY 3 1894___ 1894.

	Names of Head, and Members of Families	Amount	To Whom Paid	Witness to Payment	Remarks
1364	Petit Curry				*Patrick*
1365	Timothy				
1366	Andy	*order*			
1367	Aggie				
1368	Benjamin	1328.50	J J Patrick	Henry Eiffert	*ck Pd*
1369	Patrick Mike				*Protested that*
1370	Jennie				*Patrick do*
1371	John	797.10	Mike Patrick		*not withdraw for Maggline*
1372	Maggline	265.70	Josie Patrick	G W Benge	*Patrick By Josie Patrick*
1373	Patrick Joseph				
1374	Jennie				
1375	Florence				
1376	William				
1377	Sophie	1328.50	Joseph Patrick	Henry Eiffert	
1378	Pigeon George	*order*			*Madden*
1379	Sallie				*by order*
1380	Justice George	797.10	T.R. Madden	G W Benge	
1381	Phillips James				
1382	Lucy				
1383	Nellie				
1384	Davis				
1385	Buck John	1328.50	James Phillips	G W Benge	
1386	Patrick John J.				
1387	Alimira	531.40	Alimira Patrick	G W Benge	
1388	Petit[sic] Joseph B.				
1389	Frank	531.40	J.B. Pettitt	G W Benge	
1390	Pierce Nannie				
1391	Cornelius				
1392	Susan				
1393	Effie				
1394	Charles Jr				
1395	Claud	1594.20	Chas Price	G W Benge	

210

Starr Roll 1894

We, the undersigned citizens of the Cherokee Nation, by right of Cherokee blood, do hereby acknowledge to have received of E. E. Starr, National Treasurer of the Cherokee Nation, the sums set opposite our names respectively, in full of our shares in the per capita distribution authorized by an Act of the National Council, dated ___MAY 3 1894___ 1894.

Names of Head, and Members of Families	Amount	To Whom Paid	Witness to Payment	Remarks
1396 Petit Lucy	265.70 *order*	Walsh & Shutt	G W Benge	*W&S by order*
1397 Potts Wilson	265.70	Wilson Potts	G W Benge	
1398 Petit[sic] George W				
1399 Cherokee				
1400 Charles				
1401 Elsie				
1402 Thomas				
1403 Frank				
1404 Susan				
1405 Adda	2125.60	G.W. Pettitt	G W Benge	
1406 Petit Alex				
1407 Lizzie				
1408 Bearpaw Ellen				
1409 Tehee Henry				
1410 Nave Willie	1328.50	Alex Pettit	G W Benge	*orphan*
1411 Patrick George W				
1412 John				
1413 Ada				
1414 Alxander[sic]				
1415 Racheal				
1416 Eliza	1594.20	Geo W Patrick	Henry Eiffert	
1417 Petit[sic] Edward				
1418 Sarah				
1419 Eliza				
1420 Treat Frank	1062.80	Edward Pettitt	Henry Eiffert	
1421 Phillips Stephen	*order*			*Carlisle*
1422 Pollie	531.40	Thomas Carlile	G W Benge	*by order*
1423 Petit[sic] Thomas				
1424 Nancy				
1425 Eliza	797.10	Nancy Pettitt	Henry Eiffert	
1426 Penoskey Oo-na-tlo-ya-s-da	265.70 *order*	Brannan & Hayes	G W Benge	*B & Hayes by order*

211

Starr Roll 1894

We, the undersigned citizens of the Cherokee Nation, by right of Cherokee blood, do hereby acknowledge to have received of E. E. Starr, National Treasurer of the Cherokee Nation, the sums set opposite our names respectively, in full of our shares in the per capita distribution authorized by an Act of the National Council, dated _____ MAY 3 1894 _____ 1894.

	Names of Head, and Members of Families	Amount	To Whom Paid	Witness to Payment	Remarks
1427	Price Peggie	order			B&H
1428	Webber Ah-yos-da	531.40	Branan & Hayes	G W Benge	by order
1429	Price Mary				
1430	Hannah				
1431	Reece				
1432	Martha J				
1433	Mack E				
1434	Uudeen[sic]	paid			
1435	Price George W.				
1436	Mary L				
1437	Charles E.	2391.30	Mary Price	Henry Eiffert	
1438	Panther Rat				
1439	Tah-tah-gi				
1440	John				
1441	Lizzie				
1442	Cay-haw-ka				
1443	Thomas	1594.20	Rat Panther	Henry Eiffert	
1444	Porter Dick				
1445	Quatie				
1446	James	1088			
1447	Katie				
1448	Nancy				
1449	William				
1450	Kuh-ska-lees-kie				
1451	Porter Taky[sic]				
1452	Oo-tah-l-kie Susan	2391.30	Dick Porter	Henry Eiffert	
1453	Parris R.A.J.	265.70	G.W. Mitchell	J.C. Starr	check 68572 by order GW Mitchell AUG 22 189
1454	Proctor John				
1455	Sallie	531.40	Thomas Carlile	G W Benge	
1456	Petit William	order			R B Choat
1457	Annie				
1458	John Sr				
1459	John Jr	1062.80	R.B. Choat[sic]	G W Benge	on order

212

Starr Roll 1894

We, the undersigned citizens of the Cherokee Nation, by right of Cherokee blood, do hereby acknowledge to have received of E. E. Starr, National Treasurer of the Cherokee Nation, the sums set opposite our names respectively, in full of our shares in the per capita distribution authorized by an Act of the National Council, dated ____MAY 3 1894____ 1894.

Names of Head, and Members of Families	Amount	To Whom Paid	Witness to Payment	Remarks
1460 Prince Taylor	order			B&Hayes
1461 Jennie				
1462 Bearpaw Ellen				
1463 " Annie	1062.80	Branan & Hayes	G W Benge	by order
1464 Pernoskie John				
1465 Ella				
1466 Gee-os-sa				
1467 Nannie	1062.80	John Pernoskie	Henry Eiffert	
1468 Pruitt Mary				
1469 Sanders Samuel				
1470 Sadie				
1471 Gustavus				
1472 Richard				
Edward	1594.20	G W Fields	G W Benge	
1473 Pernoskie Tee-ki-us kie				
1474 Noley				
1475 Joseph				
1476 Annie	1062.80	Tee-ki-us-kee Pernoskie	Henry Eiffert	
1477 Parris Jack	order			W&S
1478 Hester A.	531.40	Walsh & Shutt	G W Benge	by order
1479 Petit[sic] Joseph	265.70	Joseph Pettitt	G W Benge	
1480 Pernoskey Susan				
1481 Ser des ky Sasie	531.40	J. Jack	L B Bell	
1482 Petit Mack	265.70	Edward Pallet	Henry Eiffert	
1483 Pritchett Jimmie				
1484 Mixwater Mariah				
1485 " Nancy	797.10	Susan Mixwater	G W Benge	
1486 Proctor Daniel	265.70	Daniel Proctor	Henry Eiffert	
1487 Phipps Mattie	265.70	Mattie Phipps	G W Benge	
1488 Phillips Joseph	265.70 order	Thomas Carlile	G W Benge	Carlile by order

213

Starr Roll 1894

We, the undersigned citizens of the Cherokee Nation, by right of Cherokee blood, do hereby acknowledge to have received of E. E. Starr, National Treasurer of the Cherokee Nation, the sums set opposite our names respectively, in full of our shares in the per capita distribution authorized by an Act of the National Council, dated ___MAY 3 1894___ 1894.

Names of Head, and Members of Families	Amount	To Whom Paid	Witness to Payment	Remarks
1489 Phillips Fannie	order			Madden
1490 Lillie C	531.40	T.R. Madden	G W Benge	by order
1491 Critenden[sic] Willie	265.70	J.J. Patrick	Henry Eiffert	Nov 20 94
1492 Parsons[sic] Johnston[sic]	265.70	Johnson Parson	Henry Eiffert	Nov 19/94
1493 Ross William D	265.70	W.D. Ross	G W Benge	
1494 Ross Mary J.				
1495 Howard Mary	531.40	Hubbard Ross	L B Bell	
1496 Ross E. P.	265.70 order	W.S. Nash	G W Benge	by order Nash
1497 Ross Phillips[sic]	265.70	Hubbard Phillip Ross	L B Bell	
1498 Ross Hubbard	265.70	Hubbard Ross	L B Bell	
1499 Ross Emma L.	265.70	Hubbard Ross	L B Bell	
1500 Rogers Cherokee	265.70	H.M. Rogers	G W Benge	on order
1501 Rogers Andrew L	265.70	A.L. Rogers	G W Benge	
1502 Rogers Hugh M	265.70	H.M. Rogers	G W Benge	
1503 Rogers Paul	265.70	Paul Rogers	G W Benge	
1504 Rogers Otto	265.70	H.M. Rogers	G W Benge	on order
1505 Rogers Clifford	265.70	H M Rogers	G W Benge	on order
1506 Ross John H	265.70	J.H. Ross	G W Benge	
1507 " Dannie Jane	265.70	Dannie Ross	G W Benge	Reported from orphan asylum
1508 Ross Flora	265.70	Flora Ross	G W Benge	
1509 Runyon Cora	265.70 order	Walsh & Shutt	G W Benge	by order W&S

Starr Roll 1894

We, the undersigned citizens of the Cherokee Nation, by right of Cherokee blood, do hereby acknowledge to have received of E. E. Starr, National Treasurer of the Cherokee Nation, the sums set opposite our names respectively, in full of our shares in the per capita distribution authorized by an Act of the National Council, dated _____ MAY 3 1894 _____ 1894.

	Names of Head, and Members of Families	Amount	To Whom Paid	Witness to Payment	Remarks
1510	Reese Rodman A				
1511	Marth[sic] J				
1512	Henry D				
1513	James				
1514	Ineze[sic]				
1515	Eloise B.				
1516	Charles				
1517	Rorie[sic]	2125.60	M.J. Reese	G W Benge	
1518	Riley Nancy				
1519	Linder Richard	531.40	Jack Gott	G W Benge	
1520	Rogers Connell				
1521	Kate				
1522	Gertrude W.				
1523	Ella C				
1524	Marion S.	1328.50	Connell Rogers	L B Bell	
1525	Ross Belle	265.70 ~~order~~	W.S. Nash	G W Benge	by order *Nash*
1526	Rogers George				
1527	Olie				
1528	Walter				
1529	Beatrice				
1530	Mamie				
1531	George Jr.				
1532	Fredie[sic]	1859.90	George Rogers	G W Benge	
1533	Rider Carrie	265.70	Alice Wofford	G W Benge	*Child of Clare Rider*
1534	Runyon Elsie J	265.70	W.S. Nash	G W Benge	~~By order~~
1535	Robert				
1536	Thomas	531.40	Jack Walker	G W ~~Benge~~ *Walker* *Guardian*
1537	Eraline				
1538	Minnie				
1539	Sarah				
1540	Jesse				
1541	Nettie				
1542	Lawson	1594.20	W.S. Nash	G W Benge	*by order*

Starr Roll 1894

We, the undersigned citizens of the Cherokee Nation, by right of Cherokee blood, do hereby acknowledge to have received of E. E. Starr, National Treasurer of the Cherokee Nation, the sums set opposite our names respectively, in full of our shares in the per capita distribution authorized by an Act of the National Council, dated ___MAY 3 1894___ 1894.

	Names of Head, and Members of Families	Amount	To Whom Paid	Witness to Payment	Remarks
1543	Roach Betsy	265.70	W.S. Nash	G W Benge	by order
1544	Ross William P	265.70	C.C. Lipe	G W Benge	on order
1545	Maud W.	265.70	WN Martin	Henry Eiffert	W.N. Martin
1546	Sadie B.	order			R.L. Baugh
1547	Daniel H	531.40	R.L. Baugh	G W Benge	by order
1548	Ross Edward G.	265.70	Ed G Ross	Henry Eiffert	WN Martin
1549	Rogers Theresa				
1550	Eliza				
1551	Georgia A				
1552	Serisa				
1553	Candy Almira				
1554	Susan				
1555	Fannie	1859.90	Theresia[sic] Rogers		
1556	Wetty Lydia F				Madden
1557	Roscoe H	531.40	T R Madden	Henry Eiffert	Cek order
1558	Ross William H	order			WS Nash
1559	Nannie	531.40	W.S. Nash	G W Benge	by order
1560	Ratcliffe[sic] Daniel				
1561	Annie				
1562	Richard				
1563	Houston				
1564	Racheal				
1565	Eliza				
1566	Ella	1859.90	Daniel Ratcliff	Henry Eiffert	
1567	Rogers Levi				
1568	Emma				
1569	James	797.10	Levi Rogers	G W Benge	
1570	Ross Joshua	265.70	T.R. Madden	G W Benge	Madden by order
1571	Rogers George				
1572	Peggy				
1573	Katy				
1574	Nancy				

Certificate of this payment given Peggy Rogers Dec 12/95

Starr Roll 1894

We, the undersigned citizens of the Cherokee Nation, by right of Cherokee blood, do hereby acknowledge to have received of E. E. Starr, National Treasurer of the Cherokee Nation, the sums set opposite our names respectively, in full of our shares in the per capita distribution authorized by an Act of the National Council, dated ____MAY 3 1894____ 1894.

Names of Head, and Members of Families	Amount	To Whom Paid	Witness to Payment	Remarks
1575 Hungry Charles	1328.50	Geo Rogers	Henry Eiffert	
1576 Rogers John				
1577 Emma				
1578 Katy				
1579 Charles				
1580 Cyntha				
1581 Laura	1594.20	John Rogers	L B Bell	
1582 Ross George				
1583 " Cyntha				
1584 " Betsy				
1585 " Nannie				
1586 " Maggie				
1587 " Emma				
1588 " Susan				
1589 " Annie	2125.60	T.R. Madden	G W Benge	by order
1590 Rattling Gourd Tho's	order			Madden
1591 Nancy				
1592 Sallie				
1593 Charles				
1594 David				
1595 Jennie				
1596 John				
1597 Bearpaw Samuel				
1598 Walker Jack				
1599 Rabbit Jack				orphans
1600 " Susan	2922.70	T.R. Madden	G W Benge	by order
1601 Roberson Alsie				
1602 Melvina				
1603 Lydia	797.10	Alsie Roberson	Henry Eiffert	
1604 Rain crow Betsy	265.70	JJ Patrick	Henry Eiffert	Ck
1605 Raincrow Racheal	265.70	Racheal Raincrow	Henry Eiffert	Nov 26 94

Starr Roll 1894

We, the undersigned citizens of the Cherokee Nation, by right of Cherokee blood, do hereby acknowledge to have received of E. E. Starr, National Treasurer of the Cherokee Nation, the sums set opposite our names respectively, in full of our shares in the per capita distribution authorized by an Act of the National Council, dated ___MAY 3 1894___ 1894.

	Names of Head, and Members of Families	Amount	To Whom Paid	Witness to Payment	Remarks
1606	Raincrow Joe				
1607	Mary				
1608	Eyah-tsa-ka				
1609	Cornelius				
1610	Elsie				
1611	Katie				
1612	Racheal	185.90	T.R. Madden	G W Benge	by order
1613	Rogers William				
1614	Lydia				
1615	Lovely	797.10	W$^{\underline{m}}$ Rogers	G W Benge	
1616	Ratley Wallace				
1617	Sarah				
1618	Still William	7535			
1619	" David				
1620	Sampson				
1621	John	1594.20	Wallace Ratley	G W Benge	
1622	Ross Martin				
1623	Flora				
1624	John	797.10	Flora Ross	G W Benge	
1625	Rush Isabelle	order			J.R. Skaggs
1626	Riley Jack				
1627	Belle Henry	797.10	J.R. Skaggs	G W Benge	by order
1628	Raymond Jack	265.70	N.E. Foreman	G W Benge	J.R. Skaggs
1629	Reaves Osten[sic]	order			J F Wells
1630	Horn Lillie M.	531.40	JF Wells	G W Benge	by order
1631	Rosin John	265.70	Swimmer Rosin	Henry Eiffert	
1632	Rosin Swimmer	8311			
1633	Sallie				
1634	Annie	797.10	Swimmer Rosin	Henry Eiffert	

Starr Roll 1894

We, the undersigned citizens of the Cherokee Nation, by right of Cherokee blood, do hereby acknowledge to have received of E. E. Starr, National Treasurer of the Cherokee Nation, the sums set opposite our names respectively, in full of our shares in the per capita distribution authorized by an Act of the National Council, dated ____MAY 3 1894____ 1894.

Names of Head, and Members of Families	Amount	To Whom Paid	Witness to Payment	Remarks
1635 Rogers Annie E.	order			B & Hayes
1636 William P.				
1637 Charles H.	797.10	Branan & Hayes	G W Benge	by order
1638 Running bear Betsy	265.70	Alick McCoy	G W Benge	by order
1639 Reed Mollie E.				
1640 Myrtle				
1641 Walter				
1642 Jennie	1062.80	B.O. Reed	G W Benge	
1643 Rogers John	265.70	Wm Gibson	G W Benge	by order
1644 Rogers John L				
1645 Annie				
1646 Artemus	797.10	W.W. Ross Jr	G W Benge	on order
1647 Rabbit Gent DEAD.	265.70	TE Bonham	Henry Eiffert	ck order
1648 Ross George	265.70	Geo Ross	G W Benge	
1649 Rogers Jack T.				
1650 Mary A				
1651 Susan L.	797.10	Jack T Rogers	L B Bell	
1652 Scott Walter	265.70	Walter Scott	L B Bell	
1653 Scott Bell H				
1654 " Gibson R				
1655 " Delilah			(1641)	
1656 " Emma				
1657 " John Jr				
1658 " Raphel				
1659 " Allen H	1859.90	Bell Scott	Henry Eiffert	
1660 Scott Georgia	265.70	W.A. Scott	G W Benge	
1661 Sanders Geo O.				
1662 " Lizzie A	531.40	Lizzie Sanders	G W Benge	

219

Starr Roll 1894

We, the undersigned citizens of the Cherokee Nation, by right of Cherokee blood, do hereby acknowledge to have received of E. E. Starr, National Treasurer of the Cherokee Nation, the sums set opposite our names respectively, in full of our shares in the per capita distribution authorized by an Act of the National Council, dated ____MAY 3 1894____ 1894.

	Names of Head, and Members of Families	Amount	To Whom Paid	Witness to Payment	Remarks
1663	Snyder Alice	265.70	Alice Synder[sic]	G W Benge	
1664	Smith Edith H	265.70 ~~order~~	W.S. Nash	G W Benge	~~W S order~~
1665	Swift Frank T.				
1666	" Cristie[sic]	531.40	Frank T Swift	L B Bell	
1667	Schrimsher Jasper		~~D 1042~~ 10151		
1668	" Edward L.				
1669	" Susan				
1670	" Mattiebell	1062.80	J.N. Schrimsher	G W Benge	
1671	Smith Isaac	order			W S Nash
1672	" Sallie				
1673	" Linda	797.10	W.S. Nash	G W Benge	by order
1674	Starnes John				
1675	" Thomas				
1676	" Mary	797.10	John Starnes	G W Benge	
1677	Smith Saml. L.				
1678	" Walter S				
1679	" Richard W				
1680	" Mabelle				
1681	" Willie				
1682	" Elizabeth	1594.20	Frank Smith	G W Benge	
1683	Sisson Harry	265.70	Harry Sisson	L B Bell	
1684	Smith Mahala				
1685	" Theodore				
1686	" George W.				
1687	" Lucy A.				
1688	" Mary E.				
1689	" William				
1690	" James				
1691	" Elizabeth				
1692	" Catharine	2391.30	Mahala Smith	G W Benge	

Starr Roll 1894

We, the undersigned citizens of the Cherokee Nation, by right of Cherokee blood, do hereby acknowledge to have received of E. E. Starr, National Treasurer of the Cherokee Nation, the sums set opposite our names respectively, in full of our shares in the per capita distribution authorized by an Act of the National Council, dated ___MAY 3 1894___ 1894.

	Names of Head, and Members of Families	Amount	To Whom Paid	Witness to Payment	Remarks
1693	Smithman Mary				
1694	Madden Daisy				
1695	Cox Joseph	797.10	Mary Smithman	G W Benge	
1696	Silk Charles	order			Madden
1697	" Sophie				
1698	" Nellie				
1699	" Johnston				
1700	" Charles T.				
1701	" Susan				
1702	" Sallie				
1703	Bullfrod[sic] Diannah	2125.60	T.R. Madden	G W Benge	by order
1704	Sanders Dinah	order			Madden
1705	Raincrow Charles	531.40	T.R. Madden	G W Benge	by order
1706	Sanders Levi	265.70	Mary Smithman	G W Benge	
1707	Squirrel Sequitchie	order			Gulager
1708	" Young S	531.40	Christian Gulegar	G W Benge	by order
1709	" Che-wah-nah				
1710	" Charles				
1711	" Dorcas	797.10	T.R. Madden	J.C. Starr	check on order Madden 23 1894
1712	Sanders George	265.70	Walsh & Shutt	G W Benge	by order W&S
1713	Sanders Thomas	265.70	Christian Gulegar	Henry Eiffert	
1714	Scott Chow-gah-yu-ka	order			Madden
1715	" Wah-lah-ne-ta	531.40	T.R. Madden	G W Benge	by order
1716	Sanders William N.				
1717	Annie				
1718	Eliza	797.10	W N Sanders	L B Bell	
1719	Sanders David				
1720	" Caroline				
1721	" Arthur				
1722	Ballard Belle				
1723	" Willie	1328.50	T.R. Madden	G W Benge	by order

Starr Roll 1894

We, the undersigned citizens of the Cherokee Nation, by right of Cherokee blood, do hereby acknowledge to have received of E. E. Starr, National Treasurer of the Cherokee Nation, the sums set opposite our names respectively, in full of our shares in the per capita distribution authorized by an Act of the National Council, dated _____ MAY 3 1894 _____ 1894.

Names of Head, and Members of Families	Amount	To Whom Paid	Witness to Payment	Remarks
1724 Swimmer James	order			Madden -
1725 Lorinda				
1726 Lizzie	797.10	T.R. Madden	G W Benge	by order
1727 Sanders Joanna				
1728 Mary				
1729 Polly				
1730 Annie L.				
1731 Mattie M				
1732 Sequoyah				
1733 Pigeon				
1734 Joseph	2125.60	Joanna Sanders	G W Benge	
1735 Stephens Lucy	order			Madden
1736 Cochran Maggie				
1737 " William	797.10	T.R. Madden	G W Benge	by order
1738 Sanders Josua[sic]	order			Nash
1739 " Mary E.				
1740 " Jesse				
1741 " Pearl				
1742 Quinton Cornelius	1328.50 ₁₄²⁷ W.S. Nash	G W Benge		by order
1743 Sanders Frank W				
1744 " Ellen M.				
1745 " Dewit				
1746 " Jane Ann				
1747 " Fankey[sic] E.				
1748 Sanders E Jane E[sic]	1594.20	F.W. Sanders	G W Benge	
1749 Starr Jennie				
1750 " Charles	265.70	Charlie Starr	Henry Eiffert	
1751 " Henry				
1752 Patrick Laura				
1753 " Burtha[sic] B				
1754 " Grover C				
1755 " Annie M	1594.20	Jennie Starr	G W Benge	

Starr Roll 1894

We, the undersigned citizens of the Cherokee Nation, by right of Cherokee blood, do hereby acknowledge to have received of E. E. Starr, National Treasurer of the Cherokee Nation, the sums set opposite our names respectively, in full of our shares in the per capita distribution authorized by an Act of the National Council, dated _____MAY 3 1894_____ 1894.

	Names of Head, and Members of Families	Amount	To Whom Paid	Witness to Payment	Remarks
1756	Sanders Lewis				
1757	" Maud	531.40	Lewis Sanders	G W Benge	
1758	Smith John F				
1759	" Sarah				
1760	" Susan				
1761	" Loucinda				
1762	" Harry				
1763	" Dennis				
1764	" Levi				
1765	" Richard	2125.60	John F Smith	L B Bell	
1766	Sam Creek	order			Carter
1767	" Tobacco W		8592	order with drawn	
1768	Baldridge Charlott	797.10	Creek Sam	G W Benge	orphan Creek Sam Guardian
1769	Starr Jack				
1770	" Lizzie	531.40	Lizzie Starr	Henry Eiffert	
1771	Smith Dick	order			
1772	" Katie	531.40	T.R. Madden	G W Benge	by order
1773	Sifton Frank H	order	D 1992		W&S
1774	" Emma H	"	D 229		"
1775	" James K	"	D 1993		"
1776	" Adda S.	1062.80	Walsh & Shutt	G W Benge	by order
1777	Swimmer John				
1778	" Sallie				by
1779	" Martha	797.10	Thom Carlile	G W Benge	on order check
1780	Sthee[sic] Lydia	order			B&H
1781	Sit a-wa gee Oo-da-sut	531.40	Branan & Hayes	G W Benge	orphan by order
1782	Seabolt Peggie				
1783	Spaniard Jack	531.40	Peggie Seabolt	Henry Eiffert	
1784	Smith James				
1785	" Mary				
1786	" Charles				

Starr Roll 1894

We, the undersigned citizens of the Cherokee Nation, by right of Cherokee blood, do hereby acknowledge to have received of E. E. Starr, National Treasurer of the Cherokee Nation, the sums set opposite our names respectively, in full of our shares in the per capita distribution authorized by an Act of the National Council, dated _____ MAY 3 1894 _____ 1894.

	Names of Head, and Members of Families	Amount	To Whom Paid	Witness to Payment	Remarks
1787	" Martha				
1788	" Enory[sic]	1328.50	Branan & Hayes	G W Benge	by order
1789	Smith Lizzie	265.70	James Smith	G W Benge	on Letters of Adx
1790	Sheppard Jack				
1791	" Joe	531.40	Jack Sheppard	G W Benge	
1792	Screech owl Thompson	9211			
1793	" Jennie				
1794	" Dick	9211			
1795	" Mittie	9211			
1796	" George	1328.50	Branan & Hayes	G W Benge	by order
1797	Smith Red Bird				
1798	" Lucy wife				
1799	" John				
1800	" Sam				
1801	" Susan				
1802	" Richard				
1803	" Thomas				
1804	" George				
1805	" Mose				
1806	" Kiah				
1807	" Butler	2922.70	Red Bird Smith	G.W. Benge	
1808	Still Noah	order			B&H
1809	" Levi				
1810	" Martha				
1811	" Ida				
1812	" Elias				
1813	" Polly	1594.20 9291	Branan & Hayes	G W Benge	on order
1814	Scott Susie 80 yry	8414			
1815	" Loualla[sic]	531.40	Susie Scott	Henry Eiffert	
1816	Short Mary				
1817	" Guess				
1818	" Joe				
1819	" Hugh	1062.80	Mary Short	G W Benge	

224

Starr Roll 1894

We, the undersigned citizens of the Cherokee Nation, by right of Cherokee blood, do hereby acknowledge to have received of E. E. Starr, National Treasurer of the Cherokee Nation, the sums set opposite our names respectively, in full of our shares in the per capita distribution authorized by an Act of the National Council, dated ___MAY 3 1894___ 1894.

	Names of Head, and Members of Families	Amount	To Whom Paid	Witness to Payment	Remarks
1820	Sharp John W.				
1821	" Susan				
1822	" Cornelia				
1823	" Edward				
1824	" Richard				
1825	" Rebeca				
1826	" John Jr.				
1827	" Albert				
1828	" Caroline				
1829	" Grover C.	2657.00	John W Sharp	L B Bell	
1830	Sanders Henry H.	265.70	Henry H. Sanders	Henry Eiffert	
1831	Spaniard William	order			Bonham
1832	" Amanda				
1833	" Jennie	order			
1834	" Lizzie				
1835	" Peggie				
1836	" Teacher	1594.20	T.E. Bonham	G W Benge	by order
1837	Spainard[sic] Ezekiel				
1838	Emma	531.40	Ezekiel Spaniard	Henry Eiffert	
1839	Smith John				
1840	Nellie	order			W.&S.
1841	Charles	797.10	Walsh and Shutt	G W Benge	by order
1842	Swimmer William				
1843	" Annie				
1844	" Lizzie				
1845	Rabbit Charles				
1846	Nofire Robber				
1847	Spoon Ah-ne-lah-ga-ya	1594.20	T.E. Bonham	Henry Eiffert	Ck order
1848	Sanders Mose	order 265.70	N.S. Drake		N.S. Drake
1849	Sanders Robert				
1850	" Mattie				
1851	" Daisy N.				
1852	" Claud				

225

Starr Roll 1894

We, the undersigned citizens of the Cherokee Nation, by right of Cherokee blood, do hereby acknowledge to have received of E. E. Starr, National Treasurer of the Cherokee Nation, the sums set opposite our names respectively, in full of our shares in the per capita distribution authorized by an Act of the National Council, dated ___MAY 3 1894___ 1894.

	Names of Head, and Members of Families	Amount	To Whom Paid	Witness to Payment	Remarks
1853	" Clifford	1328.50	Mattie Sanders	Henry Eiffert	
1854	Scaggs Lizzie	265.70 ⁹²⁴⁴	Lizzie Scaggs	L B Bell	
1855	Starr Joe	order			B Housebug
1856	" Ezekiel				
1857	Bearpaw Takey	797.10	Blue Housebug	G W Benge	on order
1858	Sanders Kate				N S Drake
1859	" E.B.				
1860	" Sam				
1861	" Dexter				
1862	" Jesse	paid	D 2967		
1863	Sanders Okla				
1864	" Tumpy	1859.90	N.S. Drake	G W Benge	by order
1865	Sanders John D	265.70 ⁹⁹⁰	Blackstone & Co	G W Benge	Blackstone & Co
1866	Sixkiller Mintie	265.70	Mintie Sixkiller	Henry Eiffert	
1867	Schell Charles	order			Bonham
1868	Lizzie				
1869	Cor-he-nay	797.10	T.E. Bonham	G W Benge	by order
1870	Simmons Sam	order 265			N.S. Drake
1871	Nellie	531.40	N.S. Drake	G W Benge	by order
1872	Shanks James	order			withdrawn J.R. Skaggs
1873	Jesse				
1874	Bessie				
1875	Narcessus[sic]	1062.80	James Shanks	G W Benge	
1876	Starr Addie	265.70	M V Benge	L B Bell	
1877	Smallwood William	265.70 order	W.M. Gibson	G W Benge	by order W.M. Gibson Orphan
1878	Still Robin	order			Carlisle
1879	Luella	531.40	Thomas Carlisle	Henry Eiffert	ck on order
1880	Scott Richard	265.70	Richard Scott	G W Benge	

Starr Roll 1894

We, the undersigned citizens of the Cherokee Nation, by right of Cherokee blood, do hereby acknowledge to have received of E. E. Starr, National Treasurer of the Cherokee Nation, the sums set opposite our names respectively, in full of our shares in the per capita distribution authorized by an Act of the National Council, dated ___MAY 3 1894___ 1894.

Names of Head, and Members of Families	Amount	To Whom Paid	Witness to Payment	Remarks
1881 Scott Elizabeth	265.70	M V Benge	L B Bell	on order
1882 Storker Charlott				
1883 " Ella				
1884 " Lena DEAD.				
1885 " Marvin	1062.80	Charlott Storker	G.W. Benge	
1886 Sutter George	265.70	J.R. Skaggs	G W Benge	by order J.R. Skaggs
1887 Shade Shuggs	265.70	T.E. Bonham	G W Benge	T E Bonham by order
1888 Spoon William	265.70	Wᵐ Spoon	Henry Eiffert	
1889 Searcewater[sic] Richard DEAD.				
1890 Loucinda				
1891 Ross				
1892 James	1062.80	Richard Scorcewater	G W Benge	
1893 Smith Lyda	265.70	Geo Jennings	G W Benge	
1894 Sanders Lula D	265.70	Lula D Sanders	G W Benge	
Sanders Charley	265.70	Walter Frye	G W Benge	
1895 Thornton T. Jay	order			Nash
1896 " Mollie				
1897 " Murrell H				
1898 Rogers Katie	1062.80	W.S. Nash	G W Benge	on order
1899 Thornton Lewis R.				
1900 " Ellen S.				
1901 " Clem V.	797.10	L.R. Thornton	G W Benge	
1902 Thornton Charles A.	265.70	L.R. Thornton	G W Benge	
1903 Thornton Guy E	265.70	Walsh & Shutt	G W Benge	W&S by order
1904 Thompson Elizabeth	265.70	Elizabeth Thompson	G W Benge	

227

Starr Roll 1894

We, the undersigned citizens of the Cherokee Nation, by right of Cherokee blood, do hereby acknowledge to have received of E. E. Starr, National Treasurer of the Cherokee Nation, the sums set opposite our names respectively, in full of our shares in the per capita distribution authorized by an Act of the National Council, dated ___MAY 3 1894___ 1894.

	Names of Head, and Members of Families	Amount	To Whom Paid	Witness to Payment	Remarks
1905	Taylor James E.				
1906	" Nora M.				
1907	" Dora J.				
1908	" Samuel C.				
1909	" Lyde L.				
1910	" Aenophon[sic]				
1911	" Burtha				
1912	" Emma I	2125.60	J.E. Taylor	G W Benge	
1913	Trent Mollie K.				
1914	" Georgia				
1915	" Richard O				
1916	" Martin S				
1917	" Thomas	1328.50	M.K. Trent	G W Benge	
1918	Thornton Flora				
1919	" Owen F.				
1920	" Nicholas M.				
1921	" Flora M.	1062.80	Flora Thornton	Henry Eiffert	
1922	Trippard James	265.70	Jas R Trippard	L B Bell	
1923	Thornton Cyntha	265.70	Cyntha Thornton	G W Benge	
1924	Tolan Soldier	order			Madden
1925	" Racheal				
1926	" Jack				
1927	" Lewis				
1928	" Jennie				
1929	" Walter	1594.20	T.R. Madden	G W Benge	by order
1930	Thornton Polly				
1931	Keys Maggie	531.40	Polly Thornton	Henry Eiffert	
1932	Tehee John	265.70	Banon[sic] and Hayes	G W Benge	by order B & Hayes
1933	Tolan Thompson	265.70	Tolan Thompson	Robt B. Ross	
1934	Tee hee Lee	order			W&S
1935	" Moses				

Starr Roll 1894

We, the undersigned citizens of the Cherokee Nation, by right of Cherokee blood, do hereby acknowledge to have received of E. E. Starr, National Treasurer of the Cherokee Nation, the sums set opposite our names respectively, in full of our shares in the per capita distribution authorized by an Act of the National Council, dated ____MAY 3 1894____ 1894.

	Names of Head, and Members of Families	Amount	To Whom Paid	Witness to Payment	Remarks
1936	" Charles	797.10	Walsh and Shutt	G W Benge	by order
1937	Thornton Cherokee	265.70 *order* D-199 9736	T.R. Madden	G W Benge	Madden by order
1938	Tenkiller Nancy	*order*			B & H
1939	Katie				
1940	Daler				
1941	Chic-a-lee-li				
1942	Sa-hi	1328.50	Banon[sic] and Hayes	G W Benge	by order
1943	Tenkiller Lester	265.70	Banon[sic] and Hayes	G W Benge	by order
1944	Tony Nellie	265.70 *order*	Banon[sic] and Hayes	G W Benge	B & H by order
1945	Tony Thomas	265.70 *order*	Banon[sic] and Hayes	G W Benge	by order
1946	Thornton Dora	265.70	Thomas Carlile	G W Benge	on order
1947	Tehee Kate	265.70 *order*	T.R. Madden	G W Benge	by Madden
1948	Thornton Wallace				
1949	Minnie				
1950	Wallace Jr.				
1951	Joseph				
1952	Walter				
1953	Maud	1594.20	Wallice[sic] Thornton	G W Benge	
1954	Terrell Robert M	265.70	W.M. Gibson	G W Benge	by order W.M. Gibson
1955	Terrell John				
1956	Ula	531.40	John Terrell	G W Benge	
1957	Thornton William				
1958	" Sarah				
1959	" Eliza				
1960	" Arch				
1961	" Thomas				
1962	Cola Jennie				
1963	" Elsie				
1964	" Kate	2125.60	Sarah Thornton	Henry Eiffert	

229

Starr Roll 1894

We, the undersigned citizens of the Cherokee Nation, by right of Cherokee blood, do hereby acknowledge to have received of E. E. Starr, National Treasurer of the Cherokee Nation, the sums set opposite our names respectively, in full of our shares in the per capita distribution authorized by an Act of the National Council, dated _____ MAY 3 1894 _____ 1894.

	Names of Head, and Members of Families	Amount	To Whom Paid	Witness to Payment	Remarks
1965	Terapinhead Chas	265.70	Josiah Vann	G W Benge	
1966	" Kate				
1967	" Nancy				
1968	" Stoo-is-tee	797.10	Kate Terapinhead	G W Benge	
1969	Twist Charles	order			
1970	" Nellie				
1971	" John G	797.10	John Mayfield	G W Benge	John Mayfield by order
1972	Thornton Smith				
1973	Willie	531.40	Smith Thornton	L B Bell	
1974	Tatum Alice				
1975	" Lula				
1976	" Sitting Bull				
1977	" Thomas	1062.80	Alice Tatum	Henry Eiffert	
1978	Thompson William				
1979	Frank				
1980	Nannie				
1981	Donnie			W͟m Thompson	G W Benge
1982	Thompson Lillian				
1983	Sallie	1594.20	W͟m Thompson	G W Benge	
1984	Taylor Lewis	DEAD.			
1985	Ross R.				
1986	Nannie	797.10	Lewis Taylor	G W Benge	
1987	Murphy Amand	265.70	CO Frye	J P Carter	by order
1988	Taylor John				
1989	" Booth				
1990	" Nancy				
1991	" Theodore				
1992	" John C.				
1993	" Myrthe				
1994	" James F.	1859.90	John Taylor	G W Benge	
1995	Thompson Jesse				
1996	" Emma	531.401	Jesse Thompson	G W Benge	

230

Starr Roll 1894

We, the undersigned citizens of the Cherokee Nation, by right of Cherokee blood, do hereby acknowledge to have received of E. E. Starr, National Treasurer of the Cherokee Nation, the sums set opposite our names respectively, in full of our shares in the per capita distribution authorized by an Act of the National Council, dated ___MAY 3 1894___ 1894.

Names of Head, and Members of Families	Amount	To Whom Paid	Witness to Payment	Remarks
1997 Tapp[sic] Elnora				
1998 " James				
1999 " Joseph	797.10	Elnora Taff	L B Bell	
2000 Towie Alsie				
2001 John				
2002 Petit Jennie	797.10	Alsie Towie	L B Bell	
2003 Thompson Charles	order			Carlile
2004 Oo-loo-tsa				
2005 Cor-le-sie	797.10	Thomas Carlisle	G W Benge	by order
2006 Thornton Glover	265.70	Polly Thornton	Henry Eiffert	
2007 Terrapinhead Nannie	265.70	Josiah Vann	G W Benge	
2008 Ussrey George				
2009 " Sam				
2010 " Pinkie A.	797.10	George Ussrey	G W Benge	
2011 Vann Mortar[sic]				
2012 " Mineva[sic]				
2013 " John	797.10	Morter Vann	G W Benge	
2014 Vann Araminta R.	265.70	Hubbard Ross	L B Bell	
2015 Vann William	265.70	W.S. Nash	G W Benge	by order W.S. Nash
2016 Vann Ida E.	265.70	Morter Vann	G W Benge	
				JJ Kelly[sic]
2017 Van Antwerp Avie	531.40			
2018 Vann George	531.40	J.J. Kelly	G W Benge	by order
2019 Vann Thomas	265.70	Thomas Vann	Henry Eiffert	
2020 " Jennie	265.70	T.R. Madden	G W Benge	by order Madden
2021 Dinneehead Jennie	265.70	Thomas Vann	Henry Eiffert	
				pd Check No 68570
2022 Vicary John W.	265.70	Walsh & Shutt	J.C. Starr	on order

231

Starr Roll 1894

We, the undersigned citizens of the Cherokee Nation, by right of Cherokee blood, do hereby acknowledge to have received of E. E. Starr, National Treasurer of the Cherokee Nation, the sums set opposite our names respectively, in full of our shares in the per capita distribution authorized by an Act of the National Council, dated _____MAY 3 1894_____ 1894.

	Names of Head, and Members of Families	Amount	To Whom Paid	Witness to Payment	Remarks
2023	Vann George	order			Madden
2024	" Rabbit	531.40	T.R. Madden	G W Benge	by order
2025	Vann Richard	265.70	Richard Vann	G W Benge	
2026	Vann Josie				
2027	Vann Amanda	531.40	Josiah Vann	G W Benge	
2028	Vann Buster				
2029	Betsy				
2030	Cora				
2031	Mollie				
2032	Darkie	1328.50	Buster Vann	G W Benge	
2033	Whitekiller Chas				
2034	" Delila				
2035	" Chas M.				
2036	" William				
2037	" Myrtle				
2038	" Susana	1594.20	Chas Whitekiller	G W Benge	
2039	Walker Albert	265.70	Walsh and Shutt	G W Benge	by order W&S
2040	West Nancy	265.70	M.A. Perkins	G W Benge	
2041	West Clifton P.	order			Nash
2042	" Rufus B.				
2043	" George M.				
2044	" Henry B.				
2045	" Charlie				
2046	" Morgan	1594.20	W.S. Nash	G W Benge	by order
2047	Walker Timothy				
2048	" Betsy A				
2049	" Malboy	797.10	Timothy Walker	G W Benge	orphan
2050	Wickel Mariah	order			Nash
2051	Smith Davis	D217			orphan
2052	Myrtle Samuel	797.10	W.S. Nash	G W Benge	by order

Starr Roll 1894

We, the undersigned citizens of the Cherokee Nation, by right of Cherokee blood, do hereby acknowledge to have received of E. E. Starr, National Treasurer of the Cherokee Nation, the sums set opposite our names respectively, in full of our shares in the per capita distribution authorized by an Act of the National Council, dated ____MAY 3 1894____ 1894.

	Names of Head, and Members of Families	Amount	To Whom Paid	Witness to Payment	Remarks
2053	Waters Johnston[sic]				
2054	" Sarah				
2055	" Joe				
2056	" George		Johnson Waters		
2057	Waters Thomas				
2058	" Nellie				
2059	" Akey	1859.90	Johnson Waters	G W Benge	
2060	Baldridge Eli	265.70	T.R. Madden	Henry Eiffert	T.B. Madden Orphan
2061	Willey Minnie B.				
2062	" Charey[sic] W.				
2063	" Fannie A.				
2064	" Miles J	1062.80	M.B. Willey	G W Benge	
2065	Whitekiller David W.				
2066	" Sallie				
2067	" Mary				Nash
2068	" Charles	1062.80	W.S. Nash	G W Benge	by order
2069	Waford[sic] Frank				
2070	" Clarence	531.40	Alice Wofford	G W Benge	
2071	" Mary				
2072	Ross James	531.40	Mary Wofford	G W Benge	
2073	Walker Jack				
2074	" Susan A				
2075	" Josephine				
2076	" Robert T.				
2077	" Tim M.				
2078	" Henry C.	1594.20	Jack Walker	G W Benge	
2079	Walker Richard M				
2080	" Lizzie P.	531.40	R.M. Walker	L B Bell	
2081	Walker Ollie				
2082	" Betsy J				
2083	" Rosa L	797.10	R M Walker	L B Bell	
2084	Waford[sic] Joseph				
2085	" William				
2086	" Charles				

Starr Roll 1894

We, the undersigned citizens of the Cherokee Nation, by right of Cherokee blood, do hereby acknowledge to have received of E. E. Starr, National Treasurer of the Cherokee Nation, the sums set opposite our names respectively, in full of our shares in the per capita distribution authorized by an Act of the National Council, dated ____MAY 3 1894____ 1894.

	Names of Head, and Members of Families	Amount	To Whom Paid	Witness to Payment	Remarks
2087	" Troy	1062.80	Joseph Wofford	G W Benge	
2088	Whitekiller George *or (Whitewater)*				
2089	" Ellen				
2090	" Nancy				
2091	" Sallie				
2092	" Mary	1328.50	Geo Whitewater	Henry Eiffert	
2093	Wiggans Lucy				
2094	Meeker George	531.40	Mary Smithman	G W Benge	
2095	Woodard George				
2096	" Viola				
2097	" Edwin	797.10	George Woodard	Henry Eiffert	
2098	Wilson Alice	265.70	Alice Wilson	Henry Eiffert	
2099	Whitekiller W^{m}				
2100	" Louisa				
2101	" Emma				
2102	" Caroline	1062.80	Wm Whitewater	Henry Eiffert	
2103	Wiley Quatie	*order*			*Madden*
2104	Wah le yah	531.40	*(Name Illegible)* P297?	G W Benge	*children*
2105	Watts Polly	*order* 265.70	Banon[sic] and Hayes		*B& Hayes by order*
2106	Waters Dekiney[sic]				
2107	" Eliza				
2108	" John				
2109	Girty William				
2110	Young Che-nar-ster	1328.50	Dickinny Waters	L B Bell	
2111	Waters Eva	265.70	Eva Waters	Henry Eiffert	
2112	Washington George				
2113	" Lizzie				
2114	" Lydia				
2115	" Peggie				
2116	" Red				

234

Starr Roll 1894

We, the undersigned citizens of the Cherokee Nation, by right of Cherokee blood, do hereby acknowledge to have received of E. E. Starr, National Treasurer of the Cherokee Nation, the sums set opposite our names respectively, in full of our shares in the per capita distribution authorized by an Act of the National Council, dated ____MAY 3 1894____ 1894.

	Names of Head, and Members of Families	Amount	To Whom Paid	Witness to Payment	Remarks
2117	" Blue				
2118	" Alija	1859.90	T.R. Madden	G W Benge	by order
2119	Whitewater Fannie	order			Madden
2120	" Ellen B.				
2121	" Nancy	797.10	T.R. Madden	G W Benge	by order
2122	Waters James	265.70	James Waters	G W Benge	
2123	Wicks Lizzie				
2124	George A				
2125	John A	797.10	Ostin Wicks	G W Benge	
2126	Wicks Jane	265.70	Ostin Wicks	G W Benge	
2127	Wren Theodore				
2128	" George H				
2129	" Charles R	797.10	Edwin Wren	G W Benge	
2130	Was-wah ei tah Geo.				Madden
2131	" Lucy	order			
2132	" Isaac				
2133	" Loucinda				
2134	" Sarah				
2135	" David				
2136	" Levi				
2137	" Ellis	2125.60	T.R. Madden	G W Benge	by order
2138	Watkins Sam	265.70	S A Orchard	Henry Eiffert	
2139	" Lizzie	265.70	W^m McLain	Henry Eiffert	
2140	" Ellen				
2141	" Sam Jr.	531.40	S A Orchard	Henry Eiffert	
2142	Washington John	265.70	T.R. Madden	G W Benge	Madden by order
2143	Walker Edward A				
2144	" Katie				
2145	" Eliza				
2146	" R. M.				
2147	" Florence				
2148	" John				

Starr Roll 1894

We, the undersigned citizens of the Cherokee Nation, by right of Cherokee blood, do hereby acknowledge to have received of E. E. Starr, National Treasurer of the Cherokee Nation, the sums set opposite our names respectively, in full of our shares in the per capita distribution authorized by an Act of the National Council, dated ___MAY 3 1894___ 1894.

	Names of Head, and Members of Families	Amount	To Whom Paid	Witness to Payment	Remarks
2149	" Mallie				
2150	Jennie	2125.60	E.A. Walker	G W Benge	
2151	Wildcat Goround				
2152	" Nellie				
2153	Sunday Jackson	797.10	Branan & Hayes	G W Benge	on order
2154	Wildcat William	order			B&H
2155	" Ah-ne-wa-ki				
2156	" Cah-woh-hi-loo-ki				
2157	" The-yah-ha				
2158	" French				
2159	" Alex				
2160	" Charlott	1859.90	Banon[sic] and Hayes	G W Benge	by order
2161	Wildcat Sam	265.70	Branan & Hayes	G W Benge	on order
2162	Wildcat Yo-ho-la				
2163	" Oo da yi	531.40	Branan & Hayes	G W Benge	on order
2164	" Nancy				
2165	" Snow	order			
2166	" Sallie	797.10	Brannon & Hayes	J.C. Starr	JUL 23 1894 check on order
2167	Wildcat Noley	order			B&H
2168	" Elsie				
2169	" Spade				
2170	" Benjamin				
2171	" Colston	1328.50	Branon[sic] and Hayes	G W Benge	by order
2172	Wildcat Walker				
2173	" Susan				
2174	" Goiza				
2175	Cryingdeer Dick	1062.80	Branan & Hayes	G W Benge	on order
2176	Williams Mary A				
2177	" George C.				
2178	" Edward B.	797.10	A.S. Williams	G W Benge	

236

Starr Roll 1894

We, the undersigned citizens of the Cherokee Nation, by right of Cherokee blood, do hereby acknowledge to have received of E. E. Starr, National Treasurer of the Cherokee Nation, the sums set opposite our names respectively, in full of our shares in the per capita distribution authorized by an Act of the National Council, dated ____MAY 3 1894____ 1894.

	Names of Head, and Members of Families	Amount	To Whom Paid	Witness to Payment	Remarks
2179	Walker William	order			B&H
2180	" Katie				
2181	" Charles				
2182	" Sallie				
2183	" Mesuell				
2184	" Ahli	1594.20	Branon[sic] and Hayes	G W Benge	by order
2185	Webber Nakey	order			B&H
2186	" Bullet F				
2187	" Chliloh	797.10	Branon[sic] and Hayes	G W Benge	by order
2188	Webber Suckey	order			B&H
2189	Tony John	~~D1234~~ 9840			
2190	" Yeh sli ne				
2191	" Stink	1062.80	Banon[sic] and Hayes	G W Benge	by order
2192	West Eliza				
2193	" Luella				
2194	" Burrell	797.10	Thomas Carlile	G W Benge	
2195	Watt Ezekiel	order			B&Hayes
2196	" Wah le sa	531.40	Brandon[sic] & Hayes	L B Bell	check
2197	George Arch	265.70	Arch George	Henry Eiffert	
2198	Whitmire George	265.70	Ida Whitmire	Henry Eiffert	Dead Nov 8/94
2199	" George W. Jr	265.70	J R Whitmire	Henry Eiffert	order Guardian
2200	Waters George				
2201	" Mary				
2202	" George Jr.				
2203	" Florence				
2204	" Moses				
2205	" Maggie				
2206	" Grover C.				
2207	" Nancy				
2208	" Gertrude				
2209	Starr Katie	2657.00	Geo Waters	L B Bell	orphan

Enrolled by Geo Waters

237

Starr Roll 1894

We, the undersigned citizens of the Cherokee Nation, by right of Cherokee blood, do hereby acknowledge to have received of E. E. Starr, National Treasurer of the Cherokee Nation, the sums set opposite our names respectively, in full of our shares in the per capita distribution authorized by an Act of the National Council, dated ____MAY 3 1894____ 1894.

	Names of Head, and Members of Families	Amount	To Whom Paid	Witness to Payment	Remarks
2210	Walkingstick Chas				
2211	" Mattie				
2212	" Thomas				
2213	" Loucinda				
2214	" Mack				
2215	" Jennie	1594.20	Chas Walkingstick	G W Benge	
2216	Wilson William	265.70	Robert Wilson	G W Benge	
2217	Walkingstick Jack DEAD.				
2218	" Mary				
2219	" Lucy				
2220	" Louis	1062.80	Jack Walkingstick	L B Bell	
2221	Walkingstick Levi	265.70	Levi Walkingstick	L B Bell	
2222	Wilson James W	order			Wells
2223	" James F				
2224	" Jesse A	paid			
2225	Wilson Albert M.	order			Wells
2226	" Sallie B.				
2227	" Ida F				
2228	" Robert	1,859.90	J.F. Wells	G W Benge	by order
2229	Wolf Tom	order			Bonham
2230	" Sallie	531.40	T.E. Bonham	G W Benge	by order
2231	Wilson Albert B.	265.70	Robert Wilson	G W Benge	
2232	Walker Lizzie	265.70	Lizzie Walker	G W Benge	
2233	Pig Ollie	265.70	Stephen Peak	JP Carter	Guardian orphan
2234	Walker Sallie	order			T.E. Bonham
2235	McCoy George	531.40	T.E. Bonham	G W Benge	by order
2236	Walker John				
2237	" Cora				
2238	" Mollie	797.10	Blackstone & Co	J.C. Starr	check on order JUL 24 1894
2239	Bearpaw Dave	265.70	John Bark Nov 30.96	G W Benge	Guardian

238

Starr Roll 1894

We, the undersigned citizens of the Cherokee Nation, by right of Cherokee blood, do hereby acknowledge to have received of E. E. Starr, National Treasurer of the Cherokee Nation, the sums set opposite our names respectively, in full of our shares in the per capita distribution authorized by an Act of the National Council, dated ____MAY 3 1894____ 1894.

Names of Head, and Members of Families	Amount	To Whom Paid	Witness to Payment	Remarks
2240 Wilson Robert	265.70	Robert Wilson	G W Benge	
2241 Wilson Fannie	265.70	O.L. Hayes	G W Benge	on order by JE Hays
2242 Wilson Emma				
2243 " Robert				
2244 " Gilbert	797.10	Robert Wilson	G W Benge	
2245 Wells Lourinda	265.70	John Wells	L B Bell	
2246 Wells Lila				
2247 " Emma	531.40	John Wells	L B Bell	
2248 Wade Bremis				
2249 " Clara				
2250 " Meigs	797.10	Bremis Wade	G W Benge	
2251 Winters Ida	265.70	C D Pendleton	G W Benge	Pendleton by order
2252 Waters John				
2253 " Florence	531.40	John Waters	G W Benge	
2254 Ward Ella				
2255 " Lenora				
2256 " Sadie				
2257 Smith Jack	1062.80	Ella Ward	G W Benge	
2258 Waters Mary	265.70	Mary Waters	Henry Eiffert	
2259 Young Lou M				
2260 " Willie				
2261 " Minnie				
2262 " Lucy				
2263 " Daniel				
2264 " Mary				
2265 " Jesse	1859.90	Danl Young	G W Benge	
2266 Young Thomas	265.70	Thomas Young	G W Benge	
2267 Yarbrough Lizzie	265.70	Lizzie Yarbrough	Henry Eiffert	

Starr Roll 1894

We, the undersigned citizens of the Cherokee Nation, by right of Cherokee blood, do hereby acknowledge to have received of E. E. Starr, National Treasurer of the Cherokee Nation, the sums set opposite our names respectively, in full of our shares in the per capita distribution authorized by an Act of the National Council, dated ___MAY 3 1894___ 1894.

	Names of Head, and Members of Families	Amount	To Whom Paid	Witness to Payment	Remarks
2268	Yates Ellen				
2269	" Luella				
2270	" George				
2271	" Edith				
2272	Smith Ialol				
2273	" Frank				
2274	" Arthur	1859.90	Ellen Yates	G W Benge	
2275	Young Thomas	order			Madden
2276	" Sydney	531.40	T.R. Madden	G W Benge	by order
2277	Young George				
2278	" Mary				
2279	" James	797.10	Willie or Mary Young	G W Benge	
2280	Yohola Iyah ga	265.70	Branan and Hayes	G W Benge	B&H by order
2281	Yohola Seh-on o-co				
2282	" Lydia				
2283	" Alex				
2284	" Nellie				
2285	" Nick				
2286	" Lock	1594.20	Lydia Yohola	Henry Eiffert	
2287	Young Roach				
2288	" Nancy				
2289	" John				
2290	" Jack				
2291	" Dick	1328.50	Roach Young	G W Benge	
2292	Yellow Bird				no given name
2293	" Lizzie				
2294	" Sallie				
2295	" Katie				
2296	" Kah-le-skag-wee				
2297	" Ah-y hor-ka				
2298	" Nancy				
2299	" William R.	2125.60 order	Yellow Bird	L B Bell	order withdrawn Wells

240

Starr Roll 1894

We, the undersigned citizens of the Cherokee Nation, by right of Cherokee blood, do hereby acknowledge to have received of E. E. Starr, National Treasurer of the Cherokee Nation, the sums set opposite our names respectively, in full of our shares in the per capita distribution authorized by an Act of the National Council, dated ___MAY 3 1894___ 1894.

	Names of Head, and Members of Families	Amount	To Whom Paid	Witness to Payment	Remarks
2300	Yohola Johnston	order			B & Hayes
2301	" Wah-le-sa				
2302	" Gah-gay-tie	797.10	Branan and Hayes	G W Benge	by order
2303	Yohola David				
2304	" Louis				
2305	" Woh-de-gay	797.10	David Yohola	Henry Eiffert	
2306	Yohola Nellie	265.70	T.E. Bonham	G W Benge	TE Bonham
2307	Young Lewis				
2308	" Mary				
2309	" Alice	797.10	Lewis Young	Henry Eiffert	
2310	Yohola Cumpsy				
2311	" Watty				
2312	" Quaitsy				
2313	" Daniel				
2314	" Louisa				
2315	" Jackson				
2316	Cumpsy Akey				
2317	" Stoo wee sta	2125.60	Henry Eiffert		

Tahlequah, Ind. Ter., *May 19th,* 189 *4.*

I, C. J. Harris, Principal Chief of the Cherokee Nation, and

I, E. E. Starr, Treasurer of said Nation,

Do hereby certify that the foregoing enrollment of persons to participate in the per-capita distribution of the six million six hundred and forty thousand dollars [6,640,000]. as provided by the Act of the National Council, approved may[sic] *3rd, 1894, is correct as found upon the Rolls of Illinois District in this Nation, and that the number is twenty three hundred and thirteen [2313]*

C. J. Harris
Principal Chief.

E. E. Starr
Treasurer.

Witness.
Seal of the Cherokee Nation.

****

242

Index

Index

329

Lightning Source UK Ltd.
Milton Keynes UK
UKHW041241240322
400334UK00001B/244

9 781649 680228